Citizenship in Nordic Welfare States

Citizenship in Nordic Welfare States offers an innovative analysis of the ways in which the relationship between citizens and welfare states (social citizenship) becomes more dynamic and multifaceted as a result of Europeanization and individualization.

Relations between citizens and welfare states are now to a greater extent involving issues of rights and duties, self-responsibility and choice, participation and self-government at the same time. The contents of citizenship are increasingly influenced by interactions between national and supranational levels of governance.

An interdisciplinary team (social science, law and philosophy) examines the transformation of social citizenship through a series of illuminating case studies, comparing Nordic countries and other European nations. The book deals with the following areas of national and European welfare policy, legislation and practice:

- Activation – reforms linking income maintenance and employment promotion.
- The scope for participation of marginal groups in deliberation and decision-making.
- The impact of human rights legislation for welfare and legal protection against discrimination and social barriers to equal market participation.
- The co-ordination of social security systems to facilitate cross-border mobility in Europe.
- Pension reform – efforts to make pension systems sustainable.

This book will appeal to students and researchers of social policy, comparative welfare and social work, social law, political science, sociology and European studies.

Bjørn Hvinden is Professor of Sociology at the Department of Sociology and Political Science at the Norwegian University of Science and Technology (NTNU), Trondheim, Norway.

Håkan Johansson is Researcher and Lecturer in Social Work at the School of Health Sciences and Social Work, Växjö University, Sweden.

Routledge Advances in European Politics

Citizenship in Nordic Welfare States

Dynamics of choice, duties and participation in a changing Europe

Edited by
Bjørn Hvinden and Håkan Johansson

Routledge
Taylor & Francis Group

LONDON AND NEW YORK

First published 2007
by Routledge
2 Park Square, Milton Park, Abingdon, Oxon, OX14 4RN

Simultaneously published in the USA and Canada
by Routledge
270 Madison Ave, New York NY 10016

Routledge is an imprint of the Taylor & Francis Group, an informa business

Transferred to Digital Printing 2008

Typeset in Garamond by
Taylor & Francis Books

British Library Cataloguing in Publication Data
A catalogue record for this book is available from the British Library

Library of Congress Cataloging in Publication Data
Citizenship in Nordic welfare states: dynamics of choice, duties and
participation in a changing Europe / edited by Bjørn Hvinden and Håkan
Johansson.
    p. cm.
1. Citizenship – Scandinavia. 2. Citizenship – Europe. 3. Social policy –
Scandinavia. 4. Social policy – Europe. I. Hvinden, Bjørn, 1949-II.
Johansson, Håkan, 1972-
JN7011.C58 2007
323.60948 – dc22   2006026298

ISBN10: 0-415-41489-X (hbk)
ISBN10: 0-415-47961-4 (pbk)

ISBN13: 978-0-415-41489-0 (hbk)
ISBN13: 978-0-415-47961-5 (pbk)

Contents

Contributors

Jørgen Anker (Dr) is a Researcher at the Department of Social Sciences, Roskilde University, Denmark. His main research interests include social movement theory, voluntary organizations, marginalized groups, user involvement and user participation.

Kjersti Fjørtoft (Dr) is a Postdoctoral Fellow at the Department of Philosophy at the University of Tromsø, Norway. Her research focus is political philosophy, ethics and feminist philosophy and she is presently working on issues related to citizenship, justice and democratic participation.

Rune Halvorsen (Dr) is a Research Fellow in sociology at the Department of Social Work and Health Science, Norwegian University of Science and Technology, Trondheim, Norway. His main research interests are European and comparative welfare policy, social regulation policy in the European Union and the role of European Social NGOs in European policy-making.

Karl Hinrichs (Dr) is a Senior Research Associate at Bremen University's Centre for Social Policy Research and Professor of political science at Humboldt University in Berlin, Germany. His main research focus is on comparative social policy and the changing politics in ageing societies.

Bjørn Hvinden (Dr) is Professor of Sociology at the Department of Sociology and Political Science at the Norwegian University of Science and Technology NTNU), Trondheim, Norway, and Head of Research, Norwegian Social Research (NOVA). His main research focus is on comparative social policy, European integration, disability, international migration and ethnicity.

Håkan Johansson (Dr) is Researcher and Lecturer in Social Work at the School of Health Sciences and Social Work, Växjö University, Sweden. His interests include citizenship theory, comparative social policy, European social policy and the role of European Social NGOs in European policy-making.

Stine Jørgensen (Dr) is Senior Lecturer in law at the Faculty of Law, Copenhagen University, Denmark. Her main research focus is women's perspective on social welfare, family and integration law, within the framework of the UN Convention of the Elimination of all forms of Discrimination Against Women (CEDAW).

Elsa Keskitalo is a Social Researcher and Lecturer at the Helsinki Polytechnic Stadia, Finland. Her research interests are the welfare state, comparative social policy, minimum income and evaluation of social inclusion and activation policies.

Kirsten Ketscher (Dr) is Professor of social security and welfare law, at the Faculty of Law, University of Copenhagen, and Professor in women's law and labour law at the Department of Women's Law, Faculty of Law, University of Oslo. Her main research interests include social security and social welfare rights in Denmark and in the European Union, and social, economic and cultural human rights, in particular women's rights and children's rights.

Ann Therese Lotherington (Dr) is a Researcher in political science and Head of Research at Norut Social Science Research Ltd. in Tromsø, Norway. Her research interests are related to democracy and citizenship, gender and change in organizations.

Jon Arve Nervik (Dr) is Associate Professor in political science at the Norwegian University of Science and Technology. His main research interests are public policy and implementation processes, and more specifically; quantitative dynamic study of the careers of social assistance recipients and evaluation of local activation programmes for unemployed social assistance claimants.

Stefanía Óskarsdóttir (Dr) has been working as a Researcher and Instructor in political science at the University of Iceland. She has served as a deputy member of the Icelandic parliament and carried out independent work for various governmental agencies. Her main research focus has been the impact of the economy on state polices as well as gender and the economy.

Tapio Salonen (Dr) is a Professor in social work at the School of Health Sciences and Social Work, Växjö University Sweden. His main research interests include poverty, marginality, participatory models, social policy and activation.

Øyvind Stokke is a PhD student at the Department of Philosophy, University of Tromsø. His research interests include discourse theory, normative political theory, and critical theory and globalization. He is currently working on a dissertation on discourse theory and social rights in a transnational perspective.

Katarina Thorén is a PhD student at the School of Social Service Administration (SSA), University of Chicago, USA. Her research interests include street-level bureaucracy, welfare-to-work programmes and activation in a comparative perspective.

Rickard Ulmestig is a PhD student in social work at Växjö University, Sweden. He is currently working on a Doctoral thesis on changes in Swedish labour market policies in the 1990s.

Richard Whittle is a Jean Monnet Lecturer in European Law, at the University of Leeds, the United Kingdom. His principal research interest is in EU disability law and policy. He has acted as an expert advisor to various bodies including the British Disability Rights Commission, the EU Commission and the European Disability Forum.

Acknowledgements

We are grateful for the funding provided by the Welfare Research Programme of the Nordic Council of Ministers 2002–5 for the project 'Active citizenship and marginality in a European context' (grant no 149819–599). This grant enabled us to organize six workshops where scholars from five Nordic countries, Germany and the United Kingdom presented initial ideas and later draft chapters for this book. To be able to gather scholars with backgrounds in different academic disciplines and research areas to analyze changes in social citizenship has been a rare and rewarding experience.

The project has benefited from the administrative flexibility and support of Steinar Kristiansen (senior advisor, Research Council of Norway), in his role as co-ordinator of the Welfare Research Programme.

Natalie Reid has contributed strongly to the final editing of this book. We cannot thank her enough for her skill, diligence and enthusiasm in transforming texts from Nordic English into lucid and elegant British English.

Finally, we are grateful for thoughtful and inspiring comments from two anonymous reviewers and from Anette Borchorst, John Clarke, Valerie Fargion, Sakari Hänninen, Matti Heikkilä, Janet Newman, Johannes Pakaslahti, Sasha Roseneil, Stina Johansson and Fiona Williams at seminars at the Danish National Institute of Social Research (Copenhagen), Open University (Milton Keynes), Voksenåsen (Oslo), STAKES (Helsinki), Växjö University (Sweden) and Aalborg University (Denmark).

Bjørn Hvinden and Håkan Johansson
Trondheim and Växjö, June 2006

Abbreviations

APAJH	L'Association Pour Adultes et Jeunes Handicapés
ATP	Public earnings-related pension (Sweden)
CEDAW	Convention on the Elimination of all forms of Discrimination Against Women
CES	Conseil Economique et Social
CEU	Council of the European Union
CRC	Convention on the Rights of the Child
DC	Defined contribution
DRC	Disability Rights Commission (the UK)
DS	Departmental report (the Swedish government)
EAPN	European Anti-Poverty Network
EC	European Community
ECHR	European Convention of Human Rights
EHRC	European Human Rights Committee
EDF	European Disability Forum
EEC	European Economic Community
EEA	European Economic Area
ECJ	European Court of Justice
ESC	European Social Charter
EU	European Union
FDC	Fully funded pension plan
NAP	National Action Plan
NDC	Notionally defined contribution
NGO	Non-Governmental Organization
NOU	Norges Offentlige Utredninger (Norwegian governmental reports)
OECD	Organization for Economic Co-operation and Development
OMC	Open Method of Co-ordination
OT.PROP.	Odelstingsproposisjon (Law bill, Norway)
SOU	Statens Offentliga Utredningar (Swedish governmental reports)
ST.MELD.	Stortingsmelding (Norwegian government White Paper)
TEC	Treaty of the European Community
UN	United Nations

Part I

Citizenship in contemporary welfare states

Issues and perspectives

1 Opening citizenship

Why do we need a new understanding of social citizenship?

Håkan Johansson and Bjørn Hvinden

Introduction

This book argues that ongoing changes in European welfare states, including the Nordic ones, call for a new, dynamic and multifaceted understanding of social citizenship. These changes involve new relationships between provision of income security and promotion of employment, between public and private responsibility for social risk protection (especially in old age), between rights to receive and duties to participate, between social redistribution and social regulation (especially of market behaviour), between benefit rights and the right to equal treatment and ultimately between national and supranational influences on social protection.

These transformations have made the contrasts and tensions between different aspects of social citizenship more manifest. First, the links between the rights and duties of citizenship have been strengthened, particularly in the contexts of activation reform and the integration of immigrants. Second, citizen self-responsibility and choice have been put in focus through public and private mixes of welfare provision, and more generally through the broader trend towards individualization. Third, citizen participation in deliberation, planning and decision-making has been both demanded and encouraged, most clearly under the headings of user involvement and consultation with stakeholder groups but also through public recognition of grassroots organization among marginalized citizens. Fourth, citizens are relying less on the benevolent discretion of administrators and professionals, and looking more to lawyers and the court system to secure access to welfare provisions, equal treatment and labour market opportunity.

Social citizenship as a purely national construct is under challenge, with a broad international trend towards strengthening human rights and protecting against discrimination on a number of grounds, e.g. gender or ethnicity. As these rights and protections become legally integrated at the national level, they add new dimensions to social citizenship. The decisions of national courts can under certain circumstances be appealed to supranational courts. The European Union (EU) has contributed to this process, for example through the Amsterdam Treaty and the Nice Charter of Fundamental Rights

(EU 2000). Through its various action programmes, based on the open method of coordination, the EU has also created new channels of participation for organizations of citizens, even marginalized citizens. These new channels have opened new transnational arenas and opportunities for giving citizens some influence in policy development.

The efforts to establish a single European market and the free movement of goods, services, capital and labour mean that social provisions previously available only for national citizens are now accessible to citizens from other member states and are exportable to other countries. From the perspective of the individual, this accessibility extends the rights associated with national social citizenship. From the perspective of national governments, these processes diminish their control over the design and administration of social protection systems, and to some extent over the financing of social provisions.

Yet a strong tendency exists for dealing with these changing aspects of social citizenship in isolation, as completely separate phenomena, or as issues only weakly related to one another. Without denying the ways in which citizenship is socially stratified, we focus on the ways in which several dimensions of citizenship are potentially affecting citizens *at the same time*. For most people this situation means that they face new demands, as well as new opportunities, to become *active citizens*. These demands and opportunities call for a more dynamic and complex understanding of citizenship. We need to open the existing ways in which citizenship is conceptualized and empirically approached. In particular, we ought to become more sensitive to how contrasting aspects of citizenship may be combined and reconciled in new and unexpected ways. Although recent developments in citizenship theory will be helpful for this purpose, we also need to explore these issues in concrete empirical contexts. The aim of the book, therefore, is to investigate the implications of opening citizenship, both theoretically and empirically.

Active citizenship – a conceptual map

References to 'active citizenship' are frequent among policymakers, journalists and scholars, albeit usually in a general, *ad hoc* or strongly context-dependent way. A good starting point for a more systematic treatment comes from David Miller (2000). In his discussion of the challenges that a multicultural society raises for citizenship Miller distinguishes among three main understandings of citizenship and, consequently, of active social citizenship:

First, citizenship in a *socio-liberal* sense is a relationship between the individual and the state, involving encompassing sets of mutual rights and obligations. Here, a turn towards active citizenship could imply that the state asks the citizen to more actively fulfil specific duties, e.g. taking part in different forms of welfare-to-work (activation) programmes in return for social benefits of different kinds. Similarly, immigrants who want to become permanent residents and eventually be granted state citizenship more often must go through specific introduction programmes, courses in the language and culture of the host country, etc.

Second, citizenship in a *libertarian* sense conceives of the relationship between state and individual more narrowly, with the emphasis on the self-responsibility and autonomy of the individual. The responsibilities and legitimate tasks of the state are therefore limited to guaranteeing and protecting the few but fundamental rights of the individual. Individuals should be able to exercise choice and freely enter contracts to promote their own well-being and protection against risks of various kinds. According to this understanding, a turn towards active citizenship could mean that citizens have greater scope for exercising individual choice and foresight as knowledgeable consumers in a mixed welfare market.

Third, citizenship in a *republican* sense generally focuses on the citizen's participation in the affairs of his or her community, and on the expectation that the individual is committed to acknowledging and promoting the well-being of the community as a whole. A turn towards active citizenship with this understanding could aim to achieve broader and more intensive citizen participation, both in deliberation and dialogue with relevant agencies and in self-directed activity. Increased participation might take both individual and collective forms. On the one hand, individual 'users' might engage in a dialogue to clarify the appropriate measures or courses of action; on the other hand, they might be involved in consultation and negotiation over the design and planning of new policies.

We elaborate on Miller's theoretical distinctions for somewhat different purposes than his. We emphasize that greater openness between the national welfare state and its international environment changes the meanings of all three understandings of citizenship. Transnational processes have substantial impacts on citizens' rights and duties and on citizens' scope for choice and participation. Although nation-states are still the major contexts for the discussion, formation, implementation and enforcement of social protection policy, they are increasingly constrained by decisions made at a supranational level. This development means that diverse dimensions of national social citizenship are opening up, combining and transforming in new configurations.

Why do we see a turn towards active citizenship?

The turn towards active citizenship is not a simple one-way process, where external pressures on the welfare state bring about new forms of citizenship or where new citizens' capabilities and demands force the welfare state to change. Rather we must view this change as the outcome of mutually reinforcing processes, transforming modes and structures of governance, citizen participation and self-directed activity. Many social scientists believe that the 'stateness' of contemporary welfare states is challenged 'from above', whether 'above' is called globalization, Europeanization or denationalization. They believe that this condition limits the *de facto* sovereignty of national governments, requires stricter budgetary discipline and new regulative measures, narrows the range of legitimate policy options and instruments at the state level, and shifts the balance between politics, markets and international courts as sources of material advantage, security and protection against risks.

But national welfare states clearly also face pressures 'from below'. Citizens are challenging long-established bureaucratic or paternalistic modes of administration, rigidity and inflexibility, as well as the arbitrary exercise of discretionary powers. People have become more knowledgeable, self-confident and conscious of their rights when dealing with front-line agency staff and professional helpers. They expect to have the option of influencing decisions relating to their own welfare, whether these options are expressed through co-determination, user involvement, informed consent, group consultation or freedom of choice. The emerging regime of international human rights, along with the more particular development of institutions in the European context, gives more force and legitimacy to these expectations.

Resulting from these processes are complex, sometimes paradoxical changes in the relations between state and citizens. Citizens are expected (and themselves expect) to play more active roles in handling risks and promoting their own welfare. In some respects the turn towards active citizenship corresponds to a more active role for the state; in other cases, it involves a more passive role. Increasing limitations of the scope for encompassing and redistributive welfare states (like the Nordic ones) may leave more to the agency of citizens. Individual responsibility for achieving self-sufficiency, protection against risks, and the active use of available opportunities in the market becomes more important.

The impact of economic openness and Europeanization

With a more open and globalized world market, stronger competitive pressures, and economic integration in Europe, national governments have the impetus to prevent further growth or even reduce public spending. Many argue that 'large' encompassing and redistributive welfare states (of the Nordic kind) have become too expensive – and therefore unsustainable – in a more competitive world that includes the emerging single European market. Governments attempt to reduce costs and increase the effectiveness of existing public services, in combination with changing labour market conditions (Chapter 4). Even in countries where public authorities have for a long time been the main provider of services, the governments attempt at leaving more to markets and private providers (e.g. by putting out services for open tender) and at encouraging citizens to take greater individual responsibility for social risk protection (e.g. by offering partial tax exemptions for personal pension plans).

Scholars like Majone have argued that we will see a gradual shift of emphasis from redistributive welfare provision to promoting welfare objectives through 'social regulation' (Majone 1993). Social regulation involves public efforts to influence the behaviour of non-governmental actors, especially actors operating in the market, to realize social objectives. Generally speaking, social regulation has the potential of strengthening citizens' scope for exercising active citizenship through their participation in the market as both workers and consumers.

Examples of social regulation include anti-discrimination legislation and the setting of what the EU defines as binding standards for universal design, meant to promote participation and equal opportunities for people with impairments (disabilities). Such regulative measures help to correct market imperfections or the undesirable consequences of unrestricted market competition, even if the need for correcting market failures is not necessarily the main impetus for introducing these measures (Majone 2005). Compared with the introduction of new tax-financed redistributive provisions, social regulation is more compatible with an opening and liberalization of international markets (Hvinden 2004). (The existence of observable significant weakening of the redistributive effects of national welfare schemes or of increased inequalities after taxes and social transfers resulting from European integration is a complex issue that falls outside the scope of this book.)

In the ongoing Europeanization process, the European Court of Justice (ECJ) has become an important actor. The ECJ has taken on an active role in clarifying the implications of common EU regulations for social policies (Pollack 2003; Leibfried 2005). The ECJ has made many decisions (under the single-market regulations) that have had substantial impact. For instance, one effectively extended the rights of EU citizens to have the authorities in their own country reimburse the costs of medical treatment in other member states (Ferrera 2005: Chapter 10).

The European Commission is another significant actor within the field of European welfare policy, as it has the authority to propose new European legislation. The Amsterdam Treaty of 1997 gave the EU power to combat discrimination on a number of different grounds, and the Commission later proposed two related directives in 2000, complementing earlier EU legislation against gender discrimination. The first directive implements the principle of equal treatment between persons irrespective of racial and ethnic origin (Council Directive 2000/43/EC). The second directive establishes a general framework for equal treatment in employment and occupation, covering discrimination on the grounds of religion or belief, disability, age or sexual orientation (Council Directive 2000/78/EC). Both direct member states to introduce laws – new or amended – and the administrative provisions necessary for compliance with these directives, with the Commission supervising and monitoring this process of 'transposition'.

The Commission also has the power to initiate joint action programmes in the social field (EU 1997). An ambition for several of these programmes has been to achieve greater similarity or convergence in the objectives of the social protection in member states, through what is now known as 'the open method of coordination' (Porte and Pochet 2002: Chapter 9). Although member states are to agree on overall joint objectives, especially for the direction of their social protection systems, they are free to choose the means for accomplishing these objectives. The EU, for example, has developed programmes based on the open method of co-ordination in the areas of employment, pensions and social inclusion (Chapter 9).

Following earlier initiatives from the Organization for Economic Co-operation and Development (OECD), EU employment and inclusion programmes have emphasized the need for shifting from 'passive' to 'active' policies: the primary goal of social protection systems is to promote labour market participation among people of working age. Only for those who cannot work is the main objective to be providing adequate and secure income support. A key goal is to make social protection systems more 'employment-friendly', including to 'make work pay' and to ensure that the conditions, levels and duration of benefits do not create disincentives to work.

Similarly, the EU and the OECD claim that national governments should improve the 'employability' (skills, knowledge, etc.) of those who are at risk of becoming permanently excluded from economic activity and self-sufficiency. Likewise, governments should make the continuation of benefit payments for people of working age conditional on their accepting offers to take part in employment training measures. Thus various forms of 'activation' of protection systems, of recipients of cash benefits or of unemployed citizens should play a key role in the future development of European welfare states. Reforms of this kind are highly relevant for what we have called active citizenship according to a socio-liberal understanding (Chapters 4–6).

In the case of old-age pensions, achieving 'sustainability' means ensuring that the working population will not face disproportional and unrealistic financial burdens resulting from the design of 'pay as you go systems', combined with the ageing of populations and insufficient economic growth. One way or the other, people must downscale their expectations of their future pension levels, while shouldering greater individual responsibility for securing the purchase power of their pensions (Chapter 14).

Many researchers see the aspects of EU economic integration, legislation and action programmes that we touch upon here as exemplifying new constraints on the freedom of national governments to design and change their systems of welfare provisions (e.g. Ferrera 2005; Leibfried 2005). Yet we do not wish to overstate the degree to which 'Europeanization' has diminished the decision-making capacity of member states (Cowles *et al.* 2001; Olsen 2002). Moreover, 'social issues' or 'social policy' is still marginal within the common policy-making of the EU and secondary to the complete establishment of a single (and now enlarged) European market. The focus of the EU's involvement in the 'social dimension' has mainly been to ensure that national social protection systems do not impede the free movement of goods, services, capital and labour within the single market. Member states, reluctant to give up control over their redistributive systems (e.g. social benefits, employment, health and social services) refer to the subsidiarity principle of the Maastricht Treaty, meaning that what the member states can do adequately should not be done by the EU, unless it can do it better. At the same time, several scholars have suggested that national decision-makers have not fully realized the consequences of the greater economic openness resulting from European integration (Ferrera 2005; Leibfried 2005).

The impact of incorporating human rights in national legislation

The development of an international regime of human rights and protection against discrimination has important implications for the rights, opportunities and scope of citizen participation. We will briefly point to some important examples (Chapters 10 and 12):

- The UN Convention on Elimination of all Discrimination against Women (the Women's Convention, 1979) has – through ratification by national governments – granted women stronger formal protection.
- The adoption of the UN Convention on the Rights of the Child has given children stronger formal rights than previously existed in most countries (UN Doc A/44/49 1989).
- Agreement on a draft UN convention on the rights of people with disabilities (UN 2006).
- Earlier international conventions on the rights of indigenous populations have strengthened the rights of the Sami in Northern Europe and of the Innuits in Greenland (ILO 1989). Other groups like travellers, Romani people, Kvens and Jews have similarly achieved stronger legal protection against ethnic discrimination through the adoption of the European Framework Convention for the Protection of National Minorities (ETS No. 157).

The overall impact of the emerging international focus on human rights and protection against discrimination has probably yet to be fully acknowledged, mapped and assessed. Most significantly, these developments appear to substantially improve the 'opportunity structures' (Tarrow 2003) of individuals and groups. Generally speaking, opportunity structures refer to institutional, political and legal environments that can encourage or discourage individual and collective action by affecting actors' expectations for success or failure. In our context, these structures may involve improved possibilities for achieving recognition from public authorities and for presenting claims against either public agencies or non-governmental actors.

However, this perspective – that the transnational codification and strengthening of these rights open more active forms of citizenship – presupposes that people are aware of and knowledgeable about their rights and have the necessary resources for presenting claims. A related issue is whether bodies or organizations exist for supervising implementation of, and monitoring compliance with, the duties or requirements that these rights imply (Hvinden and Halvorsen 2003: Chapter 13).

Recently researchers have argued that the emergence of transnational regimes of human rights and non-discrimination provisions challenges the democratic dimension of the relationship between the (national) welfare state and its citizens (e.g. Østerud *et al.* 2003). However, the emergence of these regimes does not point exclusively towards a weakening of the democratic basis for national welfare states. We suggest that this regime strengthens the opportunities for citizens to exercise agency in relation to the welfare state and, in particular, to strengthen the position and capabilities of minorities and others whom the previous and existing policies of nation-states have marginalized or excluded. We see a potential for enriching social and political citizenship and for contributing to improved conditions for full citizenship for a larger proportion of the total population, in terms of rights and responsibilities, freedom of choice and participation. Such a contribution is significant, not only for concerns for equality of living conditions or economic efficiency but also for considerations about democracy.

The impact of individualization

As we have seen, contemporary welfare states face various challenges 'from below'. Widely accepted diagnoses of late-modern societies see a trend towards individualization and de-traditionalization (e.g. Beck and Beck-Gernsheim 2002; Beck and Willms 2004). These complex concepts involve something greater and different from individuals becoming more egoistic, self-centred or simply occupied with their own well-being. One key argument is that traditional, more spontaneous forms of community, collectivity and solidarity between people have lost much of their practical significance. The late modern individual is increasingly becoming decoupled from these kinds of social units, while spontaneous development of community and solidarity between people is found more rarely. Beck and Beck-Gernsheim (ibid.) suggest that 'solidarity' increasingly can be achieved only through the determined and conscious efforts of individuals, based on their knowledge, skills and capacity for reflection and their ability to negotiate a common understanding of the premises for collective action. To the extent that people succeed in such efforts, the resulting community is likely to be more fleeting than more traditional and spontaneous forms of collectivity. Beck and Beck-Gernsheim picture the individual as 'manufacturing' his or her personal identity or personal biography as a 'do-it-yourself' biography. These discussions have important implications for current concerns in many welfare states.

First, by providing individualized rights, redistributive welfare states like the Nordic ones have substantially contributed to the trend towards individualization. They have thus made the individual less dependent on his or her family and kin, neighbourhood and local community as sources of help and support (Trädgårdh 1997; Esping-Andersen 1999; Supiot 2003).

At the same time individualization potentially undermines the social solidarity on which these welfare states are based. For instance, individualization can contribute to pressures for reducing the overall scope of social protection systems and replacing them with a greater reliance on individual responsibility for protection against loss of income and other risks (e.g. through different forms of individual savings or pension plans).

But individualization does not necessarily preclude popular support for and acceptance of redistributive public provisions. Rather it implies that the population regularly needs to reassess and confirm its support for such arrangements. That an arrangement is long standing is not an argument for its continued existence. To sustain their legitimacy, political and organizational rationales require renewal. Individualization will particularly challenge social benefit systems that presuppose a long-term perspective and a fairly stable joint understanding among the affected parties.

For instance, public pension systems that are not based on earlier payment into funds but that mainly operate on 'pay as you go' principles presuppose an 'inter-generational contract'. From the individualization perspective, such contracts are largely a normative fiction: the willingness of new generations to comply with the expectation that they will cover the pension entitlements of earlier generations depends on whether they perceive their financial burden as reasonable and fair. If people believe that pension arrangements entail a disproportionate redistribution across generations, their belief will contribute to the political urgency of pension reforms (Chapter 14).

More generally, the individualization perspective indicates that no one can take for granted the legitimacy of established systems of social protection, despite their having been envisioned to last for a long time. Thus governments may soon face the task of facilitating broader public participation in discussions about the premises, objectives, ambitions and time horizons of such systems. Such public participation would also make it easier for governments to avoid what affected parties would perceive as broken promises and 'changing the rules in the middle of the game'.

Second, the strengthening of human rights and protection against discrimination, combined with citizen awareness of these legislative changes, may reinforce rights consciousness and stimulate litigation. Clearly, courts are somewhat replacing politically elected and accountable bodies as arenas for deciding who should get what. Especially in the United States, some scholars warn that even Nordic countries will experience a looser link between decisions made by political bodies and the actual distribution of income and social well-being (Kagan 2001; Burke 2004). Consequently, we may witness a shift of attention from questions about the socially desirable and just distribution of resources to concerns on the part of individuals and groups about maximizing their gains. New inequities may result if welfare outcomes increasingly depend on which resources individuals and groups can draw on in pursuing their rights through the court system.

Third, we also see that a number of changes in public welfare provisions are based on notions of individualization (or justified in terms of this trend) and a growing emphasis on providing customized individual (action) plans for the special needs and requirements of each person (Chapters 4–6). Arguments for this trend are that individuals today vary more in their preferences and life situations and that many measures would be ineffective if they do not respond to these differences. By rejecting 'one-size-fits-all' provisions – especially in the area of employment, social and care services – in favour of individual plans based on negotiations between provider and user (or even 'freedom of choice'), politicians themselves may also be contributing to raising citizens' expectations and demands for individualized solutions, i.e. further strengthening the individualization trend.

The impact of self-organization

Many of the rights claimed by citizens or groups of citizens have not been bestowed upon them. Social movements of women, ethnic minorities and people with impairments have campaigned for changes in legislative and public provision. They have increased policymakers' awareness of the issues, participated in the legislation and policy process, and worked to inform their constituencies about the opportunities created by new legislation and public provision. In some cases groups of citizens have even succeeded in side-stepping their national government through transnational networks, campaigning and lobbying supranational agencies or organizations to promote their case. The inclusion of the anti-discrimination clause in Article 13 of the Amsterdam Treaty and the consequent two directives would probably not have come about without the active efforts of transnational citizen networks (Chapter 13). When such efforts succeed, reluctant national authorities then respond to pressure 'from above', i.e. from the bodies of these supranational agencies or organizations and other member states (Chapter 9).

More generally, organizations and advocacy groups acting on behalf of these broader social movements are of great significance for understanding the process of changing or restructuring social protection policies. This role of organizations, also found among groups in marginal positions, may relate to what we call the turn towards active citizenship according to a republican understanding. The organizations represent not only an immediate arena for social participation and self-directed activities but also, indirectly, a setting for building self-confidence and capability for participation in the larger society and in negotiations with representatives of public authorities (Chapter 7).

The self-activity of various citizens groups is not exclusively – or even mainly – directed at obtaining stronger rights to particular material benefits. To a great extent, their efforts are concerned with recognition and identity politics (Fraser 1995). Several groups are struggling against public policies that have exposed them to social and cultural domination, and denied them respect and dignity, even existence. They claim the right not to be made invisible and silent, but to be heard and taken seriously by governmental bodies. In many cases, such groups insist that society recognize their difference from the majority population, in terms of culture, lifestyle, and their right to express this difference.

According to some observers, concerns with recognition have somewhat replaced issues of socio-economic redistribution in late modern, multicultural society (e.g. Young 1990). Others, like Fraser, have argued that social justice requires policies of both redistribution and recognition. Even so, the international trend towards recognition politics is adding to the complexity of contemporary citizenship.

The impact of 'pressure within'

Contemporary welfare states also face substantial challenges from demographic changes. Most Western European states have ageing populations, thus adding to the demands on social protection systems, especially public pension schemes of the 'pay-as-you-go' type. Leading scholars rank demographic ageing as one of the most important 'internal' challenges to welfare states (e.g. Esping-Andersen 1999; Pierson 2001). In addition, the long-term expansion of disability income and other *de facto* early retirement systems have boosted the calls for modernization and reform. Many countries have introduced reforms aimed at improving the long-term sustainability of public pension systems, tightening the eligibility rules and administrative practices for pre-retirement plans, restraining popular demands for early leave from the labour market and even increasing the actual average retirement age (Chapter 14). Most European governments, however, have been reluctant to open greater immigration flows from non-Western countries as a means of reducing the demographic ageing. Yet without the existing immigration from these countries, the population of many European countries would start to diminish in a few years time.

Finally, additional demands fall on the social protection system as family life, patterns of partnering, and parenting and working careers become more changeable. Together with the trend towards individualization and the weakening of traditional social bonds, these changes may lead to new requirements for support from social protection systems during critical phases of adult life.

The impact of new forms of governance

The role of the state in welfare provision is undergoing change, as the state to a lesser extent is the sole or dominating provider of protection against risks. This trend is associated with the development of more complex, dynamic structures of governance over welfare provision (Johansson and Hvinden 2005; Newman 2005). In some respects, the state has taken on more active roles, e.g. combating discrimination and social exclusion, and 'activating' the unemployed. In other respects, however, the state is retreating from its previous tasks, actively encouraging individuals and market actors to provide the services and protection themselves.

We cannot simply view the new, more complex governance structures associated with these changes as a consequence of the more multifaceted emergent forms of active citizenship. Neither can we view these new forms of citizenship as simply resulting from recent changes in the structures of welfare governance. The dynamic relationship between the two is probably better captured by Weber's concept of 'elective affinity' (Ringer 1997): a mutually enabling and active resonance between two social phenomena. This resonance also reinforces the general nature of the turn towards active citizenship; it is not limited to one section or subgroup of the population.

Active citizenship: only for the poor or for the well-off?

Recent reforms in many countries have involved not only a stronger emphasis on obligations but also more explicit notions of individual responsibility, freedom of choice and contract, and citizen participation and dialogue. We expect that the practical impact of these notions on people's lives will differ by socio-economic status, gender and ethnicity. The question, bluntly put, is whether active citizenship in the socio-liberal sense is mainly for the poor and socially excluded, while active citizenship in the libertarian and republican senses are for the well-integrated and more affluent sections of the population.

We assume that the emerging patterns of active citizenship are more complex and ambiguous than this question suggests. Even people traditionally seen as socially and economically well integrated are now facing activation demands, while people with impairments are benefiting from a greater array of choices (e.g. vouchers for personal assistance, home help and transport services). Moreover, even poor and excluded groups now have a voice in consultation and negotiation with public authorities, on the basis of self-organization (Chapters 7 and 9). Nevertheless, we still need to carefully examine the implications of various dimensions of active citizenship for different sections of the population. In particular, we must discover whether, and to what respect, these implications diminish or reinforce existing patterns of marginality.

Opening citizenship – three questions for investigation

In this book we argue that we need to open social citizenship, both as a theoretical construct and as a topic for empirical research. The two main reasons are these:

First, ongoing changes in the relationship between citizens and (national) welfare states suggest that none of the traditional understandings of citizenship (socio-liberal, libertarian and republican) can fully help us to understand social citizenship. We expect this relationship to increasingly involve issues of rights and duties, self-responsibility and choice, participation and co-determination *at the same time* or *in relation to the same individuals*. Our conceptualization of social citizenship needs to be sensitive to this complexity, rather than trying to suppress or neglect it.

Second, the opening of national protection systems – both for supranational bodies' influence and for non-nationals' use – challenges existing concepts of social citizenship. The emerging international regime of human rights, the evolving transnational economic integration and the increasing cross-national labour migration are among the key aspects of this openness. Any analysis of social citizenship must include the interplay between processes at national and transnational levels, and the way in which such interactions create a new framework for social citizenship.

We therefore introduce three broad questions that the rest of the book will try to answer:

1 As a result of the transformations of societies and welfare policies described as an 'opening within', are policymakers and welfare reforms giving a stronger emphasis to the 'active' side of citizenship (as framed within each model)?
2 Are normative ideas and notions conventionally associated with different models of active citizenship – 'fulfilling duties' (socio-liberal citizenship), 'exercising choice and self-responsibility' (libertarian citizenship), 'participating in deliberation and decision-making' (republican citizenship) – combined or intertwined in practice (an 'opening between')? If so, do these hybrids give rise to tensions and ambiguities?
3 Can we observe a weakening of the strong bonds traditionally found between national welfare states and social citizenship, in that international influence or interactions between national and supranational levels of governance are increasingly determining the actual content of social citizenship? In other words, do we see a trend towards the 'denationalization' of social citizenship?

Later chapters present a number of detailed case studies dealing with important areas of welfare policy, legislation and practice. Most of the analyses focus on Nordic countries, either by studying developments within them, by comparing Nordic countries with other European welfare states, or by dealing with relationships between the EU and the Nordic countries. Reasons of both principle and pragmatism underlie this choice. While the presumed challenges to established forms of welfare provisions and understandings of social citizenship are taking place in many Western welfare states, these challenges are likely to be particularly significant in the Nordic context.

The Nordic welfare states share many characteristics that distinguish them from other welfare states. This distinctiveness is often called a 'Nordic (or Scandinavian)' welfare model (e.g. Kautto *et al.* 2001; Kangas and Palme 2005; Kildal and Kuhnle 2005). These characteristics include relatively high governmental welfare benefits, comparatively high welfare employment and public employment relative to total employment, vertical and tax-financed redistribution of resources, universal citizenship-based social rights (underpinned by public policies for maximizing employment, including female employment), and high political legitimacy for public benefits. Therefore, the Nordic countries represent natural laboratories for investigating how new and more multifaceted forms of social citizenship emerge as the net result of – or in response to – the diverse challenges we are discussing. Moreover, this book is based on research funded by the Welfare Research Programme (2002–2005) of the Nordic Council of Ministers.

Given that the research underlying this book greatly focuses on changes related to the Nordic welfare states, we ask whether we are additionally witnessing a *shift within Nordic social citizenship,* involving greater emphasis on elements from libertarian and republican citizenship and relatively less on elements from socio-liberal citizenship.

Outline of the book

One major issue in this book is the ways in which greater economic openness and integration are challenging the sovereignty of national welfare states to determine the features of their systems of social protection and, consequently, the contents of social citizenship. Although some authors relate these processes to globalization or internationalization in general (Chapter 2), most examine different implications of European integration. These include the opening of national social benefit systems to promote cross-border mobility and establish a single market for services (Chapters 10 and 11). Other examples are the efforts of the European Union to get member states to modernize and activate their social protection systems (Chapter 4), to do more to promote social inclusion of marginal groups (Chapter 9) and to combat discrimination of various kinds (Chapters 10, 12 and 13).

In contrast to the emphasis in much of the scholarly debate about internationalization and Europeanization, the authors do not merely investigate the erosion of national systems of welfare provision or social citizenship. In addition, they ask whether we can see elements of a new European system of social protection or citizenship emerging. They also seek to identify both the constraints that European economic openness and integration imply and the new opportunities that these processes create for enacting citizenship.

A second issue is the manner in which activation policies, i.e. government efforts to promote the employment of marginalized groups through active measures and a tightening of social benefit systems, impact the contents of social citizenship. Activation policies redraw the balance between the rights and duties associated with social citizenship – a major concern within the socio-liberal concepts of citizenship (Chapters 3–6).

However, both on national and European levels, policymakers have 'packaged' the introduction of benefit cuts and the reinforcement of citizens' obligations with promises of new scope for choice and co-determination, especially through participation in the formulation of individual action plans (Chapters 4–6). This packaging suggests that activation policies are also relevant for libertarian and republican conceptualizations of citizenship. At the same time the rhetoric of choice and co-determination may make citizens claiming social benefits more self-confident and less deferential. They may more easily state their reservations against requirements they consider meaningless or limiting. If the authorities try to construct marginalized citizens as their 'customers' or 'partners', these citizens may respond by demanding the freedom and scope for negotiation that such appellations imply. Activation reforms may even unwittingly contribute to social mobilization and greater visibility of marginal citizens in the public space. If so, activation reforms also become pertinent to active republican citizenship, in an unexpected and paradoxical way (Chapter 7).

A third issue is the increased role of anti-discrimination and human rights legislation in promoting the well-being of citizens, especially citizens at the margins of mainstream society. So far the impact of anti-discrimination legislation has been most obvious in the area of gender relations. A combination of human rights and anti-discrimination legislation is now covering new ground, e.g. ethnicity and disability (Chapters 10, 12 and 13). This expansion is particularly significant for citizenship because several forms of discrimination can occur simultaneously, e.g. gender and ethnic discrimination (Chapters 8 and 12). To the extent that anti-discrimination and human rights provisions are incorporated in national legislation and enforced by courts and other appropriate agencies, marginalized groups obtain new opportunities for protecting their independence, integrity and dignity.

A fourth issue is the way in which the responsibility for social protection is shifted from the collective level to the individual level. We find this shift even in the Nordic countries, where governments for a long time have established a collective responsibility for a broad range of welfare provision. The introduction of individual action plans in several areas of social protection is one example of this trend towards 'individualization' (Chapters 4–6). Both in the Nordic countries and elsewhere, pension reforms are now a major context for promoting stronger individual responsibility for risk protection (Chapter 14). The establishment of a single market in Europe is likely to give a greater role to social protection accomplished through the market and, consequently, to individual responsibility exercised through market citizenship (Chapter 10). To the extent that anti-discrimination legislation and similar forms of social regulation are more compatible with market liberalization than costly redistributive welfare systems, the European single market may also strengthen individual responsibility for implementing social protection (Chapters 10 and 13).

Finally, in Chapter 15, we draw together the main findings of the book's theoretical and empirical studies and discuss the implications of these findings for the opening of citizenship and the development of a new, multifaceted understanding of social citizenship.

2 From active states to active citizenship?

The impact of economic openness and transnational governance

Stefanía Óskarsdóttir

Introduction

This chapter examines the long-term development of citizenship in a changing political and economic context. From the beginning of the modern era, nation-states and citizenship were comprehensible only in relation to each other. This linkage reached its ultimate expression in the relations between redistributive welfare states and social citizenship in the second half of the twentieth century. Recently we have witnessed a reaction against the growth of public spending on welfare, involving efforts to privatise welfare provision and mobilize citizens' responsibility for managing their own welfare. This reaction was partly stimulated by trends towards globalization, greater openness between national economies and new forms of transnational governance, for instance through the European Union. These developments have challenged established notions of national sovereignty and citizenship.

Democracy, which refers to popular control over government, played a significant role in shaping modern states. In pre-modern times state power was synonymous with those of sovereign monarchs. But with modernization and the growth of democratic institutions states took on greater responsibilities towards their subjects while demanding greater individual contributions in terms of taxes and defence of national borders. In return, the state granted citizens various individual rights meant to enhance their economic and personal well-being.

A state's capacity to deliver security and welfare provisions depends on the steady generation of income and the compliance of the general population. Once one or both are threatened, a process leading to political reforms is usually set in motion. The welfare state is the product of political compromises between competing economic interests, for at the core of politics is the allocation of resources. The welfare state was also founded on the widely accepted idea of a collective responsibility for the more vulnerable in society. Yet to the present day the scope of this collective responsibility remains politically contested. While some put the highest value on social equality others contend that social justice is best served by safeguarding the right of people to reap the benefits of their hard work and individual initiative. For a long time these conflicting views have framed the political debate in Western countries.

This chapter will examine the links between economic and political developments that have shaped ideas about the role and scope of state power relative to its citizens. Both the rise of the welfare state and the development of democratic ideals provide a legacy that shape modern political realities. In recent years, we can detect a growing public acceptance of the capitalist ethos of profit-seeking and consumerism in all European states. At the same time, the public of Western democracies appears less trusting of governments and more cynical about the political process than previous generations. These trends, as well as public deficits and political pressures to hold unemployment and inflation at bay, have contributed to a redirection of the political discourse on citizenship. They have challenged the political dimension of citizenship, calling into question widely accepted ideas about the role of the state.

The emergence of nation-states and citizenship rights

A *state* may be defined as a political organization whose rule is territorially ordered and which is able to mobilize the means of violence to sustain that rule. The state has the power to decide whom it recognizes as its citizens. Those who live within the state boundaries are generally aware of their membership in this political community and of the rights and obligations such a membership confers. The formation of a stable political community also requires an acceptance from the community that the state elite and its institutions have a right to rule. Democratic developments have mostly been a response to pressures from below on rulers who depended on the support of the general public. The larger the scope of the state, the more pressing the issue of political legitimacy becomes (Giddens 1985). Related to this issue is the fact that the state's power rests on the state's ability to set political goals and carry them out. Those goals are dependent on economic resources and the ability to secure compliance.

Efforts to secure borders from invading armies, stemming from the ability to raise money to buy provisions and arms and, not the least, to pay loyal troops, were probably the trigger that set off the development towards the modern day nation-state. Extending the tax base was necessary, in turn calling for the development of means to account for all citizens, registering them and assigning them certain duties and rights. By contrast, the removal of liberties, or the threat of their removal, became standard disciplinary practice in the emerging nation-states in Europe (e.g. Giddens 1985). Efforts to extend the tax base and increasing administrative efficiency also involved attempts at standardizing language and customs. Such efforts contributed to a sense of a national identity within the state, thereby reproducing political legitimacy.

The modern project of nation-state building required a standing professional military that could defend national sovereignty, or even assist in expanding existing state boundaries. This undertaking required material resources. Increasing commerce and industrialization helped in this regard, because both contributed to economic growth. Merchants benefited from the widening trade made possible by a unified economy in which local barriers to commerce were reduced. They also earned profits from trade with the newly opened lands in Asia and the New World, a trade that in turn stimulated local production. The state gained from the tariff revenues derived from large trade, from the sale of monopolies, from the development of strategic industries and from the general economic growth that provided a firm economic base for national power (Fusfeld 1986).

On the eve of the industrial revolution, mercantilists argued that states created national wealth by ensuring that theirs did not flow out of the country. To this end they argued for protecting national industries, keeping foreign imports to a minimum and acquiring colonies to increase the size of the 'home market' and the tax base. By the eighteenth century, however, many were sceptical of mercantilism. In particular, British liberal economists attacked restrictions on international trade and fought for an end to tariffs, monopolies and regulations. Their arguments had wide implications for the development of democratic values and citizenship rights and called forth counter-arguments from those who held different views. All this, in turn, helped these concepts evolving.

Liberal economists based their argument on the social theory that individual motives, however selfish, resulted in benefits to society as a whole. They found the source of wealth neither in trade nor agriculture but in human labour. Only through individual effort, they argued, does production take place and human needs receive satisfaction. The labour theory of value did not emphasize wealth or the aggrandisement of national power as ends in themselves. Wealth was wealth because it made people better off. The production of wealth, furthermore, depended not on the fertility of the soil or on favourable trade balances but on the individual incentives of ordinary people. The motive to work was the need to provide food, clothing, shelter and comforts. The greater the incentive to work, the greater would be the production of wealth, and the faster humanity would move toward prosperity (Fusfeld 1986: 17).

Economic liberalism was closely linked to a political theory that called for civil liberties and the curbing of state power. Proponents argued that *natural law* dictated that all men were created equal and had inalienable rights to life, liberty and property, none of which could be taken away without due process of law (early liberal theory did not include women in the notion of citizenship, see Pateman 1988). The rights to life, liberty and property became the central focus of ideas of liberal citizenship. John Locke, in particular, developed this line of thinking in the second part of the seventeenth century. He, and later economic liberals, argued that the first requisite for national economic growth was the protection of private property, for unless the right to property was sustained, the incentive to work was reduced and the production of wealth would decrease (Fusfeld 1986: 18). This argument supported the claim that people could not be taxed unless they gave their consent and had a say in how tax revenues were to be spent. Representative government became a rallying cry of liberals who fought conservatives on this issue.

The theory of the *social contract* was no less important for the evolution of democratic thought. Since Thomas Hobbes, the theory of the social contract implied that at some point in history people gathered together and created the state, giving its ruler certain powers which they could take back if the ruler betrayed their trust (Kymlicka 2002: 61; Kelly 2005: 21). According to social contract theory, the government was created by the people, for the people and (should be) of the people, as stated in Abraham Lincoln's Gettysburg Address. The social contract theory gave all citizens a stake in the running of the government and subjected the ruler to supervision from below. This republican notion of citizenship views the political community as the creation of citizens, whose engagement in the political process gives them a social meaning.

These ideas, that natural law and the social contract transferred the source of state power from the divine to the popular masses, proved powerful weapons in the fight for creating representative legislatures and extending voting rights. The concept of *citizenship* evolved as these ideas were debated and put into practice. Citizenship rights eventually fell into three separate categories: civil rights, political rights and social rights (Marshall 1965): *civil rights* grant individuals the right to associate freely with one another, to live where they want, and to enjoy freedom of speech and justice in accordance with the rule of law. *Political rights* give citizens the right to participate in the political process and exercise political power. *Social rights* concern the right of everyone within the state to enjoy a minimum standard of life, economic welfare and security. The acceptance of these rights, often written into formal constitutions, transformed the political processes within states. Organized political parties and interest groups emerged, becoming an integral part of interest intermediation. Their role became that of articulating particular interests and pushing for their realization within the parameters of a stable government.

These political and economic theories set the stage for modern politics. Different emphasis on citizenship rights is usually a litmus test for adherence to political parties. Political parties situated on the left of the political spectrum have traditionally focused on social rights. They have campaigned for an active state that guarantees that all citizens enjoy an acceptable standard of living. Parties to the right of centre have been more reluctant to support such claims. They have, in the tradition of the liberal economists, generally argued that by accepting such a responsibility the state is encroaching upon the private sphere – mostly by taxing private incomes and property beyond acceptable levels – with the result that people lose the incentive to work and try to avoid paying taxes.

Sovereignty in the age of economic openness

The democratic evolution described above was anchored in the belief that citizenship is inherently linked with the existence of a sovereign state which '... entails that there is a political authority in the political community which has undisputed right to determine the framework of rules and regulations in a given territory and to govern accordingly' (Held 1989: 215). Respect for sovereignty in the international system has also traditionally meant that foreign powers refrain from interfering in a state's domestic affairs. But developments in recent decades have seen important changes in the abilities and mechanisms of sovereign states to deal with their political agendas and manage their conflicts and resources. For example, in an increasingly global marketplace, companies have the option of escaping high taxes and restrictions on their operations by moving them to other countries, with the consequent loss of local jobs and state revenues. National governments are already dealing with the impact of such moves. In many instances this has led to the increasing co-operation between governments on the inter-state level and an emerging regime of international or transnational governance.

Various international treaties and organizations affect the ability of states to retain exclusive power over how they conduct their domestic affairs. Admittedly, states are usually bound only by treaties and conventions they have voluntarily signed and agreed to uphold. In this formal sense, sovereignty is still the constitutive principle of international law. In practice, however, the voluntary acceptance of treaties and conventions leads to a substantial degree of self-binding on the part of a national government, for instance because lack of compliance is associated with loss of either international standing or economic gains.

Diplomacy, international organizations and public international law are not alone in shaping the regulatory regime states find themselves in. Networks among agents and norms – standards of expected behaviour – that are widely accepted among agents also shape outcomes in the international sphere (Keohane and Nye 2000: 19). In reality states find themselves operating in a co-operative web of a compromised sovereignty. A case in point is the fast-evolving co-operation among European states in the post-WWII period. Right after the war the American administration attached to its aid package to Europe (the Marshall Plan) certain conditions for receiving aid. Similarly, the creation of the North Atlantic Treaty Alliance (NATO) took defence issues out of the hands of partners to that treaty. Furthermore, a closer institutional integration through which a semi-sovereign West Germany was accepted back into the regional system set the stage for the creation of the European Common Market. Within this dual framework of Atlantic and West European institutions, West European states rebuilt their national legitimacy through providing stable government, welfare and prosperity to their citizens (Wallace 1999: 85). Since then European states have pursued even closer ties through the European Union and a single European market.

Scholars and politicians alike do not agree whether these developments have undermined the sovereign foundation of such states; thereby affected the principle of popular control over government. Some argue that states have simply pooled their sovereignty to cope with various economic and political pressures and to deliver political promises. Their reasoning is that the transformation of Europe's economy and society in the 1970s and 1980s pushed West European states into sharing previously sovereign powers over policy. The economic recession in the 1970s marked a period of economic adjustment in which international companies moved from national to transnational manufacturing. Progress in communications facilitated this shift by allowing the development of Europe-wide marketing, consequently extending nationally based services across national boundaries. Improvements in physical communications, combined with rising affluence, sparked a parallel surge in individual border crossing – both short-term and long-term – for pleasure, work, study or retirement (Wallace 1999: 89). In response to these changes, establishing closer international co-operation became attractive to governments hard pressed to serve their citizens' interests.

Inevitably, the increasing importance of trade, capital movement and other economic transactions across borders has had ramifications for the ongoing debate about the social rights of citizenship (Moses 2000; Pierson 2001). Those who see sovereignty as undermined maintain that the internationalization of production, finance and other such resources has eroded the capacity of the state to control its own economic and social agenda. They point out that technology has increased the mobility of economic units and the sensitivities of markets (and societies) to one another, thereby reducing the possibility of a national economic policy. They believe that government efforts to co-operate on the inter-state level have not helped sovereign states maintain their capabilities to carry out independent policy-making. Leibfried and Pierson (1995: 70), for example, show that

> ... the European Union intervenes in the social polices of member states in two ways: First, by enacting some significant social policies of its own and, secondly, by striking down features of national systems that are deemed incompatible with the development of the single market.

Their conclusion is that the process of European integration has consequential impacts on the social polices of member states because the economic policies of the European Union, and the responses of social actors to those policies, pressure national welfare states to modify their social programmes.

Despite their disagreements about what increasing international policy co-ordination means for formal state sovereignty, most scholars agree that these developments are changing our perceptions of the political community, the role of the nation-state and the future of democracy. Some years ago, Held (1989: 214) noted that political theory, which assumes that one can understand the proper nature of the polity by reference to the nation-state, was under strain in the face of major twentieth century developments. These developments are already testing the meaning of democracy. For example, if political decision-making is removed from governments, the relevance of active political participation at the national level will likely be questioned. The apparent erosion of national political accountability has in all likelihood already had political ramifications. In all developed countries, traditional political participation, such as voting and joining political parties, is on the decline, and citizens are showing less faith in their elected leaders (Ingelhart 1997). But the legitimacy of the modern welfare state rests not only on its claim to be democratically governed but also on its ability to settle political conflicts. The development of an active state in the post-WWII era was the product of various political settlements between competing socio-economic interests.

Economic goals and redistributive welfare provision

The welfare state provides mechanisms for stabilizing the flow of income and basic services for people at risk of serious income loss (Hicks 1999: 13). Public services and income schemes also aim at facilitating class mobility, educating the work force, equalizing opportunities and contributing to better health among its citizens, thereby increasing political and social cohesion within the community and promoting economic growth within the nation-state.

When the modern welfare state developed after WWII, many believed that achieving both economic growth and political stability was possible through ensuring the economic inclusion of all citizens. That political climate assumed the rights of citizens to a secure livelihood. Citizens could now depend upon the state or upon local governments to provide for them when they failed to do so themselves (Marshall 1965), as part of a bargain between the tax-paying public and the state. In recent years this bargain, however, has begun to come under some strain.

Although the responsibility for deciding how much money governments must raise and how they are going to spend it rests with elected leaders, negotiations between various interests also shape the content of economic policies. Of the interest groups with influence over economic policies, employers' associations and trade unions have been the most powerful. The bargaining among these groups and the outcome of negotiations have affected the development of welfare polices and socio-economic entitlements. This has been the most apparent in countries where *neo-corporatist* arrangements have characterized the relationship between trade unions and the state. Neo-corporatism refers to a process of interest intermediation, which involves policy negotiations between state agencies and interest organizations arising from the social labour divisions. Historically, countries like Sweden, Norway, Denmark, the Netherlands, Japan, and more recently, Ireland and Iceland have relied on neo-corporatist bargaining. The process arrives at and helps implement policy through the collaboration of interest organizations and their willingness and ability to secure the compliance of their members (Grant 1985). Neo-corporatism effectively means that unions and employers associations receive some of the state's traditional powers for making economic policy. At the same time, it often has allowed the state to gain greater influence over the workings of the market.

Various theories have been advanced to explain why neo-corporatism arises. One theory holds that Fordist mass production methods contributed to the establishment of centralised bargaining and neo-corporatist public policy-making structures. Katzenstein (1985), however, has argued that neo-corporatism is likely to develop in small states, which are dependent on foreign markets for selling their products and need to import a huge variety of goods, i.e. open economies. He posits that insulating the economy from global market fluctuations calls for small states to create buffers that protect the livelihood of citizens and avoid political upheavals – hence the development of the welfare state, with its centralised bargaining structures and extensive welfare provisions.

Centralised bargaining over wage agreements requires highly centralised associations of both trade unions and employers. Some argue that under such conditions, producers' groups can negotiate agreements not only involving agreements on wage increases and the working conditions of those directly involved but also sometimes linking these to state promises to compensate incomes in other ways. Such compensation might include changing taxes, increasing social benefits or combating inflation. The incentive for state participation in such negotiations is that they might aid the state in achieving its economic goals, e.g. keeping inflation under control, maintaining employment levels and securing economic growth. State involvement in wage negotiations implies the consideration of wider interests – such as those of the unemployed, people with impairments or retired persons – partly because workers at some point are likely to find themselves in one or more of these conditions. Thus policies that have arisen from neo-corporatist wage bargaining have affected the whole of society and contributed to the expanding web of policies aimed at attaining various economic, social and political goals.

In countries where neo-corporatist mechanisms were not so strong the institutionalization of an active state in the post-WWII era was aided by a wide political acceptance of an economic theory called after the influential economist, John Maynard Keynes. Keynesian economics were founded on the hypothesis that by using monetary management and an active fiscal policy (i.e. government spending and taxing policies) economic growth could be sustained. The theory had implications for the development of the welfare state because it promoted social policies emphasizing the redistribution of income. The theory held that the way to avoid a serious economic recession, like that of the 1930s, was to invest in public works and to follow a monetary policy that makes borrowing money easier by lowering interest rates in an economic downturn (Keynes 1936). Keynes also claimed that the redistribution of wealth was healthy for the economy and helped keep recession away. Maintaining high demand levels would keep production from falling and would secure employment levels. Thus Keynes argued that deficit spending was not a problem in a depressed economy but actually the very cure; and besides deficits would disappear in more prosperous times.

Keynesian economics remained popular well into the 1970s, until a 'stagflation' hit much of Western Europe and North America. Suddenly, despite generous welfare transfers many countries found themselves suffering from high inflation and high unemployment rates, both of which strained public finances. Moreover, political leaders discovered that tax increases were increasingly difficult to carry out without public support. In addition, the internationalization of trade and finance made it easier for companies to escape local taxes and high labour costs. Keynes' economic theory seemed less appropriate to provide the right answers for an increasingly global economy, where inflation may be imported and capital is mobile, therefore it came under attack, most notably from neo-liberals who argued that deficit spending was costing the economy dearly because it kept up interest rates, making all investment more expensive and causing inflation. They also claimed that *demand-side* economics, which both social democrats and conservatives had practised since the 1930s, only exacerbated economic problems. Instead they called for *supply-side* economics, which – rather than attempting to keep production up by providing incomes subsidies – focused on using monetary policy to enhance production. Consequently, governments were advised to curb public spending and cut taxes.

In the economic and political climate of the late 1970s, neo-liberalism gained political momentum, as best witnessed by the electoral victories of Margaret Thatcher in 1979 and Ronald Reagan in 1980. Both Reagan and Thatcher saw deregulation and the privatization of public companies as the most effective ways of cutting back state spending, and other states soon followed their lead. These new policies signalled a political change that put traditional social democracy and the welfare state on the defensive.

Apart from the impact of increasing internationalization of capital, the political and economic effects of new production methods and the decline of the power of trade unions contributed to the changing political climate. Changing production methods meant that product lifetimes were becoming shorter, and technology and innovations were playing a larger role. New forms of working conditions created a demand for highly skilled workers and more flexible work hours. Such a labour force is less likely to be unionized than the more traditional working force. This in turn undermines union strength during collective bargaining and in national politics.

Another contributing factor to the decline of faith in Keynesian economics was the rivalries between public and private sector unions and a wage drift among public employees (Katz 1993). Keynes had assumed that, in prosperous times, governments would reduce public spending and minimize its interference in the market – a practice that had trouble materializing, because political and economic realities make firing public workers and rolling back public programmes on short notice very difficult. Contrary to Keynesian thought, public agencies tend to expand rather than shrink. By the 1980s, businesses were increasingly arguing that wages in the public sector were driving up costs in the private sector, making it harder for them to compete in global markets. Thus a growing number of people increasingly began viewing taming the welfare system and cutting welfare spending as important political priorities. This attitudinal change set the stage for governments to attempt welfare reforms.

From active states to active citizenship?

The breakdown of the consensus regarding the benefits of generous welfare spending led to substantial changes in political programmes in many developed countries. In particular, parties wanting to appeal to the political centre, where in fact a lot of votes are to be found, have been experimenting with programmes meant to put brakes on ever-increasing public spending. The implementation of some of these programmes has been promoted under the banners of private responsibility and individual choice. The terminology of '*active citizenship*' is closely related to such political efforts. Seen in this context, active citizenship appears as the antithesis of the active state, i.e. a state that actively intervenes in the market with the aim of promoting social goals.

Although neo-liberals spearheaded the movement against an overly active state, other political forces have come to agree with many of their claims. In various countries, social democratic parties have changed their traditional stance, realizing that their old platforms, steeped in the tradition of the interventionist state, would not get them elected in the new political and economic climate. The British Labour Party, for example, found the Conservative Party – who stood for less state interference in the economy – repeatedly defeating them at the polls. Those interested in modernizing the Labour Party and increasing its electoral appeal began campaigning for a renewal of social democracy. The reforms centred on curbing the increasing rigidness and bureaucratization of the modern welfare state which, as was argued, had begun to undermine the public support on which it rests. Among those calling for this kind of renewal was Anthony Giddens (1998). He argued that social democratic parties could no longer rely on the support of the working class for re-election, because the traditional working class is shrinking while the middle class is expanding. Giddens called his solution the 'Third Way', which he saw as a compromise between neo-liberal criticism and traditional social democratic values.

When the government of Tony Blair, under the banner of New Labour, took office in 1997 after 18 years of rule by the Conservative Party, it set out to reform the welfare state. One important goal was to cut the number of welfare recipients. The government viewed education and 'welfare-to-work' programmes as the most effective ways of getting the unemployed and the dependent into the workforce. By fostering a renewal of civic awareness and a turn towards a more active citizenship, leading politicians hoped to help people out of dependency. A former senior Labour government minister, David Blunkett, put it like this:

> The Government must continue to fundamentally redefine its relationship with the people it serves, and empower communities and boost active citizenship ... I am looking to promote a form of positive consumerism where to get something back from society; we need to encourage people to put something in ... We are truly free when we act together as members of a community to shape our own lives. That is what real democracy is all about – the participation of citizens in the society in which they live, with an enabling state providing the resources, legislation, framework and accumulation of assets and capacity building, to equalize the chance of this becoming a reality for those without wealth or access to sources of personal advancement ... There are many challenges to achieving this – particularly the modern dilemma of how to engage people in mainstream politics.
>
> (Blunkett 2003)

The concern here is that citizens may have come to take state services for granted and lost sight of the fact that they share the public sphere with the rest of the community. This is evidenced by a decline in political involvement and civic awareness. Some attribute this to modernity itself, arguing that it fosters individualism and indifference to public life. In a very large comparative study Ingelhart (1997) outlined a development that points to a fundamental change in cultural values in industrial societies. His study shows that a new world-view is gradually replacing the outlook that dominated industrializing societies since the Industrial Revolution, transforming the basic norms governing politics, work, religion, family and sexual behaviour. An emphasis on quality-of-life issues is replacing older class-based social cleavages. The new outlook (or post-modernization) deemphasizes all kinds of authority, whether religious or secular, allowing a much wider range for individual autonomy in the pursuit of subjective well-being. Ingelhart claims that these changes in values also lead people to reject hierarchical, bureaucratic, centralized, big government (Ingelhart 1997: 79–80). It is this new electorate that political reformers are addressing.

In some ways Ingelhart's findings support the theory that de Tocqueville advanced in *Democracy in America* (published in the 1830s), in which he claimed that indifference to public life and active citizenship resulted from the development of highly centralized administrative methods for enacting modernizing reforms (Maletz 2003: 17). Criticism of the rigidities of modern bureaucracies that provide social benefits has been one of the concerns of welfare reformers. Beck (1999: 70–71), for example, argues that governments increasingly delegate public policy-making to experts who bypass or pre-empt the democratic process. Thus he calls for the opening of the public sphere and an active involvement of the general public in issues affecting their livelihood and survival. Likewise, Giddens maintains that the

> social welfare state is essentially undemocratic, depending as it does upon a top-down distribution of benefits. Its motive force is protection and care, but it does not give enough space to personal liberty. Some forms of welfare institutions are bureaucratic, alienating and inefficient and welfare benefits can create perverse consequences that undermine what they are designed to achieve.
>
> (Giddens 1998: 114–15)

To circumvent these problems, welfare reformers are increasingly looking for ways to cut down on red tape and remodel public services so that they become more receptive to the needs of their users. One such way is to allow competition within the public service sector, while continuing its public funding. In this model, the consumer of public services is expected to make informed choices about which services to use in much the same way individuals have traditionally made their choices in the marketplace. By making room for choice within the public service system, policymakers hope they can achieve two things: introducing the efficiency of the market economy into the public sector and sustaining the public commitment to social justice.

In the 1990s European welfare reformers looked to the United States for inspiration. When Bill Clinton was elected the US president in 1992, the Democrats had been out of power for a long time, mainly because voters feared that their policies promoted big government and tax increases. To win back public trust, Clintonites argued that limiting deficit spending was very important for the health of the economy. Clinton's solution was to combine targeted tax cuts, aimed at the middle class, with measures to activate people on welfare by offering them assistance in improving their skills and making it easier for them to re-enter the labour market. The guiding idea was that public spending on things like education was a necessary form of public investment, helping Americans stay competitive in world markets and contributing to higher economic growth (e.g. Reich 1998). The belief was that an active civil society would not only save public money but also invigorate government through the creation of dense networks of individual relationships, which in turn would create the bonds essential for civic engagement and effective democratic governance (Katz 2001). These attempts were viewed with interest by many European policymakers who were also starting to experiment with various ways to activate their citizens.

The political shift away from the active state has included the privatization of public companies and the deregulations of industries. The result has been the transfer of control over decision-making away from politicians to private owners and consumers. Inevitably, this change alters the content of politics, because many important economic decisions no longer take place in the political arena but in the market. But the shift has also given the state a new, important function as a *regulator* of the economy ensuring that the market operates fairly, according to principles usually defined through collective channels. Ideally, the regulatory state watches over both the market and services that decentralized public agencies provide. Increasingly, European governments have been moving away from their traditional modes of governance as interventionist states to regulatory ones, with rule-making replacing taxing and spending (Majone 1997).

The failure of active fiscal polices to secure economic growth, the process of privatization, and the growing importance of the single European market, which requires clearly defined ground rules and the capacity to enforce them clearly contributed to the rise of the regulatory regime (Majone 1999: 309). Interestingly, the 'deregulation' associated with the building of a single European market has simultaneously led to new forms of regulation – re-regulation, now often carried out at the European level of governance. The regulative framework is the most apparent within the realm of economic and social policies. *Economic regulation* is usually a response to some form of a market failure and often centres on controlling price, demand or supply. While *social regulation* may also be a response to some forms of market failure, it often is an attempt at achieving wider social goals (Majone 1993). It attempts to change the behaviour of enterprises, organizations and individual decision-makers to promote social goals, e.g. to prevent discrimination. Systems for economic and social regulation often co-exist and interact.

Even if governments increasingly seek ways to opt out of directly providing public services, reliance on state oversight will likely continue to grow. In this more passive role the state becomes the venue for determining and settling issues of fairness and quality, while mostly market forces produce goods and services. Whether these changes will be more cost-effective, however, is unknown. Undoubtedly, theorists, politicians and the general public will continue to debate the issue and suggest new ways of managing our collective problems and responsibilities.

Concluding remarks

This chapter has suggested that as the active engagement of the state in the economy has been reduced, calls for active citizenship have become louder. Economic and political developments convinced many that welfare reforms were necessary because established practices did not seem to fit new realities. These realities include the effects of the internationalization of capital and increasing inter-governmental co-operation, as well as changes in production methods, the class system and changes in values. European welfare states are challenged by neo-liberal ideas about the scope of the state and demands for opening the public sphere to allow more personal autonomy and, at times, more democratic decision-making on issues that concern citizens.

These challenges have resulted in the ongoing redefinition of the relationship between the state and citizens, and a reconfiguration between the public and the private. As these developments call for reshaping policies and practices, they are perhaps changing the content of what it means to be a citizen. This chapter has argued that the concepts *state* and *citizenship* are intertwined. They have developed in relation to each other throughout a history characterized by the expansion of democratic forms of government, statebuilding, the advance of industrialization, international competition, and more recently, attempts to enhance national well-being and international security by the strengthening of international or transnational governance.

While we are witnessing a weakening of some elements of social citizenship associated with redistributive national welfare states (as in the Nordic countries), attempts to build institutions of transnational governance are simultaneously introducing new elements of social citizenship. These new elements will likely be mainly of a kind that is compatible with regulatory provisions, such as strengthening human rights and non-discrimination legislation. All in all, these changes suggest that we also need to revise and expand our understanding of citizenship.

3 What do we mean by active citizenship?

Håkan Johansson and Bjørn Hvinden

Introduction

In public discourse, civic engagement, political activism, community self-help, volunteering and neighbourhood associations are examples of 'active-citizenship'. Nonetheless, despite these positive connotations, active citizenship is an essentially contested concept. This chapter, therefore, contextualizes active citizenship within more general approaches to citizenship.

First, calls for active citizenship come from both conservative and radical standpoints. Conservative politicians appeal to the moral duty of well-to-do or affluent people to help the less fortunate, by giving money and time (Lister 1990, 2003; Marquand 1991). At the other end of the political spectrum, social movements like feminism and environmentalism have stated goals about active citizenship responsibility, reflecting efforts to create inclusive, caring and sustainable societies. Similarly, movements for poor or disadvantaged people view active citizenship as mutual aid and collective self-help, involving efforts to create themselves as subjects, not as objects for others (Williams 1998). Kymlicka (2002) refers to contemporary arguments that passive acceptance of citizenship rights need supplementing or replacing by the active exercise of citizenship responsibilities and virtues, including economic self-reliance, political participation and civility.

Second, the distinction between 'active' and 'passive' modes of citizenship is generally under debate. Turner (1990, 2001) distinguishes between passive and active citizenship, with the passive citizen a mere subject to absolute authority and the active citizen an active political agent. He relates this conceptualization to the origins of citizenship: granted 'from above' (from the state) or achieved 'from below' (through political and social struggle against the absolute state). Siim (2000), however, maintains that Turner's use of the active-passive dimension does not cover the historical exclusion of women and marginalized social groups from the public sphere. She therefore redefines the active-passive axis to include both the activities of various social groups (i.e. formal and informal associations in civil society) and their degree of inclusion in, or exclusion from, the public sphere.

Turner and his co-workers later partly accommodated this criticism in a study of the role of voluntary associations in providing welfare (Brown *et al.* 2000). Despite admitting that not all such association is able to include marginalized citizens, they conclude that voluntary associations seen as intermediary institutions give the brightest hope for making active citizenship a reality. Yet Turner (2001) is pessimistic about the prospects for active citizenship, based on what he claims to be the demise of work, military service and reproduction as three separate sources of citizenship entitlements and channels of active citizenship. Nonetheless, he sees potential for three forms of 'post-national' (active) citizenship – ecological, aboriginal and cultural – and links this potential to the growing salience of international human rights.

Third, the notion of active citizenship includes a range of citizen activities. Janoski and Gran (2002) delineate the active citizen as one of six types of political 'citizen-selves' or citizens' subjectivity. According to them, an active citizen participates in many political activities, has concern for people belonging to the same group, identifies with altruistic goals, opposes established elites, and pursues some form of social change. Faulks (2000) lists active citizenship as one of several aspects of what he calls 'thick citizenship', together with elements like mutually supportive rights and duties, participation in a political community, interdependence of public and private, and civic virtues. Similarly, Habermas (1994) sees active citizenship as analogous to membership in a self-determining ethical community.

In this chapter we are seeking a more systematic treatment of the different notions of active citizenship and their interrelationships. Rather than giving a complete review of the literature on citizenship, we focus on those directions that seem most relevant as a theoretical backdrop for the empirical studies in later chapters. As we suggested in Chapter 1, much of the significant variation in contemporary perspectives on citizenship is evident within a matrix of socio-liberal, libertarian and republican understandings of citizenship, and their active and passive modes. We start, therefore, by outlining the main features of citizenship in the liberal and republican traditions.

Citizenship in the liberal tradition

Liberal citizenship is generally identified as a legal status. A common liberal assumption is that everyone recognized as a member of a given community is also entitled to a set of rights (and duties), protected by common law and that community's government. Liberal citizenship is closely linked to the emergence of the modern Westphalian nation-state, as the status of citizenship became analogous to having nationality in relation to a given territory. Liberal citizenship meant that the individual shifted status from being a subject under the rule of the church and the king into that of holding the status of citizen with equal rights.

Liberal citizenship involves a set of basic rights and liberties, such as freedom of religious, political, ethical and philosophical beliefs, which allow for pluralism of conceptions of 'the common good'. These rights are basic to liberal reasoning because of their fundamental position, i.e. they have absolute priority over other political values and cannot be sacrificed or negotiated. The liberal dilemma concerns what kind of rights are to be included and what their scope and character should be (Janoski and Gran 2002; Schuck 2002; Smith 2002).

Another central feature of liberal citizenship is the idea that freedom, while belonging to all people by birth, is precious. Although the main way to protect citizen freedom is by granting citizens rights, citizenship rights may never (at least ideally) overrule the individual's freedom of self-determination and autonomy. Thus rights tend to be civil or political, in opposition to interventions of different kinds (by the state or by fellow citizens). Yet another key liberal value is equality of opportunity (as opposed to a society having fixed social positions). An important issue is to what extent 'negative freedom' (Berlin 1969) is sufficient for promoting equality of opportunity. For some liberals, equality of opportunity is equal to the absence of restrictions on individual freedom, thereby leading the argument in the direction of a neo-liberal or libertarian position. However, for other liberals this identification is inadequate, since ensuring equality of opportunity presupposes state regulation to promote fair or even real equality in opportunity, leading the argument in the direction of a socio-liberal position.

Liberal citizenship, involving a special relation to the public and to participation in public affairs, draws a sharp line between the public and private spheres. According to the liberal stance, the public has no essential or independent meaning, as it comprises the many residents of a given community. Even though political rights are important, the main emphasis is on providing citizens legal protection of their right to pursue their preferences, including the right to participate if they wish. For instance, no citizen is obliged to take part in public deliberation, vote or stand for elected positions. Furthermore, liberal citizenship assumes that participation in public affairs will not necessarily change individual preferences.

These propositions relate to an 'ideal-type' of liberal citizenship – to what we for the sake of simplicity call the 'original liberal position'. As we will discuss later, neo-liberal or libertarian citizenship has taken these assumptions one step further, claiming that rights – by definition – must not interfere with the rights of each citizen and that the state must limit duties of any kind. By contrast, socio-liberal citizenship is much more willing to accept state intervention, redistribution and more extensive notions of citizens' duties.

A socio-liberal understanding of citizenship

With his seminal essay on 'Citizenship and social class' (originally written in 1950), T. H. Marshall played a particular role in formulating the socio-liberal conception of citizenship (Marshall 1965). Many have later read him solely as a liberal concerned with the development of three types of individual rights – civil, political and social rights – over the last 300 years. This reading is partly accurate, as Marshall in many respects stood firmly within a British liberal tradition. Indeed, a key theme in his essay is the compatibility of the emerging equal status of citizenship for all inhabitants, with the continued existence of substantial class differences in income, wealth and living conditions in liberal capitalist economy.

At the same time, however, Marshall the sociologist fully accepted the main premises and assumptions of the dominant sociological paradigm of the mid-twentieth century, and its concern for the conditions for societal integration and social inclusion. This paradigm maintained that generally shared norms for action, based on a fundamental consensus on values, serve as integrating mechanisms. Socialization (internalization of values and norms) and social control (rewarding and sanctioning of behaviour) would ensure people's acceptance of and compliance with these norms. This preoccupation with integration and inclusion involved a stronger collectivist orientation than typical liberal thinking. Moreover, this belief in the significance of norms and a reciprocal or 'organic' relationship between individual and society emphasized both 'duties' (the action prescribed by shared norms) and 'rights' (the action to be expected from others, given these norms).

Marshall treated the emerging relationship between the modern state and the individual as a special instance of the general relationship (as viewed through the sociological lens of his day) between the societal community and its individual members. The rights and duties on the part of the individual also corresponded to those of the state. Some might be of a formal, legally enforceable nature (e.g. the right and duty for schooling, the duty to pay taxes or do military service, the right to receive social benefits in specified circumstances). Other rights and duties involved legitimate social expectations (e.g. for citizens to not only work but to work as well as they can, to be interested in political affairs, to vote). Talcott Parsons and other leading representatives of the sociological paradigm of that time easily absorbed Marshall's work into their own (Parsons 1967, 1971; Bendix and Rokkan 1971).

Although Marshall argued for a balance between rights and duties, he noted with some regret that rights had proliferated more rapidly than duties in the modern welfare state. Moreover, welfare states' possibilities of keeping alive an effective sense of duty – when people perceived the state as a distant and abstract construction – had become more difficult. Similarly to Durkheim (1947), Marshall suggested that the state should aim to develop people's sense of rights and duties in the context of intermediate institutions, e.g. the local community or workplace.

Marshall's depiction of socio-liberal citizenship parted ways with the original liberal position on several points. Marshall emphasized the duties of citizenship much more strongly. He saw not only civil and political rights but also social rights – guaranteeing all citizens a reasonable standard of living, level of knowledge, health, etc. – as fundamental for citizenship. Moreover, he claimed that these three forms of rights were interdependent; without one of them, the other two could not be fully realized. In a certain way, therefore, Marshall's socio-liberal citizenship is a hybrid of liberal individualism and civic republicanism (Marquand 1991).

Public education held a unique role in Marshall's analysis, not only as a social right and duty for the child but also as a means of enabling the future adult to realize the other aspects of citizenship both knowledgeably and competently. The value of civil and political rights would be limited for an illiterate person, with his or her ability to fulfil community duties severely circumscribed. Marshall the liberal followed the original liberal position in describing citizenship as a *status*, something one either has or has not, while Marshall the sociologist saw citizenship as *practice*, something one does (e.g. education).

Socio-liberal citizenship, as codified by Marshall, contained considerable complexity and even ambiguity. This complexity has led to a great variety in later interpretations of socio-liberal citizenship and provided ample opportunities for selective 'reading in' of what one likes or dislikes in Marshall's essay. We will be commenting briefly on some of the later, and particularly relevant, readings of Marshall.

A libertarian understanding of citizenship

The libertarian stance takes an individualistic direction when elaborating on the importance of freedom. It is opposed to any form of coercion, aggression or forcing people to do what they do not want to do. Although similarities to the original liberal position are obvious, the question remains whether the libertarian position is a variation of liberal citizenship or a more fundamentally different approach to society and citizenship (Freeman 2002).

The notion of libertarian citizenship is a paradox, because it sees society as comprising individuals and their preferences and values, through exchanges in the market or voluntary and contractual relations with like-minded individuals. To the extent that we can meaningfully speak about a libertarian understanding of citizenship, we see that it relies on the inviolable freedom of the individual, with every other action continuously weighed against individual rights (e.g. Hayek 1960; King 1987; Schuck 2002). Several different libertarian or neo-liberal positions exist, e.g. Hayek's argument that liberals have not adequately considered people's right to make their own decisions. We will focus on the thesis of Robert Nozick in *Anarchy, State and Utopia* (Nozick 1974).

Nozick claimed that citizens' rights have a 'natural' dimension, in the sense of being pre-political. This argument had far-reaching consequences, as it presumed that citizens' rights could never be replaced by or subordinated to political decisions or arrangements of public distribution. Hence Nozick argued in favour of a minimal state, saying it would best respect individual freedom, i.e. a negative conception of freedom – that a state exists only to defend the basic liberties of individuals and, above all, their property rights. Not surprisingly, the objectives for this minimal state were to ensure law and order by handling issues such as street lighting, police and public defence. A state that assumes objectives beyond these tasks would be violating individual freedom and individual rights. When Nozick defined the legitimate existence of the state as merely securing basic liberties and properties, this position placed him in opposition to several of the main twentieth-century liberals, especially John Rawls. Other libertarians have argued for something beyond the minimal state, such as Hayek's Hobbesian argument in favour of poor relief, which he claimed was instrumental for preventing theft and disorder (Hayek 1960: 285–86).

What further separated Nozick from liberalism was his claim that property rights were among the fundamental rights of citizens. This claim has important consequences: property gains a higher value for political consideration than issues such as justice or needs, leading to a strict opposition between the right to property and issues of public distribution: every form of distribution (or redistribution) of goods rests on an allocation of resources and will thereby undoubtedly violate individual freedom and the right for individuals to uphold property.

According to Nozick, liberals and socio-liberals make a general mistake when they assume the existence of a collective budget or a social pot that can spend money on public issues. On the contrary, policies of distributional justice would force people into actions against their will, and the most obvious example is taxes for social redistribution. Nozick did not define policies for distributional justice as immoral per se, as he firmly believed in every individual's right to decide how to live his or her own life. If people wanted to constitute a community based on certain assumptions (such as representative democracy), he found this choice fully acceptable, because this community would be based on a set of private contractual relations, i.e. when everyone completely and voluntarily accepted these arrangements. People would, however, be equally right in leaving this kind of community. With regard to welfare issues, Nozick made a similar argument. As everyone had a total right to decide about his or her own property, people also had the right to decide about giving to charity or to groups of people (a voluntary transaction).

Markets have great importance for libertarians. Most liberals also see markets as important institutions, above all because they allocate productive resources. For libertarians, however, a market is a space where the individual can act freely and rationally, following his or her own self-interest. They therefore reject the socio-liberal assumption that markets might be subordinated to political considerations, since any kind of political regulation would interfere with the property rights argument. Rather, markets are to be fully self-regulating, as individuals exercise their freedom to enter into contracts with other individuals. Consequently, the liberal value of equal opportunity is of no significance to libertarians, who find it acceptable that people might encounter discrimination in market situations, as these activities are by definition part of private contracts and arrangements.

Libertarians also justify markets for other reasons. They argue that the market is by definition apolitical, resting on a decentralized form of decision-making, and that it empowers the individual as a consumer. Thus, they view all market outcomes as just. All social relations are defined as contractual: individuals know the premises for entering into an agreement and have the possibility of opting out if the transaction or service does not fulfil the agreed-upon conditions. This contractual rationale leads to a narrow concept of citizenship. A citizen according to the libertarian position is very much synonymous with being a market participant and consumer, exercising choice and the power to enter into and terminate contracts. The implication here is that the government apparatus works essentially a business enterprise.

Citizenship in the republican tradition

The republican tradition of citizenship has represented a clear contrast to the liberal tradition. This section discusses some general features of the republican understanding of citizenship, emphasizing those features that will help us to analyze current changes in the relationships between states and citizens.

Citizenship in the republican tradition dates back far longer than any liberal conceptualization of citizenship, to ideals from ancient Greece. These ideals are still prominent in contemporary versions of republican citizenship, although now in a more generalized form (e.g. Taylor 1989; Faulks 2000), attributing key roles to the public realm and citizen participation. Republican citizenship focuses on the direct participation of citizens in the public realm and in deliberation and decision-making related to common affairs. The public realm is identified as a space open for everyone. Participation in this space is complex and multidimensional, since it is neither constituted by nor equal to the number of people participating: it is the representation of society as a whole, taking people out of their private lives and bringing them together. Because participation is a key aspect of life, being a republican citizen thus means being connected with the *polis*, public sphere or space, or community.

These classic ideals of the Greek *polis* have served as a normative model for political theorists, e.g. Hannah Arendt. Like many other civic republicans, Arendt (1958) expressed concern that political activity had been overwhelmed or even invaded by the forces of modernity (mainly through liberal capitalist culture), resulting in a loss of civic togetherness. She suggested that modern society had moved away from the civic republican vision of citizen debate and deliberation, resulting in the erosion of political citizenship and activity. Later Habermas (1984–87) would express a similar argument with his thesis of a 'colonization of the life-world'.

For Arendt the public sphere was a space not only for political activities but also for coercion-free communication, deliberation and decision-making among equals. Arendt's definition of the public sphere entailed the participation of the entire voting public, as opposed to democratic models of representation, where only elected officials make the decisions. Rather, she defined the public sphere as an activity-oriented place where citizens exchanged opinions and debated differences. In this sense, political activity had a clear spatial dimension, constituted by face-to-face interaction among citizens. Wherever people met to discuss and engage, Arendt saw the manifestation of the public sphere.

The notion of the public sphere also had the broader meaning of a space for forming citizens, constituting a world 'we have in common' or a world transcending the individual. Arendt argued that appearing in the public sphere gave individuals the opportunity to leave behind their private identities and establish themselves as citizens. The importance of participation in the meetings, discussions and interactions in the public sphere was to strengthen citizens' capabilities for hearing their fellow citizens' points of view in discussion and debate. In Arendt's view, the public sphere could not be put aside even for a while, as it was fragile, existing only as a potential when people got together, not as a necessity, and not lasting forever. Without the public sphere, a democratic society could very well turn into a totalitarian society.

Against this backdrop, we can point to some general features of a republican citizenship (Oldfield 1990; Marquand 1991; Dagger 2002). Civic republicanism contains a tendency to romanticize participation, failing to recognize that the public sphere has always been based on the exclusion of 'the other', e.g. women. Participation has been seen as a civic duty resting on the premise that citizens are those who, by their thoughts and actions, are able (and willing) to pursue the common good.

Republican citizenship is closely interlinked with issues of political socialization, citizen education or the general idea that one is not born a citizen: citizenship is something one achieves. Arendt, for example, identified participation in the public as the general way of becoming a citizen. Other scholars have likewise emphasized the empowering effect of participation (e.g. Pateman 1970). Citizens are socialized to become citizens, a point also emphasized by Marshall and reflected in current efforts to provide 'education for active citizenship' (Britton 2001). Similarly, most civic republicans today would agree that although enjoyment of basic civil, political and social rights are necessary, they are not enough for enabling citizen participation.

Since the capacity and competence for being a good citizen are unevenly distributed, realizing the ideals of republican citizenship depends on stimulating people's *capabilities,* that is, their effective freedom to act and govern themselves. In contemporary social theory, this issue is systematically developed within the human capabilities approach, as developed in slightly different ways by Amartya Sen, Martha Nussbaum and Robert Salais (see Chapter 8). However, their frame of reference is not republican citizenship but rather John Rawls' theory of social justice and, in Nussbaum's case, Aristotelian and Marxist theories of human nature. In the contexts of social inclusion (Sen 2000), European employment promotion (Salais and Villeneuve 2005) and improvement of the situation of women in developing countries (Nussbaum 2000), these scholars have sought to clarify how to stimulate the development of human capabilities. Nussbaum has gone further than the two others in specifying such conditions, in this case conditions for ensuring the recognition of women and their being treated as human beings with dignity and integrity. Nussbaum has developed a list of human capabilities, of which political participation is only one. Her intention has not been to constitute a full-fledged definition of the human good but to offer a radical approach to people's effective freedom to act by creating the conditions for developing their capabilities.

All in all, the ideals of republican citizenship view the relationship between the individual and the community as entailing engaging practices and participation in time-consuming deliberation. These ideals depict individuals as more than simply embedded in their social, cultural and political context; they depict citizens doing so as the way things *should* be. Republican citizenship is closely associated with bottom-up processes, as citizens' activities, practices and self-governance are the key words in an ideal 'republic'. Faulks (2000) calls this 'thick' citizenship. By contrast, liberal versions of citizenship (whether broad or narrow) emphasize citizenship as a matter of status or contract, i.e. involving *thin* citizenship. While republican citizenship is presumably the inner core of our lives, liberal citizenship is its outer frame.

New dynamics of citizenship

Recent social and political changes have helped to manifest *underlying active and passive dimensions* in all three 'pure' understandings of citizenship. Moreover, current welfare reforms illustrate how elements from socio-liberal, libertarian and republican citizenship may be *mixed* in sometimes surprising ways. We postulate that most of the literature on contemporary citizenship has missed these two implications of social and political change. The following discussion concentrates on the first of these: the need to widen established understandings of citizenship to allow for the active-passive dimension (an opening of citizenship models). From the case studies that follow, we will later examine the combining of ideas from the three models of citizenship in current policy reforms.

However, we first have three points to stress: first, the terms 'active' and 'passive' have strong normative connotations, where active is usually understood as the more positive, virtuous and desirable. Pinning the label 'active' on a policy is an effective rhetorical device. Yet we will show that even 'active' policies may be normatively ambiguous. Second, passive and active modes of policy or citizenship are not necessarily poles apart; they can also co-exist. Third, although recent ideologies of welfare reform try to convince us otherwise, the movement from passive to active is not always obvious. Some current expressions of active citizenship may not be strictly 'new'; they may instead reflect a return to policies and goals pursued previously in the welfare state in question but later marginalized or eroded from lack of continued implementation or from competition from more recently adopted policies and goals. Over time we may observe a fluctuation between active and passive dimensions of citizenship, rather than a clear progress from the one to the other.

Active citizenship in a socio-liberal understanding

T. H. Marshall's analysis of modern citizenship has been heavily criticized with some of the most important criticisms coming from feminist scholars (e.g. Pateman 1988; Siim 2000; Lister 2003). Marshall focused almost exclusively on the historical development of citizenship for men. This neglect of women had a number of implications. He did not deal with women having attained civil and political rights much later than men. Nor did he consider women's subjugation to male dominance, oppression and control, especially within the context of marriage and the family, despite the increasing proportion of men who were said to have become 'free individuals'.

Marshall followed the original liberal position in drawing a sharp line of division between the public and the private sphere, therefore covering only issues of individual rights and duties insofar as they related to the public sphere. Similarly, he focused on participation in paid work as a fulfilment of obligations toward society and a contribution qualifying for being granted social rights. He included men having the duty to perform military service. However, he ignored the significance of motherhood – i.e. giving birth and nurturing and raising children – as essential for the continued existence of society. Care, housekeeping and other unpaid work in the private sphere did not figure in his reasoning about balancing rights and duties. He failed to ask whether social citizenship rights, including an individual's right to economic security and independence, applied to women who were caregivers and housekeepers for the greater part of their adult lives. All in all, women were largely invisible in Marshall's discussion, leading us to doubt whether they really enjoyed socio-liberal citizenship as he codified it.

Since the mid-twentieth century, gender relations and the situation of both women and men have changed dramatically in most Western countries. On the one hand, women's increased labour market participation, greater economic independence and stronger presence in politics and other decision-marking arenas – reinforced by women's higher level of education –

suggest an equalizing of the conditions for women's and men's citizenship, along the lines of a socio-liberal understanding. On the other hand, women still take greater responsibility for unpaid work (both care and household work), even if younger men now take more of an active part in childcare and raising children. Clearly, the issue of whether – and how – to recognize motherhood and unpaid care as social contributions qualifying for full social citizenship rights, e.g. in the form of care credits in earnings-related pension schemes (Chapter 14), remains unsettled. The issue of whether – and how – to enforce activity requirements for the daily care of young children for unemployed single women is likewise unresolved. Some feminist scholars have proposed 'Basic Income' – a state-guaranteed minimum income – as a way of breaking the link between the gendered division of labour and economic security in and out of paid work (Dahl 1984; Pateman 2003).

Another major criticism of Marshall's socio-liberal citizenship has been that he excessively emphasized individual social rights, especially formal and enforceable rights, while saying too little about citizens' duties or responsibilities (e.g. Marquand 1991; Turner 2001). This criticism appears less well founded than the feminist criticism, because reciprocity and balance between rights and obligations were indeed central themes in Marshall's codification of socio-liberal citizenship.

So what has stimulated this reading of Marshall? First, the original ambitions, in some welfare states, of balancing rights and obligations were eroded in practice. Findings from Norway and Sweden indicate that front-line welfare workers in the later decades of the twentieth century interpreted eligibility rules fairly leniently, rarely sanctioning citizens who did not actively seek work or who rejected job offers (Hvinden 1994; Johansson 2001). Second, writers within social policy analysis have contributed to a one-sided understanding of social citizenship, because they focused only on the expansion of rights. For instance, Esping-Andersen (1990: 21–23) made a direct link between 'decommodification' and Marshall's concept of social citizenship. Here, decommodification means that '... citizens can freely, and without potential loss of job, income or general welfare, opt out of work when they themselves consider necessary'.

For some critics, Marshall seems to have served as the straw man for a more general criticism of how generous redistributive welfare arrangements, especially social benefit systems, supposedly had an adverse effect on citizens' attitudes towards self-reliance, paid work, and responsibility for personal welfare and risk protection. They argued that the proliferation of unconditional social rights, underpinned by welfare provisions, has led to widespread passivity – even economic and social exclusion – and a weakening of the work ethic (e.g. Mead 1986, 1997a).

More than ever, these arguments are linked to the external and internal pressures facing contemporary welfare states. All European welfare models, including the Nordic model, have to be slimmed down to keep from being a liability in a more globalized, competitive market. Ambitions to provide tax-financed redistributive welfare need reduction, while individuals and families need to take greater responsibility for protecting themselves against risks. Out of these arguments come calls for new conceptions of citizenship, involving a better balance of individual rights and duties. Whatever the label ('Third Way' or 'Communitarian'), a substantial common core links these concepts (e.g. Levitas 1998; Dwyer 2000; Lister 2001), exemplified by the slogan 'no rights without responsibilities' (Giddens 1998: 65).

Regardless of how appropriate these views are as a criticism of Marshall's socio-liberal citizenship, they have gained wide resonance within contemporary welfare reform. Many welfare states have initiated reforms, aiming at giving stronger or renewed emphasis to citizen duties and responsibilities, most clearly in the 'activation' of social protection systems for working age people (Chapters 4–6) and in pension reform (Chapter 14). In both cases the focus is very much on promoting participation in paid work, by providing stronger financial incentives and, for activation reform, also by combining sticks and carrots.

Participation in activities not oriented towards paid employment (or seen as 'stepping-stones') are rarely recognized as fulfilment of citizen duties in current welfare reforms, although some cross-national differences exist. The Danish and Dutch governments have to a greater extent accepted participation in voluntary social and cultural work, self-help activities, and organizational, co-operative or 'social economy' work as alternatives for people distant from the mainstream labour market. In most other countries, fairly narrow conceptions of socially useful activity have dominated recent welfare reform. Unpaid care in the family receives only limited recognition.

All in all, governments seek to achieve what is now perceived as an appropriate balance between rights and duties, much in line with what Marshall would probably have favoured. The issue for empirical investigation is whether the duties now enforced are 'new' or simply a reawakening of duties that have lain dormant for a while. We expect that the answer will vary according to which welfare programme and which country we are examining.

To summarize, a turn (or return) to active socio-liberal citizenship implies that people should not only enjoy the rights associated with citizenship but also fulfil their obligations. The focus has been on the citizen's duty to be self-sufficient and responsible for obtaining a means of livelihood through gainful employment. Significant changes in social benefits legislation or, more generally, governmental attempts to switch from passive to active forms of social protection reflect such concerns (Table 1).

The active dimension of socio-liberal citizenship has hardly replaced the passive dimension. Cash benefits mainly substituting for labour market incomes ('passive benefits'), still play an important role in Nordic and other European welfare states. Many benefits ('hybrids') are in the middle ground between 'pure' passive and active provisions. Some provisions labelled passive may give greater room for individual autonomy, self-determination and agency than those labelled active. Moreover, governments are likely to direct

Table 1 Different constructions of passive and active aspects of social citizenship

	Passive dimension	*Active dimension*
Socio-liberal citizenship	Focus on receiving and claiming of rights to benefits and services	Focus on fulfilment of duties, especially in return for entitlement to benefits and services – conditional rights
Libertarian citizenship	Focus on welfare consumerism on the basis of managed and circumscribed 'user choice' or quasi-markets	Focus on the fulfilment of individual self-responsibility and exercise of choice in the private market
Republican citizenship	Focus on managed participation in terms of user involvement, informed consent or agency-directed self-help	Focus on self-governed activity, combined with co-responsibility for and commitment to participating in deliberation and decision-making on common affairs

their efforts to promote active citizenship in the socio-liberal sense toward certain sections of the population. For instance, the long-term unemployed, economically excluded people and social assistance claimants are key target groups for activation reforms. Because marginal groups have to comply with a predefined and imposed set of duties, the turn toward active socio-liberal citizenship may involve a 'deliberalization'. From the view of the marginalized, they are subjected to paternalistic policies that reduce their personal autonomy and freedom of choice, and some of these may resist the turn toward active socio-liberal citizenship, paradoxically promoting a turn to active republican citizenship (Chapter 7).

Active citizenship in a libertarian understanding

Political ideologies associated with a libertarian understanding of citizenship, the 'New Right', had a remarkable renaissance in the 1970s and 1980s. These ideological strands had a strong impact on welfare reform in the United States, the United Kingdom and New Zealand. Business models have recently been introduced in the management of welfare states; e.g. the actual undertaking of services has, if possible, been put on tender or contracted out. In general, the important thing is the price and quality of the 'product', not who (the public or private sector) is providing it. These changes naturally have profound implications for the conception of citizenship, if people's role is mainly to be consumers exercising choice, entering and exiting contracts with providers, and eventually expressing their dissatisfaction through complaints or demanding a change of provider. Active libertarian citizenship involves a 'marketization' of citizenship (Crouch *et al.* 2001).

The core of the turn towards the libertarian understanding of active citizenship is the belief that people should take responsibility for their own well-being and protection against risks by exercising choice in the market and in relation to public provisions (Table 1). Active citizenship here implies a greater scope for contracts as the basis for provider-consumer relations in markets or quasi-markets. Perhaps the clearest examples are found in the area of pensions, where many Western countries have introduced substantial reforms (Chapter 14). Likewise in education and health and social care services, the right to choose and freedom of contract have received ideological emphasis through policy changes, both nationally and locally (Le Grand 2003; Edelbalk and Svensson 2005; TemaNord 2005a, 2005b).

The active dimension involves individual self-responsibility and exercise of choice in a full-fledged private market situation. It differs from the passive dimension mainly in the degree of individual independence from public provisions and political decision-makers. Policy instruments for promoting individual choice in welfare – like vouchers, quasi-markets and managed 'user choice' – are mainly associated with the passive dimension. Again, mixes of the active and passive dimensions do occur, suggesting that active libertarian citizenship will often complement rather than replace passive libertarian citizenship.

Active citizenship in a republican understanding

Republican citizenship has experienced a revival, especially through the criticism of socio-liberal citizenship as being based too strongly on top-down processes and paternalism. Partly to accommodate such criticism, different levels of government have tried to promote active citizen participation in different ways. Policymakers have also acknowledged the inability of public and professional agencies to solve many contemporary social problems on their own, along with the need for the involvement, motivation and commitment of ordinary citizens. Finding new and more effective ways of combating social and economic exclusion and preventing health problems related to modern lifestyles are two examples of such problems. This awareness has stimulated government attempts to mobilize citizens to solve and prevent problems – both their own and those of others.

The stated rationale for involving and mobilizing citizens in this way resembles the ideas behind republican citizenship, despite some differences (Marquand 1991). What is common is the emphasis on citizen participation: citizen activity, direct involvement, co-determination and even self-government. In the present context, this emphasis often appears in calls for broader participation in deliberation, decision-making and dialogue with relevant agencies, as well as in self-directed activity. Moreover, these calls stress that citizens should not only have the theoretical possibility of participation in discussions and decision-making affecting their future well-being but also receive help and stimulation for actually using these opportunities.

At the same time the scope for participation, co-determination and self-government that public authorities seek to provide varies: often they limit the scope to the more narrow status of 'user' rather than to the more general status of 'citizen'. Nonetheless, in some cases governments also acknowledge self-organized and self-governed activity as an alternative or complementary channel for participation in processes affecting citizens' welfare and well-being (Table 1).

Our general argument is that we have witnessed a development towards a participation-led welfare state, which takes many forms. As regards policy-making, organizations of citizens, especially those already receiving welfare state provisions, are to a greater extent involved in negotiation and consultation about the design and development of services. As regards implementation, governments encourage individuals to engage in dialogue with agency staff about the measures or activities for their case, about formulating treatment or action plans, about rearranging service packages, etc. For this purpose citizen organizations or particular groups of beneficiaries achieve not only recognition but also financial assistance and practical support for their work, from public authorities at either national (Chapter 7) or supra-national (Chapter 9) levels.

To a varying degree, these policy changes can be linked with different conceptions of active participation on the part of citizens. Within general social and political theory, distinctions between different ways in which citizens can become more active (Isin and Turner 2002: 19) allow us to relate those differences to other understandings of active citizenship and their hybrids.

First, we have demonstrated that republican citizenship embodies a *communitarian* ideal that lately has undergone a striking revival. Scholars have directed a general criticism at the liberal conception of citizenship for being solely occupied with individual rights (e.g. Bell 1993; Tam 1998; Etzioni 2000). They argue that we cannot analyze individuals as separate entities but in their social settings. Accompanying this sociological reflection are normative proposals to the effect that citizenship requires a definition of the common good. Essential to these arguments is the assumption that Western liberalism has too loosely defined what it means to be a member of a community and that generous social entitlements result in a number of social wrongs, such as moral decay, idleness, dependency and freeloading. One main advocate of the communitarian agenda has explained that a major task for communitarians is to curb the language of rights, because 'rights talks' fosters a disregard for social responsibility (Etzioni 2000).

The solution to these problems, mainly spelled out by Etzioni, is a greater role for individual responsibilities, especially in relation to the duties and virtues of community. However, the 'community' in question is not synonymous with the welfare state. Communitarians claim that the true values of the community are embedded in the traditional social structure of the family, civil society and voluntary activity of different kinds. In this sense communitarians adopt one aspect of the republican tradition – that of seeing civic participation as a means of finding the true or inner meaning of social life – while contradicting the arguments for civic republicanism put forward by Arendt and others. The main activity that communitarians call for is charitable, voluntary or unpaid efforts, as an expression of how the individual forsakes his or her own interests for the common good. Some versions of the new communitarianism actually resemble active socio-liberal citizenship in their arguments for enforcing individual responsibility through work requirements and for putting a premium on economic self-reliance through paid work (e.g. Levitas 1998; Dean 1999).

Second, and in contrast to this emphasis, several scholars have paid increasing attention to another aspect of republican ideals. At the centre of their arguments are proposals of participation, deliberation or dialogue as the key notions for a revival of the republican tradition. These proposals, which in the 1980s revived debate about the nature of democracy, go to the heart of republican citizenship. The best known of these proposals comes from Habermas, in his theory of *deliberative democracy*, which builds upon '. . . a person's capacity to be swayed by rational arguments and to lay aside particular interests and opinions in deference to overall fairness and the common interest of the collectivity' (Miller 2000: 10).

The link between republican citizenship and deliberative democracy is evident, because political actions are public. Each form of democratic participation is made in public, implying that giving, weighing, accepting or rejecting arguments is open and transparent for all participants. The deliberative understanding of citizenship expresses full trust in the competence of citizens: if citizens receive possibilities for dialogue on equal terms, they will jointly agree by the strength of rational arguments and for the sake of the general will that individual preferences are by definition less important. More exactly, the deliberative understanding of citizenship activity may be expressed in citizen panels or citizen juries, as well as in dialogue between authorities and users about the premises, outline and organization of welfare arrangements. However, whether the dialogue can really remain unaffected by the underlying structure of power and dominance is doubtful.

A more fundamental criticism of current forms of citizen participation and dialogue comes from a number of scholars who seek to follow up the work of Michel Foucault (e.g. Dean 1995; Rose 1996). They have argued that the growing complexities of modern society mean that government can effectively control citizen conduct only if the citizens operate under the illusion that they are autonomous, able to pursue individual preferences, make choices and influence the ways in which the decisions of others affect their lives. As a result, discipline in modern society is increasingly taking the form of self-discipline, a way of governing citizens 'at a distance' (ibid.). From this perspective, participatory dialogues with representatives of public agencies have mainly a disciplinary function. They serve to persuade these citizens to take responsibility for changing their own situations by thinking and behaving in the way that these agencies find desirable or, specifically, by complying with the norms of active citizenship (e.g. Warburton and Smith 2003).

Another criticism of the deliberative democracy approach is that it pays too much attention to deliberation as a formal process, without reference to the social and political context in which participation usually takes place. Critics argue for rejecting the idea of a taken-for-granted community as the starting point for participation and viewing participation as a process of identity building and mobilization.

The main proponents of this 'radical notion of participation' have been Laclau and Mouffe (1985). They claim that participation is an act occurring in a social structure of power relations. In their daily lives, citizens are continuously engaged in political action, expressing their views and resisting identities or issues imposed on them. Democratic participation is in this respect not a simple, linear or homogeneous act limited to a specific public arena. The boundaries for participation are not pre-drawn; they are rather the very objects of contestation and political action, as illustrated by the struggles of social and political movements or of different user organizations to make their voices heard and to gain a position within the general public debate. Consequently, radical citizenship is a map for struggle and conflict, not something that can be reduced to a procedural vision (Mouffe 1992). Neither are political activities actually for the sake of the common good, as there is no kind of 'essence' to being a citizen. Democratic participation involves a dialectic relation between making differences and forming identities.

Conclusion

The chapter has sought to clarify the main meanings of active citizenship against a background of three fairly distinct approaches to citizenship: socio-liberal, libertarian and republican. We have argued that all three approaches have underlying active and passive dimensions, and that current changes in society and welfare policy have stimulated a new or renewed emphasis on the active dimensions. Whether these shifts represent a genuine new turn or a return to older ideals and principles will probably vary by country and the kind of welfare provision under consideration. In much discussion of welfare policy, a fairly narrow or rights-dominated ('passive') version of socio-liberal citizenship has predominated, especially in the Nordic context. We argue that recent changes in European welfare states, including the Nordic ones, necessitate adopting a more open, multifaceted model, involving libertarian and republican citizenship ('opening between') and including both active and passive dimensions of each ('opening within').

More specifically, we have pointed to a much stronger focus on the duties associated with socio-liberal citizenship, in terms of both policy analysis and practical policy. At the same time this concern with a balance between rights and duties has also received an individualistic twist, related to arguments about the need for reciprocity between the state and the individual where both parties have duties towards the other. Simultaneously, we have witnessed a stronger focus on individual self-responsibility, self-reliance and choice relative to private markets – in other words, an equation of the citizen with the consumer or market actor (active libertarian citizenship). Finally, we claim that active republican citizenship has gained new importance through a stronger focus on self-governed activity, participation in deliberation and decision-making related to common issues of welfare. The discussion shows the need for theoretically reconsidering well-established perspectives on citizenship and the ways in which different perspectives on active citizenship may gain support from empirical studies of specific areas of welfare policy.

Part II

Towards a new balance of rights and duties

Activation reform

4 Nordic activation reforms in a European context

A distinct universalistic model?

Håkan Johansson and Bjørn Hvinden

Introduction

This chapter argues that recent reforms in social protection have led to a significant shift in social citizenship for people on the margins of the labour market. After 1990 all the Nordic countries – Denmark, Finland, Iceland, Norway and Sweden – introduced changes in policy and legislation to strengthen the integration of unemployed people into the regular labour market. These changes have redefined the relationship between rights and duties for unemployed citizens, in the interest of promoting active citizenship in the socio-liberal sense (Chapter 3).

The Nordic countries, however, have not been alone in introducing a closer link between income maintenance systems and employment-promoting services. Encouraged by the Jobs Strategy Programme of the Organization for Economic Co-operation and Development (OECD 1995) and the European Employment Strategy of the EU, many governments in Europe have adopted similar activation reforms since the early 1990s (e.g. Goetschy 2003; Barbier 2005). Existing models in comparative welfare research suggest that the policy legacies and institutions underpinning the Nordic concepts of social citizenship would give such reforms distinct contents in the Nordic countries. Researchers describe the Nordic welfare states as providing all citizens with the same rights to income security and social services, regardless of their previous income or occupation (e.g. Kangas and Palme 2005). This universalistic and inclusive citizenship is supported by a political culture combining solidarity and a passion for social equality. Many scholars claim that this universalistic and egalitarian culture is also reflected in the kind of activation policies pursued in the Nordic countries (e.g. Esping-Andersen 2002; Ferrera and Hemerijck 2003; Barbier 2004).

In our view, these claims are based on a simplistic understanding of the Nordic system of social protection, the actual contents of the new activation policies and the social position of their target groups. We will substantiate this argument by examining the policy efforts directed at unemployed citizens, including the citizens with the most marginal position in relation to the labour market: people claiming social assistance (means-tested income support).

To give the necessary background for the particular focus and contents of activation reforms aimed at this group, we will start by outlining: (i) the main features and trends of the Nordic labour markets; and (ii) the dual structure of the Nordic systems of social protection and their target populations. Next we will discuss the ideological reasoning behind the activation policies and the ways in which Nordic governments have adopted this rationale in relation to an increasingly diverse target population. Finally, we will return to the issue of whether 'universalistic' is an appropriate label for Nordic activation policies, making them distinct from the policies adopted in Europe more generally.

Winners and losers in the Nordic labour market

After WWII the governments of the Nordic countries sought to maximize labour market participation and keep unemployment at a minimum (Lindqvist and Marklund 1995; Midré 1995; Junestav 2004). Despite slogans like 'the whole people in work' and 'full employment', for several decades policymakers understood these goals in a male-biased way, being primarily concerned with the employment of male breadwinners (although less so in Iceland and Finland).

After 1970 female labour market participation increased in all five countries, stimulated by demand for labour in the expanding services sector, especially the public welfare sector (education, health and care). Greater availability of publicly provided childcare services facilitated the participation of mothers with small children. Similarly, the expansion of public services for people needing care related to impairments (disabilities) or age enabled more women to take part in paid work.

Largely as a result of these developments, the Nordic countries have a higher ratio of people aged 15–64 in employment and a smaller difference in the employment ratios of women and men than Europe as whole, as of 2003 (OECD 2005b). Moreover, the Nordic countries have been relatively successful in keeping older workers in the labour force. The gap between the employment ratios of people aged 55–64 and the whole working age population aged 15–64 is smaller in the Nordic group than in Europe as a whole (ibid.). Obviously we find some variations within the Nordic group; e.g. Iceland has an exceptionally high employment ratio while Finland has the lowest ratio of the five countries. Nevertheless, a high overall employment ratio and small gender and old-age gaps are major achievements of the Nordic employment model.

In two other respects, the Nordic employment situation is less impressive. First, all governments (except the Icelandic) have during the last three decades struggled with fairly high unemployment. In Denmark unemployment rose after the first oil crisis in 1973, reaching peaks in the early 1980s and the early 1990s. Norway went though moderate and temporary increases of unemployment in the early 1980s and then again from the late 1980s to the early 1990s. Sweden and especially Finland experienced dramatic increases in the number of people out of work from the early 1990s, and still have not returned to their pre-1990 unemployment levels. By contrast, Iceland has maintained low levels of unemployment. Consequently, we find greater contrasts in unemployment rates within the Nordic group than between the Nordic group and Europe as a whole (OECD 2005b).

Second, the Nordic labour markets do not succeed particularly well in integrating immigrants, people with impairments or young people. The gap between the labour market participation rates of nationals and foreigners is larger in the Nordic group of countries than in Europe as a whole, for both men and women. Similarly, the difference between the unemployment rates of nationals and foreigners is greater in the Nordic group than in Europe as a whole (e.g. EC 2003; Garson and Loizillon 2003). Comparative data about the employment situation of people with impairments are scarce. The few data we have suggest that the gap between the employment ratios of people with and without impairments is roughly the same in the Nordic group and in Europe as a whole (OECD 2003b). Finally, the difference between the unemployment rates of young people aged 15–24 and the whole working age population is only marginally smaller in the Nordic group (OECD 2005b). Immigrants, people with impairments and young unemployed people have therefore been target groups for activation reforms in the Nordic countries, albeit to different extents, since the early 1990s.

The dual structure of the Nordic systems of social protection

Governments provide social benefits in different ways. Two main types of provisions are 'social assistance' and 'social insurance' (e.g. Ferrera 2005). Minimum subsistence benefits and means-tested housing allowances are examples of social assistance. Social assistance involves a test of 'need' and the person's financial resources or 'means', as well as (sometimes) those of other family or household members. Social assistance is usually financed through general taxes.

By contrast, social insurance (or 'contributory benefits') involves compulsory membership for a specific population, e.g. all wage earners. Social insurance is based on the idea that contributions or premiums paid by members (and/or also by their employers) give these members clear entitlements to benefits in cash or kind (e.g. medical treatment). Social insurance is typically oriented towards protection against some specified 'risk' (e.g. illness or unemployment). The need for financial support is presumed to result from the occurrence of one of the specified risks, thereby eliminating a reason for directly testing the person's need for financial support.

The long-term aim of the Nordic governments has been to move away from social assistance and towards social insurance (and hybrids of these two) as the main elements of their cash benefit systems. Social assistance has become a residual income support, partly as a last-resort provision, partly as a supplement for citizens with insufficient entitlements to social insurance. Yet in the early 2000s, means-tested benefits still amount to about 5 per cent of the total social benefits expenditure of the Nordic countries, while the corresponding figure for Europe as a whole is 8 per cent (Eurostat 2006).

In the Nordic group as a whole, slightly less than 5 per cent of the population over 18 received social assistance in 2003 (NOSOSCO 2005). People aged 18–24 years are strongly over-represented among recipients of social assistance, especially since they rarely have enough work experience and earnings to qualify for unemployment insurance benefits. The same factor, in combination with a higher risk of unemployment, explains why immigrants are receiving social assistance more often than the native population. Generally, Nordic social assistance is administered by the municipalities (local authorities). The scope for local and professional discretion in administering social assistance varies considerably between the Nordic countries, with the largest in Norway and Sweden and the smallest in Denmark and Iceland (ibid.). Social insurance and hybrid benefits are administered by a range of different bodies, in some cases by local offices of central government agencies (Finland, Iceland, Norway, Sweden), in some by separate and autonomous union-run administrations (Denmark, Finland and Sweden) and in some by local authorities (Denmark).

Employment services that provide unemployed citizens with guidance and practical assistance in finding jobs are mainly operated by the country's central government. As part of activation reforms, governments have emphasized the duty of unemployed citizens to accept all offers from these employment services, including offers of courses for improving their qualifications. People claiming social assistance from the municipalities are also required to seek the assistance of staff in local offices of the employment services. Thus two separate public agencies have a joint responsibility for putting into practice the political goal of activating this target group.

A recurring problem within this divided administration is that the employment services have been less successful in helping social assistance recipients than in helping recipients of unemployment insurance. The staff in employment offices have complained that many unemployed citizens receiving social assistance are too distant from the labour market or that employers do not view them as attractive job candidates, even after agency efforts to assist them. This complaint shows that policymakers' high ambitions for active policies of social protection do not always resonate with the perceptions, job orientations and experience of the staff who must put these ambitions into practice (e.g. Hvinden 1994; Johansson 2001).

Assumptions behind the Nordic system of social protection

The Nordic countries have a long tradition of constructing the citizen primarily as a worker. The Nordic governments' strong commitment to promoting maximum participation in paid work (the 'work-line') has clearly aimed at turning all adult citizens into workers. Governments have considered high rates of employment essential for ensuring sufficient tax revenues to finance an expanding set of welfare provisions, both cash benefits and services. They view employment-promoting policies as important tools for increasing productive capacity and for using available resources as effectively as possible.

In addition to such instrumentalist reasoning, a strong popular belief in the moral virtues of work has supported the promotion of the work-line. The Nordic work ethic has much in common with the Protestant ethic. For instance, from their early beginnings, the Nordic labour movements gave the duty of contributing to the common good a moralistic overtone. Trade union banners encouraged members to 'perform your duty, demand your rights!' – in that order of priority. Similar norms were later incorporated in the emerging system of public welfare provisions, e.g. in the form of the close link between previous records of employment, earnings and contributions on the one hand and entitlements to social insurance benefits (e.g. unemployment insurance) on the other.

With Sweden as a pioneer, Nordic governments adopted the same kind of mixed rationale when they initiated programmes of active labour market policy immediately before and after WWII. Policymakers saw active measures as instruments for improving overall labour productivity, hastening the restructuring and modernizing of economic life and limiting the impact of downturns in the business cycle. On the individual level, policymakers thought offers to participate in active measures would function as 'work tests' for unemployed people claiming social benefits: were they available for the labour market and really motivated to work?

Governments also appealed to a norm of reciprocity between effort and reward in the context of active measures, for instance through a combination of incentives (e.g. additional benefits, mobility grants) and sanctions ensuring compliance (e.g. withdrawal or reduction of benefits, forced labour market mobility). In principle, the authorities should exhaust all possibilities for making citizens economically independent through measures like vocational rehabilitation, retraining or mobility assistance before granting them long-term benefits. Thus active labour market policies served the dual purpose of streamlining the labour market and supporting (and controlling) the individual unemployed citizen.

This brief review demonstrates the dualism underlying the Nordic systems of social protection for people of working age (Marklund and Svallfors 1987). The rights to social benefits that citizens of working age enjoy need understanding in the light of the duties (past or current efforts and contributions) they are expected to fulfil. For a long time this dualism has been most evident in the Nordic systems of social insurance (e.g. unemployment insurance). The right to relatively generous benefits of fairly long duration has presupposed that the individual is more than a mere member of an insurance plan, with a sufficient record of contributions. In addition, an unemployed individual must be prepared to do what he or she can to return to work as soon as possible. This duty includes registering at the employment office, actively seeking work, and accepting all suitable jobs or offers for participating in labour market measures. Similarly, sickness and disability insurance benefits combine conditions in the form of sufficient prior earnings or a contributions record and the willingness to comply with current requirements.

For citizens receiving social assistance, the rationale for the activation policy is more complex. These citizens are almost by definition unable to fulfil the reciprocity requirements related to past efforts, performance or contributions that could give them sufficient access to social insurance benefits. They may or may not have been involved in socially valuable activities like education, voluntary work or unpaid care for children or other dependent family members. Nevertheless, in return for social assistance, their obligation is mainly to comply with current requirements, e.g. participating in training courses and/or actively seeking work.

We have previously seen that young unemployed people and immigrants are over-represented among recipients of social assistance in the Nordic countries. Throughout European welfare states as a whole, public opinion studies show that these two groups are generally regarded as the least deserving (e.g. van Oorschot 2006). Recipients of social assistance are easily seen throughout Europe as at least partly to blame for their lack of sufficient income. They are identified as less responsible, capable or competent than other citizens in terms of finding and holding on to regular paid work.

Therefore, social assistance recipients may be subject to paternalistic policies, rigid or meaningless obligations, and practical constraints of their scope for self-determination, all of which are justified in terms of vague notions of normalization and behavioural change necessary for inducing responsible citizenship. These factors suggest that activation policies aimed at social assistance recipients will focus more on control and discipline than activation policies directed at other groups of citizens (e.g. those receiving unemployment or disability insurance benefits). The next section will consider whether recent activation reforms in the Nordic countries have demonstrated this kind of differentiated design and focus.

Reinvention of activation policy in the Nordic countries

After 1990 the governments of the Nordic countries (except Iceland) introduced major activation reforms, albeit with different timing and speed. One important factor fuelling these reforms was the extra pressure on public budgets resulting from diminished tax revenues and higher government spending on social benefits during periods of high unemployment. Equally significant has been the practical functioning and effectiveness of the social protection system for working age people. Policymakers and outside experts concluded that the agencies administering this system had become excessively oriented towards the rights of the citizens they were supposed to help, at the expense of citizens' obligations to do their part to enter or re-enter paid work (Chapter 3). Many policymakers and experts argued that the original policy goals and assumptions underpinning the social protection system had been eroded, and that the Nordic governments needed to reinstate them as the basis for practical policy.

We emphasize here that the Nordic governments – at least in principle – had different policy options at this early stage of the reform process. The first main option was simply to make cuts in existing social benefit provisions: to tighten the criteria for eligibility for benefits, reduce benefit levels and shorten the duration of benefits. These cuts would potentially reduce public expenditure in the short-term and improve incentives to work, i.e. 'make work pay'. The second main option was to provide resources to unemployed citizens, giving them the opportunity to improve their qualifications and skills. Participation in 'capacity-building' (training and education) might potentially speed up the entry or return of these citizens to paid work, widen their range of relevant jobs and increase their attractiveness to employers.

Leading figures in comparative welfare research suggest that the Nordic countries primarily have favoured the capacity-building option, because of their institutional legacies and the universalistic and inclusive nature of Nordic social citizenship (e.g. Esping-Andersen 2002; Ferrera and Hemerijck 2003; Barbier 2004). These scholars argue that the second option, cutting social benefits to make work pay, is typical for other European countries, especially liberal welfare states. However, detailed studies show that since the early 1990s the Nordic countries have indeed chosen both options, in different combinations (e.g. Hvinden *et al.* 2001; Johansson 2001, 2006). In addition, cuts in social insurance systems have made more citizens dependent on social assistance, i.e. reinforced the dual structure of the Nordic social protection systems.

Among the Nordic countries, Denmark has undergone the most explicitly ideological repositioning of the status of unemployed citizens. From the reforms introduced in the early 1990s, the Danish government has repeatedly emphasized that unemployed persons have both a right and a duty to be activated. For instance, to increase individual incentives, the government has institutionalized this norm through changes in unemployment insurance. Principally, the Danish government divided unemployment insurance into a passive part (years during which the unemployed could receive unemployment benefits) and an active part (years during which the unemployed had to actively participate in 'activation' measures). Later, the Danish government extended the active part and reduced the passive part. Thus Denmark has revised a previously very generous unemployment insurance system in a major way and implemented stricter eligibility rules and shorter duration of benefits (Halvorsen and Jensen 2004; Torfing 2004).

Similarly, Finland enacted a set of major labour market reforms, and activation policies remain at the top of the political agenda. The Finnish government has introduced a special national programme for employment.

After the deep economic recession that started in the early 1990s, the Finnish government argued that their dual objective was to activate the 'passive' social benefit system and to activate passive unemployed individuals. The government described existing active labour market policies and local employment projects as both ineffective and insufficient for tackling the risk of social exclusion among the young and the long-term unemployed. More recently, reforms have mainly focused on changing the institutional settings and patterns of inter-agency co-operation, above all between public employment services and social services (Chapter 5).

Because of Iceland's high level of employment participation and low level of unemployment, the issue of reforming activation policy has not been as central here as in the other Nordic countries. Nevertheless, Iceland introduced a new act on labour market measures in 1997, and the country has experienced a growth in the number of participants in active labour market measures since 2000 (NOSOSCO 2005). Icelandic trade unions have called for a stronger government emphasis on active support (advice and counselling) and the provision of education and training for unemployed citizens (Mósesdóttir 2004, 2005).

From the late 1980s leading Norwegian politicians and policy experts expressed growing concern about the steep increase in social benefit expenditures and the number of people receiving benefits. Expert committees and government departments presented proposals for both tightening the social benefit system and providing new resources for activation measures. The ruling Social-Democratic party emphasized the need for keeping the social protection system from unintentionally contributing to social and economic exclusion. Since the early 1990s, a number of reforms changed the rules for benefit levels, duration and/or eligibility for a number of social insurance benefits (e.g. unemployment, sickness, disability and single parent's benefits) modifying the regulatory framework for social assistance.

Among the Nordic countries, Sweden has a tradition of stricter work conditions in the unemployment insurance system, combined with a large, expensive activation programme. Against the backdrop of the economic recession, the Swedish government created even stricter qualifications for receiving unemployment insurance and curtailed recipients' chances of renewing their entitlement to unemployment insurance through participation in different forms of labour market programmes. Unemployed citizens met stronger demands for geographical and occupational mobility as conditions for receiving benefits, with the benefit level reduced after the first 100 days. In the public debate, the government defined these reforms as incremental reforms (corrections of previous failures or anomalies), not fundamental ('paradigmatic') reforms, as in Finland and Denmark.

Broad changes in ideology and policy, such as the reinvention of the work-line and its normative rationale or the construction of a sharp discursive division between 'passive' and 'active' policies, have led to a renewed emphasis on the duties dimension of the Nordic systems of social protection system –

and not only within social assistance. For instance, all the national systems of unemployment insurance have been modified in the direction of stricter eligibility rules (e.g. required prior work and earnings record), shorter benefit periods and, in some instances, decreased benefit levels.

In tandem with these reforms, the Nordic countries expanded their activation programmes, with the focus and detailed design differing in each country. However, while the Nordic governments originally had portrayed the male working class as the primary target for active labour market policies, the new activation programmes explicitly embraced a much broader range of groups at the margins of or outside the labour markets: both men and women, including people with impairments, single mothers, immigrants and young people with low qualifications. This change does not necessarily mean that all these groups participated in the same programmes. A number of activation measures are designed for particular groups, partly because they have different sources of income (social insurance or social assistance), and partly because policymakers believe that different groups have different needs and requirements. However, despite these internal differentiations, all unemployed Nordic citizens receiving social benefits now have a general duty to be 'active' according to the interpretation that the public authorities give the term.

Activating Nordic systems of social assistance

Nordic systems of social assistance have been in flux since the mid 1980s. In some countries, we have witnessed a trend towards standardization, making eligibility less dependent on local and professional discretion and social assistance payable as a fixed amount. Finland has included a right to a minimum income support in its constitution. Both Finland and Sweden have national standards for basic or subsistence payments to reduce local variation in outcome, while in Denmark and Iceland the governments have created standardized rates for payments. Only the Norwegian social assistance has retained most of its traditional characteristics, as a system based on local self-determination and, at best, locally agreed-on rates for social assistance payments (NOSOSCO 2005).

On the other hand, in all five countries decision-makers at the municipal level are exercising wide discretionary power over the design, focus and contents of their own activation programmes. The establishment of municipal activation programmes is partly a response to the employment services' lack of enthusiasm for and commitment to assisting unemployed citizens receiving social assistance. In addition, the staff in municipality administrations believe that they needed special activation measures to accommodate the particular background, situation and needs of some social assistance recipients. For a minority of their recipients, the municipalities in all the Nordic countries have adopted special work-for-benefit measures ('workfare'), involving particularly strict activity requirements for the person in question (Lødemel and Trickey 2001).

If a person fails to comply with the activity requirements stipulated by the municipality, or if he or she drops out of an activation measure, the municipality has the legal right to impose sanctions, e.g. reduce social assistance payments. However, since social assistance is a provision of last resort and for many recipients the only source of income, a complete withdrawal of benefits could have adverse personal consequences. Moreover, under the legal acts regulating this area, the municipalities have a duty to provide the minimum necessary for subsistence. Apart from reducing the amount of money granted to the person, a municipality can in principle require that the person call at the office to receive a small daily allowance or benefits in kind (e.g. food stamps).

While the practical tasks that activated recipients of social insurance and social assistance have to carry out are not necessarily that different from before, the context – social assistance as last-resort support and the more restrictive requirements and sanctions that municipalities can impose – tends to give activation measures aimed at social assistance recipients a more compulsory, punitive character in the Nordic countries.

The Danish Act on Active Social Policy (1998) regulates in detail the rights and duties of both public authorities and social assistance recipients. The Act gives municipalities a legal duty to give all recipients an activation offer and an individual action plan. Recipients younger than 30 years are to be activated within 3 months of unemployment (12 months for those above 30 years); individual and personal interviews are to take place within 2 months on social assistance. Activation offers can include guidance, job training, individual job training or vocational training (e.g. Torfing 1999, 2004).

Recently, the Danish government has introduced additional changes in the social assistance system, more directly targeting non-Western immigrants for labour market integration. The government has argued that these new measures will create stronger financial incentives for entering the labour market and strengthen the policy rationale of 'something for something' as part of a general 'agreement' between the welfare state and the unemployed recipient. According to the 2005 programme 'A new chance for everyone', young social assistance recipients (under 25 years) must go back to school, otherwise they risk losing their income support. In relationships where both spouses receive social assistance, the government has suggested replacing the cash assistance of one of the spouses with a lower 'spouse allowance' if the spouse has not had ordinary paid work for 300 hours in the preceding 2-year period (Danish Ministry of Refugee, Immigration and Integration Affairs 2005).

Finland introduced its Rehabilitative Work Experience Act in 2001. The target group for the reform was the young and the long-term unemployed who received either labour market support (a means-tested benefit, complementary to the unemployment insurance) or social assistance. The Act regulates in detail the rights and duties of the unemployed, all of whom are to be activated after a certain period on means-tested benefits. Unemployed citizens younger than 25 years are targeted earlier and more vigorously; they have to be activated after 4 months of social assistance. Those older than 25 years have to be activated after 12 months, and each has to complete an individual action plan, a key instrument in the reform (Chapter 5).

The Swedish system of activating social assistance recipients shares some features with the Danish and Finnish models but also differs in some important respects. The Social Services Act of 1998 (revised 2001) gives municipalities the legal option of requiring participation in activation programmes in return for social assistance. Municipalities can demand that young recipients (under 25 years) participate in different forms of local programmes. If recipients fail to comply, the municipality can decrease or deny their right to social assistance. Neither the revised Act nor other official documents give detailed regulations for the implementation of these rules, leaving municipalities room to determine the contents and focus of activities. However, the Act does not give municipalities the duty to provide activation for social assistance recipients or give recipients a right to activation (Johansson 2001).

The Norwegian system of activating social assistance recipients is even further away from the Danish and Finnish models. As early as 1991, the Norwegian government introduced a new Social Services Act with a clear emphasis on work and activity, as opposed to 'passive' provision of social assistance. The municipalities have wide scope for requiring particular forms of activity from social assistance recipients (e.g. active job search). As a result of the official Norwegian commitment to local self-governance, the Social Services Act provides merely a general framework, regulating in broad terms the circumstances for granting or refusing social assistance. The Norwegian government has not stipulated a binding national activation programme for local municipalities to implement or specified regulations for local programmes. Decisions on focus, contents and target groups are left to local politicians and municipal staff. Moreover, local authorities have the right to decide to what extent they use sanctions for non-compliance.

These Nordic social assistance reforms share the introduction of stronger legal duties on the part of the unemployed recipients, including the obligation to participate in different kinds of activation and the possibility of sanctions for those who do not accept activation offers. We have seen, however, that activation is only a duty, not a right, for social assistance recipients in Norway and Sweden. The weak legal regulation of activation in Norway and Sweden emphasizes the differences in power between municipal authorities and unemployed citizens claiming social assistance.

By contrast, Danish and Finnish social assistance recipients have obtained stronger legal rights to activation. These institutional differences are also reflected in the degree to which the governments have specified the municipalities' scope for applying incentives and sanctions. Finland and Denmark have regulated this scope in detail, while Norway and Sweden have largely left it to local and professional discretion.

A neglected aspect of activation reforms is the possibility they provide for voice and participation in deliberation and decision-making. As we have seen, activated recipients tend to have very limited possibilities for leaving activation programmes by choice (unless they are willing to risk losing their benefits). Some countries do, however, provide activated recipients with some power of influencing the contents of their activation offers. Among the Nordic countries, Finland has most explicitly focused on the joint development of individual action plans as an instrument for dialogue, co-operation and self-determination. In the Finnish reform, individual action plans can also be a tool for pressuring social workers and employment officers to consider the views of the client (Chapter 5). Individual action plans and personal interviews are also central to Danish social assistance reforms, becoming one way of ensuring recognition of individual perspectives.

Compared with their Finnish and Danish counterparts, neither the Norwegian nor the Swedish governments have instructed municipalities to develop such plans as part of their activation programmes. Although the employment services in Norway and Sweden have adopted individual action plans, they have not explicitly linked them to the activation of social assistance recipients. To what extent these joint meetings, discussions and action plans provide unemployed citizens claiming social assistance with real possibilities for individual voice, autonomy and self-determination is an issue for empirical research (Chapters 5 and 6).

However, the administrative landscape of activation is changing in three of the Nordic countries. Finland, followed by Denmark and Norway, has initiated major reforms at the interface between central and local administrations of income maintenance and employment promotion. To achieve better co-ordination or integrated approaches to activation, these reforms aim at introducing 'one-stop' models by restructuring and merging previously separate agencies. The division between agencies administering social insurance, social assistance and employment assistance will partly disappear through mergers, and partly diminish through the sharing of office facilities or mandatory inter-agency team models.

Governments hope that these administrative reforms will improve both the effectiveness of activation measures and prospects for social assistance recipients to find work.

Conclusions

In this chapter we have discussed the claim from leading scholars in comparative welfare that recent activation reforms in the Nordic countries bear the stamp of the overall universalistic, egalitarian and inclusive logic of a distinct Nordic model of citizenship. The Nordic countries are supposed to have favoured widening the access to capacity building for all citizens on the margins of the labour market, and to have rejected the other main policy option – that of making cuts and in other ways tightening the benefit system through stricter eligibility criteria, lower benefits and/or short duration of benefits. We have argued that this presentation of Nordic activation reforms is far too simplistic and one-dimensional, disregarding important divisions within both the labour market and the social protection system of the Nordic countries.

First, we have seen that when it comes to the labour market integration of young people and people with impairments, the record of the Nordic group is essentially the same as that of other groups of European countries. As for integrating immigrants in the labour market, the Nordic countries are less successful than most other European countries. Given the higher overall affluence and more favourable labour market conditions of Nordic countries, this result is not particularly impressive.

Second, the thesis of a distinct universalistic and egalitarian Nordic activation policy fails to acknowledge the dual structure of the social protection system of Nordic countries, most clearly expressed in the division between social insurance and social assistance. This division greatly carries over into the Nordic activation programmes, creating a two-tiered system: one administered by the state-run employment services, the other by the municipalities.

Several factors tend to make the municipalities' activation programmes more restrictive and punitive than those of the employment services. Unemployed citizens receiving social assistance are more exposed to the suspicion that they themselves are to blame for their situation and to the belief that they need control and discipline, if the government is to prevent fraud and abuse of public funds. Young people and immigrants, who are over-represented among social assistance recipients, are generally regarded as the least deserving of social benefits. Since social assistance is a support of last resort, the sanctioning of non-compliance with activation requirements through reduction in or termination of payments is likely to have particularly adverse effects for recipients. Their marginal position in the labour market, reinforced by employer prejudices or scepticism makes receiving public benefits their only legal source of support.

Third, our outline of actual policy changes in the Nordic countries shows that, on the one hand, the Nordic countries have provided widened access to capacity building, by channelling more resources to training and educating unemployed citizens. On the other hand, Nordic governments have also considerably tightened their systems of social benefits for working age people. Like many other European governments, the Nordic ones view the expansion of activation measures and the introduction of cuts and stricter eligibility as complementary, not alternative, options.

Therefore, our main conclusion is that a thorough analysis of Nordic activation reforms and their broader labour market and social policy context does not support the idea of a distinct universalistic, egalitarian and inclusive type of activation policy, i.e. one that has more or less left the pre-existing form of Nordic social citizenship unaffected and intact. On the contrary, the recent activation reforms have substantially shifted the focus of social citizenship from the *rights* to the *duties* of unemployed citizens, particularly those receiving social assistance.

Yet, even this picture is not unequivocal: governments accompany their stricter enforcement of duties and requirements with promises of giving unemployed citizens scope for voice and co-determination through individual action plans. This participation has the potential for strengthening unemployed citizens' effective freedom, i.e. for becoming a means for empowerment. Just as possibly, however, joint discussion of plans may become new instruments for controlling and disciplining unemployed citizens – or, perhaps, merely empty promises?

5 Individualizing welfare provision

The integrated approach of the Finnish activation reform

Elsa Keskitalo

Introduction

This chapter discusses individual action plans as a new way in which to assist unemployed citizens to find work. Individual action plans were a key aspect of the 2001 activation reform in Finland. The government implemented this reform through a new integrated approach involving mandatory co-operation between local employment offices and social welfare services. The mandatory co-operation gave the public services the duty of providing substantial practical assistance, thereby presumably strengthening the rights of unemployed citizens, whom the public services had previously often offered only cash benefits.

The question is whether the reform changed the position of the citizens it was to assist and whether they received new scope for agency and negotiation relative to these public agencies. How did staff in the two services and the unemployed citizens experience the way in which the reform was put into practice? This chapter highlights these issues on the basis of a case study involving interviews and observations in a sample of Finnish municipalities.

Activation as individualization of welfare policy

The Finnish government introduced the reform at a time when the country's labour markets had been undergoing profound change. Greater economic openness and increased variability and volatility of labour markets were exposing citizens to greater risks and uncertainty (Kiander 2002). Work was increasingly becoming an individual concern, demanding individual flexibility, choice and effort.

In this new 'risk society' (Beck 1992), more people experienced periods of unemployment and the need to keep changing qualifications and occupations. According to Beck and Beck-Gernsheim (2002), risk society is associated with a trend towards individualization. While clear norms, roles and given trajectories – related to class, gender and local community attachment – governed most people's lives in the earlier phase of modernity, individuals are now forced to construct the course of their lives by exercising choice.

However, both the individual's particular background (and capacity) and current social conditions will constrain his or her choice in certain ways. Structural changes in the labour market involve a long-term shift and diversification for the qualifications that employers demand.

In Finland these new risks and constraints are clearly evident. A deep economic recession in the early 1990s left a large number of people unemployed. Since the mid 1990s the economic development has been rapid, while unemployment has decreased more slowly. At the same time the labour market has gone through structural changes and become increasingly more flexible and uncertain. Although both young and qualified people have gained access to employment, individuals from groups made redundant from traditional workplaces have had a hard time finding work (Kiander 2002).

Governments have succeeded only partially, through general or standardized measures, in including long-term unemployed people in paid employment. More targeted and differentiated measures, taking into account the particular situation of the unemployed individual, are necessary. Such measures entail personalized or tailored solutions, involving individual choice for the unemployed, because individuals are unequal in their capacity to benefit from the same general labour market services:

> In order to combat this inequality, equal access to services and treatment according to his or her need is required. If it proves necessary, each person must receive a specific kind of help, differing in quality and quantity from that given to others.
>
> (Salais 2003: 333–34)

One way of achieving this kind of personalized employment assistance is for public welfare services and the unemployed citizen to jointly formulate and commit themselves to an action plan for improving the citizen's labour market prospects through practical steps like training. As in the Finnish activation reform, this plan must grow out of a thorough assessment of the unemployed person's needs and prospects. The individual is expected to take part in developing the activation plan and its follow-up; otherwise, he or she risks sanctions like reduced payments. The planning process thus involves a new type of contractual arrangement between the public agencies, represented by front-line staff and the unemployed citizen. Individually adjusted forms of assistance have been important in social work for a long time. However, the distinct agreements between the state and citizens (implied in the joint formulation of an action plan, combined with the more explicitly stated sanctions), introduce new elements in social work with unemployed citizens (Lødemel and Trickey 2001; Mosley and Sol 2005).

This type of activation approach is a major recent development in European labour market policies (Hvinden *et al.* 2001; Clasen and van Oorschot 2003). Several authors have criticized this approach for ignoring the conditions of high overall unemployment, structural changes and regional differences (e.g. Julkunen 2001), and for implying that unemployment is no longer a structural problem but a question of individual employability. Although activation policy is mainly a supply-side strategy, aimed at activating unemployed citizens by improving their qualifications and skills, it also relates to wider innovations in human resource management, particularly as applied in the European context (Theodore and Peck 2001).

The 2001 Act on Rehabilitative Work Experience codified locally developed approaches to activation. More significantly, the Act created a new setting for welfare policy: mandatory co-operation between local offices of both the national employment administration and the local government social welfare services. These agencies were now to operate on the basis of one coherent legal framework. The central government gave quite detailed regulations for procedures and roles at the local level, while leaving decisions about the contents of individual action plans to the discretion of local actors – the unemployed citizen and the representatives of the two welfare providers. By introducing the individual action plan, the reform also changed the relationship between the state and the citizen and the balance between rights and obligations. One important aspect of the Finnish reform is that it activated not only unemployed citizens but also the public agencies providing them services.

Individual activation plans may provide scope for negotiation and informed participation on the part of the citizens involved (Van Berkel and Roche 2002). The action plan approach promises to put the perspective of the unemployed citizens into focus, treating them as competent actors able to negotiate the direction of their lives (Valkenburg and Lind 2002). At the same time this process places demands on both citizens and front-line staff. The negotiation over the action plan does not occur between equals but rather in a context of structural inequality. Not only does unemployment disproportionately affect citizens who have low vocational qualifications or are otherwise marginal (Kortteinen and Tuomikoski 1998), but their income also depends on staff decisions. While obligatory participation in the action plan process is meant to give unemployed citizens new opportunities and improved access to public resources, the citizens may not view participation in this light or be convinced of its value.

Tensions, therefore, were likely to arise between the formal framework of the activation plan process (a result of political aims) and the way in which unemployed citizens experienced the process. We need to empirically examine how both staff and individual citizens handled – and possibly solved – these tensions: Did the mandatory activation plan process give citizens opportunities for a negotiation process accommodating both their and society's interests (which the staff of public agencies represented)? Did the process allow individual choice and co-determination, enabling unemployed citizens to act as competent participants (Van Berkel and Roche 2002)? Did the overall process create new possibilities and opportunities, rather than only new constraints?

Research design and data

From 2001 to 2003, STAKES (National Research and Development Centre for Welfare and Health) conducted a broad study of the content and effectiveness of the reform (Ala-Kauhaluoma *et al.* 2004). The overall study applied a representative sample of 51 Finnish municipalities to examine the outcomes of the reform. This chapter primarily uses an intensive approach to focus on the relationships between front-line staff and citizens, with data from four municipalities of different size and geographical location, thereby allowing variation in the factors influencing local practices. The data consist of interviews with 17 staff members and 15 unemployed citizens about their experiences with activation plans. The staff involved social workers and their managers, who co-ordinated local actions. To meet given criteria for different ages and genders, the social workers selected the unemployed citizens from their registers. In addition, the study included observations of nine meetings of staff and unemployed citizens discussing activation plans. Collecting the data in 2002 and again in 2004 allowed further investigation over time.

Aim and design of the reform

The aim of the integrated activation model in the Act on Rehabilitative Work Experience was to improve the efficiency and targeting of activation measures. Many of the unemployed registered in state employment offices and municipal social welfare offices were the same people. Co-operation between the two administrations was irregular, depending on the activity of local actors. The Act therefore mandated inter-agency co-operation, and this mandate created a new framework for local activation efforts.

The Act required co-operative preparation of the activation plan by the employment office, the social welfare office of the municipality and the unemployed citizen. The plan was meant to form a tailored pathway to employment, involving labour policy measures, employment and social services, and rehabilitative work experience as a last resort. The reform introduced rehabilitative work experience – a new 'work-for-benefit' measure to be provided by local municipalities – and this measure lent its title to the Act. The Act specified the categories of unemployed citizens whose participation in the activation plan process it required as follows:

- Persons under the age of 25 had to participate after having received social assistance for 4 months.
- Persons over the age of 25 had to be activated after having received 12 months of social assistance.
- Recipients of labour market support under the age of 25 had to be activated after 180 days; all others, after 500 days.

Unemployed citizens meeting these criteria had to participate and follow the measures they agreed to in the plan. If they did not comply with these two requirements, they might be subject to sanctions. The sanctions included a temporary 20 per cent reduction of social assistance (if the behaviour was repeated, then 40 per cent) and a temporary withdrawal of labour market support. The offices had to impose these sanctions whenever an eligible person did not participate without 'fair reason' (as spelled out in the Act), i.e. if he or she did not follow the agreed-on plan. Although the Act clearly stated the principles of sanctioning, front-line staff made decisions about enforcement case by case. Moreover, within the legal framework of the Act, the content of individual activation plans and measures included in them was decided through local co-operative practices.

Staff perceptions of the sanctioning of non-compliance: variability and ambiguity

Front-line staff basically welcomed the integrated model because it made them more goal-oriented and productive, and because participants could more easily get access to the resources that they provided. Staff no longer had to refer an unemployed citizen to another office, because measures like workplace training could be agreed on immediately. Further, they now found it easier to deal with the various barriers to working and to negotiating individual routes towards employment. Staff maintained that without the new legal framework, putting the integrated activation approach into action would not have been possible.

Many social workers interviewed believed that activation would not work on a voluntary basis and that without an obligation of unemployed citizens to participate activation would be 'watered down'. They therefore tended to look favourably on obligatory participation, but they were more cautious about enforcement and the use of sanctions. Some social workers viewed sanctions as necessary for enforcing the duties of the unemployed citizens and for stressing to the individual the importance of his or her own efforts in finding a job. Others were more sceptical, arguing that sanctions hardly ever helped in individual cases.

The sanctioning policy differed between the employment offices (administering labour market support) and the social welfare offices (providing social assistance). The differences largely derived from the legislation for labour market support and social assistance. While the sanctioning rules for labour market support were categorical, the rules for social assistance left more to staff discretion, e.g. the staff could consider individual circumstances and fairness. Moreover, the staff had to apply social assistance sanctions in a way that did not endanger the necessary subsistence that the Finnish constitution guaranteed. Staff, therefore, could only reduce – and not completely withdraw – social assistance payments. The distinct considerations of the two groups of staff on the matter of sanctions clearly reflect the difference in legal frameworks, as these comments illustrate:

> We've never used a reduction in social assistance, since rents are high in the area, and the assistance is hardly enough for living. We've used it only once in the case of one young person. Sanctions don't motivate people.
>
> (social welfare officer)

> Sanctions do have an important role. If participation is totally voluntary, not everyone would be motivated at the early stage of these activities. As for the employment administration these sanctions are in line with the compulsory character of our other activities.
>
> (employment service officer)

The Act on Rehabilitative Work Experience made unemployed citizens more aware of their rights and duties. The letter of invitation to the meeting about the activation plan informed the unemployed citizens about the rights and duties of participation. Compared with the established discretionary practice in social services, this routine clarified rights and duties for the citizen. A social worker described the invitation process in the following way:

> In this letter of invitation we emphasize that they have to come to the appointment. If they don't come, you need to have a sick note from a doctor. We explain to the participants that if they are not active, they are not entitled to the labour market support. For all those who have received the letter, we did not need to emphasize these sanctions so strongly.
>
> (social worker)

Only a small minority of the unemployed citizens invited to meetings refused to participate in the planning process or in the agreed-on measures. Non-attendance at activation plan meetings without prior notification or drop-outs from the measures happened slightly more often. Although no available national statistics on the extent of applied sanctions are available, the social workers estimated that they adopted sanctions in about 5 per cent of all cases (Ala-Kauhaluoma *et al.* 2004). Of all labour market support recipients invited to an activation planning meeting, 3 per cent were sanctioned (Ministry of Labour Statistics 2003). Given local staff's scope for discretion, their actual adoption of sanctions probably varied substantially among municipalities.

Although participation in the activation plan process and the measures (as agreed upon in the plan) was mandatory, staff sought to avoid using sanctions if possible. They stressed that although they were obliged to comply with their legal duty under the Act, the important thing was to create an atmosphere of trust and co-operation with the unemployed citizens. Social workers described basing their decisions on individual discretion and considerations about the nature of non-compliance, imposing sanctions more or less only if participants were not 'willing to do anything'. Therefore, the possibility of sanctioning operated as a work test (Lødemel and Trickey 2001: 15–22).

The views of participants on the activation process

According to the views expressed by participating unemployed citizens, the idea of the activation plan as an individual-oriented process worked. Even if participation was compulsory, they tended to see the planning process as based on negotiation and co-determination, with the possibility of stating their opinions and preferences in the plan's formulation. Broadly speaking, all the interviewees shared these perceptions. However, the planning process had different meanings to different people, depending on their age and previous work history. For long-term unemployed citizens, participation could help to break a vicious circle:

> Yes, it was not all good – now when I think about it – being unemployed for eight years. That time has gone quite fast, but so many years, that's a long time. Was it that I got used to it? Was it going to be this way in the future, when nothing seems to appear? Then came this suggestion [from the social worker] and things changed totally. Now you can perceive that period of being unemployed totally differently from before, when you lived through that period in your life. This has really been a good choice.
>
> (unemployed citizen)

For unqualified, young and unemployed individuals, participation in the activation plan could open a route to a training course or create the motivation to apply for further education. Participation in the activation planning process in this way contributed significantly to their future career.

The integrated approach to activation also dealt with other barriers that kept participants from finding work. For instance, the process helped some participants to get access to health care and social services as part of their plan. The planning process dealt with not only the lack of a job but also other – and sometime complex – life problems.

For a few other participants, although the counselling part of the process was insignificant, the activation plan worked as a gateway to employment measures. Given the limited resources of the employment services, participation in the activation plan opened access to labour market policy measures. 'It is through [the meetings about activation] one gets into [the subsidized] work, one can't just go there and ask for it; it is a complicated route' (unemployed citizen).

Basically, involvement in the planning process made it easier for unemployed citizens to obtain information about available opportunities and access to the various measures. The process served as a new mechanism for rationing scarce goods; through this process, staff selected the unemployed citizens who would enter training and other labour market measures. The activation reform thus shifted the relative position among eligible unemployed citizens, because not all of them were invited to take part in such activation measures.

The participants attributed great significance to their experiences of interacting with the staff in the activation planning process. They felt that the competence and responsiveness of the staff were decisive for the outcome. However, mandatory participation can also be associated with paternalism – inferring with a person, against his or her will, with the justification that the interference will lead to a better result (Mead 1997b). Therefore, some tensions arose:

> [The activation plan] is a sensible idea, but the first time I felt it was like being forced into working life, that they forced you into a situation although you were not ready. You had a feeling that the city wanted you to move from welfare to the state, to go under the care of KELA [the Finnish national insurance institution]. The second time I felt it as a fresh start, providing a new thinking. The second time I met another staff member, she received me in a different way, as a person, not as an ineffective unemployed person.
>
> (unemployed citizen)

Although the participants' opinions and preferences were supposed to be the starting point for formulating the activation plan, the staff had to weigh these preferences against the availability of practical possibilities, resources and measures. The specific situation in the local labour market and the opportunities it offered determined the scope for choice. Participants acknowledged this limitation.

Participants' perceptions of the use of sanctions

Few interviewees perceived the mandatory character of the activation plan process as important for them personally. Although they were aware of its compulsory nature, they understood it either as a part of the familiar 'rules of the game' in the employment services or as part of a policy that was primarily providing new opportunities and accommodating their preferences. Since their experiences with activation measures were generally positive, they did not perceive obligation as a major problem. Some of the participants, however, felt that the compulsory nature of the plan gave the policy a negative image that contradicted the spirit of negotiation, choice and individual commitment, leading them to resent the entire policy:

> The first reaction for everybody is – for sure – that when you are forced ... nobody likes the word obligation. You go and [wonder] what

will take place there. This obligation is negative for the idea of the activation plan, invalidating the idea and preventing one from seeing immediately that it is good.

(unemployed citizen)

Other participants saw the obligation to participate as a normal feature of employment policy but one at odds with the conditions of structural unemployment and job shortage in Finland. That some of the eligible recipients did not get access to the activation plan was also seen as contradicting the notion of compulsory participation. Participants questioned the reason for compulsion if not everybody could receive the service: 'One just wonders, why they oblige some, while the others are not good enough?' (unemployed citizen).

Interestingly, the interviewed participants in part accepted the overall justification for activation policy, implying that compulsion would promote a participation that would otherwise not occur:

I do not know whether I have understood it right – that the activation plan is not drawn up with the short-term unemployed but with the long-term unemployed and social assistance recipients. Although one can never generalize, a great number of people surely need a kick-start. If there wasn't the threat of sanctions, many would not go or take it seriously. The number of participants would have been smaller and the number of cancellations larger, if it wasn't [obligatory]. I see it as more of a good thing anyway, that is how I see it.

(unemployed citizen)

Yet the participants were more critical about the use of sanctions than about obligatory participation. They emphasized that obligations and sanctions should not be applied to sick and mentally vulnerable people, because these steps would only lead to drop-outs and a worsening of exclusion. Some argued against imposing sanctions because of the economic hardship that reductions in payments would cause. But others, on the basis of their own experience, were more accepting of the use of sanctions.

If unemployed citizens were dissatisfied with the staff's decision to reduce their social assistance payments because they had refused to participate in the activation plan or agreed-upon measures, they had the right to appeal. For social assistance, citizens were able to appeal first to the municipal social welfare board and then to the regional administrative court. However, none of the participants interviewed in this study had ever appealed.

Interactions between participants and front-line staff

During the formulation of the individual activation plan, the interaction between the staff and citizens was decisive in four municipalities in the first year of implementation, when co-operation practices were still developing. The practical course of the interaction depended on the specific situation of the participants. The social worker represented expertise on social services provision, and the employment officer provided information about employment services. In practice, however, one staff member did the interviewing while the other was drafting the plan. The meetings lasted from an hour to an hour and a half. According to the STAKES' survey, the formulation of the average activation plan, including the preparatory work, took about 2 hours (Ala-Kauhaluoma *et al.* 2004).

The activation planning process started with a discussion of the unemployed citizen's situation and his or her wishes and preferences. The staff presented different opportunities in terms of work, training and other measures, from among which options the participant was required to choose. The staff tended to push for a clear decision. In some cases, this ambition manifested itself as pressure on the unemployed citizen to make a decision on the basis of the options that the staff had outlined. At the end of the meeting the staff members presented a draft and asked whether the unemployed citizen approved it. If he or she objected to something in the plan, that part was changed. In the end, the activation plan was to be signed by both the authorities and the unemployed citizen.

In the following illustrative exchange, the unemployed citizen had refused the staff's first suggestion but had agreed to a second one. The exchange shows the influence of the unemployed citizen on the outcome:

Q: Are you interested in this job?
A: There might be other jobs available.
Q: You are not excited about this job?
A: Isn't it summer workers who pack those parcels?
Q: These are the subsidized placements that we are able to provide for a half year. But it seems that you are not willing to do that. You want that additional training in your own business?
A: Yes.
Q: In principle we are able to provide that training for a half year, since other jobs are not available and you have been unemployed that long. On account of that, we might consider that option, too, on the condition that you are able to find that kind of place of training yourself.

The staff took the unemployed citizen's preferences as the point of departure for the discussion while using their discretionary power when outlining the available options. Although they expected the unemployed citizen to choose between these options, he or she had some scope for negotiating the outcome, especially as no agreement could be signed without the approval of all participants. Even if the planning process was framed by an imbalance of power, unemployed citizens still had a say in it.

The overall experience with activation plans

The statistical material from the survey indicates about how often different measures were included in the activation plans. As the regulatory framework implies, individual plans strongly emphasized job search activity and participation in active labour measures, most of which derived from the employment administration. Local staff used these measures to try to reintegrate both the young and the long-term unemployed citizens into the regular labour market, thereby including municipal activation – a tailored rehabilitative work experience – only in a smaller number of plans. The policymakers' objective of giving priority to labour market attachment was thus put into practice.

As part of the overall reform, the rehabilitative work experience scheme was voluntary for those aged 25 and older. The findings of the STAKES' survey showed that most of the participants were over 25, meaning that they started voluntarily. Non-governmental organizations, public services and different workshops for young people offered placements for rehabilitative work experience. An advantage of the rehabilitative work experience was that participants could influence both their placement and their working hours by tailoring the length of the contract. If the placements were well tailored and the work tasks found to be motivating and meaningful, participants tended to be positive, seeing the work experience measure as improving their confidence and overall activity. Nonetheless, some participants viewed their lack of status as a regular employee as negative in their experience with the placements.

Overall the survey shows that the participants viewed the drawing up of the activation plan as important (Ala-Kauhaluoma *et al.* 2004: 125–27). Just after they had completed their plan, as many as 83 per cent rated the formulation of the plan as personally significant. Many expected that their plan would give them access to regular work. Survey findings also show that about half the participants lacked vocational qualifications. Renewing a job search was the single most frequent option for the participants. The second most important option in the plans was participation in labour market measures, e.g. practical training, subsidized work or subsidized training. If no other measures were applicable, rehabilitative work experience was usually the final choice. Rehabilitative work experience was in the activation plans of 18 per cent of the participants. In practice, however, only about 10 per cent actually began rehabilitative work. About 15 per cent of the plans included assistance from the social and health care services. In general, the plans included several optional measures (Ala-Kauhaluoma *et al.* 2004: 131–34).

The first study of the participants' situations took place immediately after the drawing up of their activation plans, with individual follow-ups after 6–8 months. The results of the follow-up study show that 50 per cent of the participants were unemployed 6–8 months after they had been involved in drawing up the activation plan. The other 50 per cent were in most cases involved in various labour market policy measures. If these measures were related to work, they contributed to the participants' economic and social well-being (ibid. 147–49, 166–78).

The follow-up indicated that participation in the activation plan process did not have any great impact on participants' prospects for finding regular employment in the short-term. Even though finding work was the first option agreed on in the activation plans, a high overall unemployment rate (with considerable regional variation) meant that the chances of finding work were not good for many participants. Only 8 per cent were employed in the open labour market during the 6 months after their plan was drawn up, although almost all of them had high expectations immediately upon completing their activation plan. When the plan did not lead to employment in the open labour market, these expectations diminished (Ala-Kauhaluoma *et al.* 2004: 157–61).

Although the process of drawing up the activation plans worked as intended, the functioning of the local labour market limited the participants' success. In addition, the implementation process revealed a shortage of training and other labour market measures. Between 2001 and 2003 (the evaluation period for the outcomes of the activation reform), the overall unemployment level in Finland remained high, severely limiting opportunities for gaining access to the regular labour market. For an activation policy to be successful, both a dynamic labour market and available entry-level jobs are necessary (Theodore and Peck 2001). However, such was not the case in Finland in the early 2000s. All together, these findings illustrate the substantial limitations of a supply-side strategy of activation.

Conclusions

The new Finnish activation approach – based on the integrated efforts of employment services and social welfare services and mandatory individual activation plans – was well received by the staff and the unemployed citizens in this study. The new approach generated a coherent institutional framework for local activation and promoted standardized practices, without fully removing the scope for local discretion and variation. Both the staff and the unemployed citizens tended to view obligatory participation as a positive feature, with only a minority of unemployed citizens refusing to attend activation plan meetings. All in all, from the perspective of the unemployed citizen, the integrated activation approach increased the predictability of both the process and the outcome.

This chapter earlier posed the question of whether the mandatory activation plan process gave citizens opportunities for a reflexive process that could accommodate the interests of both the unemployed citizens and society, as represented by the staff in public agencies. The answer is *yes*. When staff presented options that the unemployed citizen regarded as unsuitable, he or she always had the chance to argue against options that he or she did not find meaningful or helpful. Both the interviews with participants and observations of activation plan meetings indicated that the process offered unemployed citizens some scope for individual choice and co-determination, enabling them to act as competent participants. In this sense, participation in the process promoted active citizenship.

Did the unemployed citizen experience the overall process as creating new possibilities and opportunities, not only new constraints? Yes, at its best the formulation of the activation plan meant a new start and opened up new opportunities for the unemployed citizen. Moreover, the strength of the rehabilitative work experience was the tailoring of the placements to individual needs and interests. Negative features were the role of participants as a secondary labour force in regular workplaces and the controversial title of the Act. Critics argue that the title implied that the government viewed unemployment not only as an individual problem but also as one that carried a stigma.

Although the integrated approach and the activation plan process meant that many citizens who had been unemployed for a long time now received the attention and interest of public agency staff, the process also contained a risk of further marginalizing the participants. The greatest risk was that of the participants becoming absorbed in the activation plan process and various measures without realistic prospects of ever gaining access to regular paid work.

The range of options that the staff presented in the planning process was contingent on available resources and on local labour market conditions. Within these limitations the reform offered participants new possibilities and opportunities, in particular through improved access to labour market measures and other services. All in all, while the Finnish activation reform was able to promote the employability and social inclusion of unemployed citizens, only to a limited extent did it improve their access to regular paid work, at least in the short-term.

6 The challenges of decentralized delivery of services

The scope for active citizenship in Swedish and Norwegian activation policies

Rune Halvorsen, Jon Arve Nervik, Tapio Salonen, Katarina Thorén and Rickard Ulmestig

Introduction

Since the 1990s, European welfare states have come to emphasize individual or personalized approaches to unemployment. An individual approach, on the one hand, implies an ambition to involve the individual on his or her own terms in a dialogue on how to handle unemployment, from both short- and long-term perspectives. Individual circumstances therefore become the starting point for social interventions, with presumed reciprocity between individual job seekers and agency staff, as they negotiate a common agreement on activation measures. This presumption places great pressure on both the individual and the public services. On the other hand, an individual approach means strengthened individual responsibilities and obligations, i.e. public welfare provisions become conditional on the individual fulfilling these obligations. Whether this approach recognizes the individual as a subject with legitimate views and with the rights to influence the activation process is debatable, because the state uses either strong financial incentives or monetary sanctions to bring people into gainful employment.

The practical outcome of the individual approach to activation is likely to depend upon various factors. These include the division of labour and goals between national public employment and local social services, the institutional design of welfare provisions, the ideology and professional competence of activation officers, and the nature of the regulations and instruments that may safeguard the rights of the individual vis-à-vis the discretionary powers of public authorities and professionals. This chapter therefore explores the meanings of an individual approach to activating unemployed citizens claiming social assistance. Our empirical context will be municipality activation policies in Sweden and Norway, i.e. activation mainly exercised within a separated system of activation.

The previous chapter focused on Finland's integrated approach. Here, instead, we examine the local systems of activation in Sweden and Norway. In brief, the situational context is one in which unemployed citizens receive social assistance payments from the municipality's social services authorities but must get practical job-finding help or training through the central government's employment services authorities and/or through the local municipalities' activation services. We ask how a separated system of activation affects the scope for exercising active citizenship:

- First, as a decentralized, fragmented and discretionary system of welfare provision is likely to create much local variability, can we identify a clear status of active citizenship, involving a consistent set of rights and duties, for unemployed people claiming social assistance?
- Second, to what extent do local activation approaches give possibilities for tailored solutions, or are the measures more standardized? Do they encourage voice, influence and choice on the part of participants?
- Third, to what extent do unemployed citizens remain passive or active, given these situational constraints? Is the individual able to resist participation in measures that he or she sees as useless or degrading?

Discussing the effect of participation in local activation measures on the person's likelihood of leaving social assistance and/or entering the mainstream labour market is outside the scope of this chapter. However, recent evaluation studies show contradictory results (e.g. Nervik 1997; Lorentzen and Dahl 2005). We argue that if the demonstrated effect is weak or nonexistent, we have reason to examine more closely what occurs within the scope of local activation, especially whether the operation of activation measures is compatible with broader notions of active citizenship, human dignity and freedom of choice.

Methods and sources of data

We draw on findings made in the following studies of social assistance and activation in Sweden and Norway:

- Johansson (2001) studied the changing rights and duties of people claiming social assistance in Sweden during the 1980s and the 1990s, analyzing legal acts and the decisions of administrative courts, national boards and two municipalities.
- Salonen and Ulmestig (2004) carried out an extensive survey of the activation programmes of Swedish municipalities in 2002, highlighting both the extent to which the municipalities had initiated activation measures and, if they had, the kind of measures.
- Thorén (2005) studied a large activation programme with between 100 and 150 daily participants in one Swedish municipality, through fieldwork and observation of the interaction between staff and participants. A small interview study by Thorén and Ulmestig later supplemented this research.

- Vik-Mo and Nervik (1999) investigated the labour market measures of Norwegian municipalities in the late 1990s, combining a survey of all municipalities with qualitative interviews with staff and participants in five of them.
- Halvorsen (2002) carried out an in-depth study of how unemployed citizens coped with the changing administration of social assistance in Norway, both individually and collectively (Chapter 7). In 2004, to supplement this study, he made a set of qualitative interviews.

Because the foci and exact design of these studies have been heterogeneous, we will not be strictly comparing the ways in which local activation affects the scope for active citizenship in Sweden and Norway. Rather, we seek to identify a set of common themes that this pool of complementary data highlights.

National activation policies in local contexts

The background to changes in Norwegian and Swedish activation policies have been previously clarified (Chapter 4). However, despite recent changes, we know surprisingly little about how, and to what extent, municipalities in Norway and Sweden have adopted activation measures. As the measures are decided locally, with considerable variation, collecting comparable data across and between countries is difficult. Our empirical study, however, allows us to point to some broader trends, along with some peculiarities of activation in such a divided and discretionary model.

To begin with, since the beginning of the 1990s we have witnessed a general policy shift among Norwegian and Swedish municipalities From arguing that providing labour market measures for unemployed people was largely a task for employment services, municipalities have generally acknowledged the importance of becoming involved and operating projects on their own (Johansson 2001). That municipalities expect social assistance recipients to participate in locally organized and financed projects is no longer unusual. This shift does not mean that all municipalities have been involved in such activities or that only municipalities have set up activation measures, because some municipalities have for different reasons chosen not to engage in labour market measures at all. However, among those engaged in activation activities of this kind, some have developed them in co-operation with local offices of the national employment service. As a consequence of a decentralized model, both volume and type of activation measures differ substantially among municipalities, as the following findings indicate:

- In Sweden, Salonen and Ulmestig (2004) found that 82 per cent of the 288 municipalities were engaged in activation measures and projects in 2002. In 168 of them, 527 local activation measures involved about 12,000 people. This number corresponded to 10 per cent of the total number of recipients of social assistance and about 10 per cent of the number of participants in national labour market programmes.

- In Norway, Vik-Mo and Nervik (1999) found that 44 per cent of the 435 municipalities operated activation measures and projects in 1998. Only 13 per cent used activation measures exclusively, while 42 per cent used some of them to encourage work in return for social assistance payments ('workfare'). All in all, only 22 per cent of the municipalities demanded 'workfare'. An earlier study suggested that, since 1995, slightly more than one-third of the municipalities requested work in return for social assistance payments for at least some of their recipients (Lødemel 1997).

These studies also indicate that some municipalities mainly used short-term strategies to relieve the beneficiaries of immediate financial hardship (an 'emergency' strategy), while others adopted a more long-term perspective, seeking to improve the social skills, capabilities and labour prospects of the participants. While some municipalities provided positive incentives in the form of additional grants for participants ('motivation grants'), others have used threats of withdrawing or reducing the social assistance allowance (Salonen and Ulmestig 2004). These differences raise several questions about the rights and duties of unemployed citizens claiming social assistance in Norway and Sweden, and make it disputable whether we can identify a single or consistent model of active citizenship for this group.

Activation offers – tailored or standardized?

The picture of local activation becomes even more complex when we turn our attention to the internal and professional practices in local municipalities. In principle, the discretionary and flexible system of local social services appears well suited to tailor solutions for unemployed citizens – as indeed was the case in many municipalities. However, other studies show that in some municipalities, front-line staff developed work practices that largely negated the tailored approach.

In Sweden, Thorén (2005) found that front-line staff in the activation programme she studied had developed numerous procedures and practices that effectively standardized work. One of her most striking findings was the way in which front-line staff selected and categorized clients before their participation in activation programmes: this categorization then justified the different attention and treatment clients received. Thorén identified the use of four different categories: people considered motivated and willing to work; people perceived as being motivated to work but lacking sufficient capacity; people perceived as not serious and lacking any real motivation to work; and people temporarily excused from participation in activation measures. The categorization enhanced the effective processing of people and affected what kind of activation programme (training or job placement), if any, the staff offered the individual.

Front-line staff also standardized and rationalized their encounters with unemployed citizens. The first contact with each individual tended to be short, dominated by a mapping of his or her 'competence profile'. The unemployed citizen filled out standardized forms and answered routine questions about his or her interests, ambitions and goals. In the activation programme that Thorén studied, the job coaches used forms with pre-determined job alternatives, as they wanted to gain information that was easy to respond to, not information that required additional resources. The activation programme had a general shortage of training and education opportunities to offer its clients. Moreover, the job coaches had no particular education or knowledge about the labour market. As a result, they tended to simplify the options they offered.

The aims and ambitions of unemployed citizens often conflicted with the way in which the activation programme operated. In their encounters with unemployed citizens, front-line staff generally approached the individual from a 'work first' approach:

> ... we do not offer or encourage clients to participate in education and training as the first alternative for clients ... clients shall find a job initially ... it's later on that we suggest training and education and other programmes that are the responsibility of the employment services.
>
> (job coach)

Among other things, this attitude indicated that when unemployed citizens tried to negotiate practical training or education, job coaches often discouraged or even refused their requests, instead emphasizing the work-first approach. Similar lack of responsiveness characterized the contents of the available activation measures. Beyond these formal meetings, job coaches rarely engaged in conversation, discussion or dialogue with unemployed clients. The activation programme that Thorén studied mainly offered unemployed citizens 'do-it-yourself' provisions – e.g. access to computers, phones, copying machines, faxes and lists of vacant jobs – even though any participant could use these resources without any guidance from a job coach.

Admittedly, these findings are from one particular municipality committed to 'tough' activation policies. Nevertheless, the study exemplifies what might occur within a decentralized and divided model of activation. The actual substance of this model would be under strong influence from the way in which front-line staff exercises their wide scope for discretion. Thorén also demonstrates how some municipalities used local and professional autonomy in a manner that conflicted with either a more individual approach or, at the least, the stated government ambition of considering individual preferences and wishes.

A somewhat similar picture of standardized measures emerges from research undertaken in Norway (Vik-Mo and Nervik 1999). In one of the localities studied there, participants referred to the work training as a 'waste of time' or 'slave work'. Complaining about too few work tasks, they did not view the activation measures as helping to increase their qualifications or improve their opportunities to achieve paid work ('we just sit there'). Front-line staff rationalized this situation as the result of an unfortunate shortage of externally procured work assignments. Not surprisingly, this locality was characterized by strong tensions between staff and participants, contradictory accounts of how well the measures functioned, and frequent threats about stopping the benefit payments of participants seen as not complying with their obligations.

In a similar vein, interviews by Halvorsen uncovered a discrepancy between the stated ideals of tailored solutions and actual practice. Despite a limited supply of measures and resources, opportunities existed for modifying the conditions for participation. In practice, however, case-workers had limited time to help each individual and therefore used more routine practices to shelter themselves from an indefinite workload (Hvinden 1994). Additionally the municipalities' activation measures served purposes other than improving an individual's capabilities. Staff in this municipality used participation in their own elementary measures to check whether people were willing to work and able to meet with them at regular working hours before allowing them to participate in measures that other agencies offered (Midré 1995).

Even if these examples from Sweden and Norway are somewhat unusual, they nevertheless raise doubts about the extent to which activation measures in the two countries succeeded in enabling individual participants to exercise choice, access tailored solutions and reject offers they considered useless or degrading. In contrast, professional practices by front-line staff in activation organizations tended to follow well-known patterns of 'street-level bureaucracy' (Lipsky 1980; Brodkin 1990), including the way in which job coaches developed coping mechanisms for handling external demands that they decrease unemployment among social assistance recipients. Front-line staff also adopted various coping mechanisms to simplify tasks, control clients and shift responsibility from the public agency to the individual.

As expected, given their professional ethos and training, many social workers argued that they worked for the benefit of their 'clients'. However, from the point of view of many unemployed citizens, social workers mainly represented the authorities. Some claimants even referred to social workers as 'oppressors' or 'enemies', because they controlled access to money. Clearly, the contradictions inherent in the structural position of the social workers as both gate-keepers to cash benefits and providers of other support and advocacy created ambivalence on both sides. Therefore, it was not surprising that participants were generally more satisfied with social workers who worked only with local labour market measures than with those who also assessed applications for financial support.

Social workers who worked only with labour market measures and closely followed up participants (e.g. by means of counselling, information and home visits) were not experienced as exercising a lot of social control. Instead, participants perceived their actions as help when the actions corresponded to the participants' ideas of 'meaningful' and 'useful' and when the actions clearly were in line with their own interests. Therefore, social services offices that separated the vocational training and activation measures from the administration of the cash benefits were more successful in achieving co-operation and dialogue with these unemployed citizens.

Similarly, social workers who worked only with labour market training tended to present their work as less problematic and as offering more choice and scope for agency. They could more easily present themselves as advocates of the unemployed citizens. Social workers who controlled access to financial and other resources more often referred to acts and regulations that limited their discretionary powers, thereby quite clearly appearing – and being – gate-keepers to scarce resources (Vik-Mo and Nervik 1999).

Interaction, negotiation and control in local activation processes

A significant feature of the Norwegian and Swedish models of local activation is the lack of national central regulation of the contents of the process or the structuring of the interaction between front-line staff and unemployed citizens. Policymakers apparently regard front-line staff's professional competence and exercise of discretion as sufficient for handling citizens' interests. The governments of Sweden and Norway have only to a limited extent given municipalities and their staff legal obligations for providing appropriate activation offers to unemployed citizens. By contrast, Finland has made an explicit attempt to activate municipalities and institutionalize new working procedures, not only to promote co-operation between social services and employment services but also to regulate the interaction process between front-line staff and the unemployed citizen in great detail. As Keskitalo has shown, individual action plans received a central role in securing the proper involvement of the individual in the activation process (Chapter 5).

Given these characteristics of local activation in Sweden and Norway, we ask:

- What meaning did front-line staff and participants attribute to work and activation measures?
- What did they think about the scope for negotiation, self-determination or choice in the activation process?
- What significance did individual action plans have in the Norwegian and Swedish contexts?

Attitudes towards work and activation measures

Interviews in Norway suggest that the dominant attitude towards work and activity among the social workers was that any activity was better than no activity. To help unemployed citizens to keep up more or less the same daily rhythm and routines as employed people was considered a goal in itself. People claiming social assistance were often assumed to lack the necessary competence to make their own choices. Therefore, social workers had to motivate them to participate in measures that others designed or even controlled.

Several of the social services offices operated work training programmes where claimants carried out regular work tasks. To ensure participation, the offices combined work training with incentives, sanctions, or both. Despite objections from some members of staff, the use of threats of cuts in benefit payments was not uncommon. Although professional social workers tended to be sceptical of using workfare as a separate measure, they were less reluctant to reduce financial support as an incentive for participating in work training and other activation measures. Given that unemployed citizens were considered able to participate in vocational training and work practice, staff in several social services offices considered workfare appropriate. They were less inclined to enforce participation in cases where they assumed the beneficiary had legitimate reasons for rejecting the job opportunities that he or she was offered.

The interviews with unemployed citizens claiming social assistance gave a different but complex picture. With few exceptions, participants accepted the premises for the official work-first approach and expressed willingness to fulfil the requirements of participating in labour market measures. At the same time many expressed strong reservations about the contents of activation measures provided by municipalities. As already indicated, some claimants largely appeared to participate only to avoid reductions in their social assistance payments (Vik-Mo and Nervik 1999). Findings in Sweden were similar; e.g. claimants said that they did not know anyone who got a job through job-related activities in one activation programme (Thorén 2005). Thus both Norwegian and Swedish studies suggest that participants perceived local activation programmes as a means for public agencies to conduct work tests, check that they were willing to work and ensure that they did not have undeclared paid work.

Nuances in this picture emerge if we look at the municipalities adopting more generous approaches. For example, in the Norwegian studies, participants were more satisfied, less sceptical and more co-operative in cases where the municipalities granted additional financial support ('motivation grants') to those who participated in the labour market measures. In Sweden participants expressed more positive attitudes towards local activation programmes that had more resources, that did not enforce strict and punitive rules and that involved them in decision-making or gave them the opportunity to choose among different offers.

The use of sanctions in local activation processes

The use of sanctions had a substantial impact on participants' scope for negotiation, self-determination or choice in the activation process. In both countries, the use of sanctions and incentives was exempted from legal or centralized regulations. For instance, even though the Swedish government had introduced a national standard for social assistance, decisions whether and how payments should be reduced or withdrawn was an issue for local professional discretion. Our studies of the interaction between social workers and participants in activation programmes indicate that the use of sanctions took many guises and served different purposes.

According to the Norwegian studies, participation in the labour market measures was presented as more voluntary by social workers – and particularly by the heads of the offices – than participants perceived. The 1998 Norwegian survey suggested that 66 per cent of the municipalities practising workfare regularly used reductions in payments as sanctions. Nevertheless of the municipalities that did not request such work efforts in return for social assistance, only 25 per cent used such sanctions (Vik-Mo and Nervik 1999: 89). The use of threats or actual cessations of cash benefit payments (up to NOK 500 [63 euro] per month) was not infrequent in cases where the claimant hesitated or refused to participate (interviews by Halvorsen).

Social workers used sanctions both to recruit participants and to make sure they continued to participate in the measure ('we have to push them a bit by holding back money'). By ensuring that claimants were more compliant, sanctions helped to reduce their workload. The alternative – to motivate people to participate by reasoning, coaching and counselling – was considered more time-consuming. However, compared with unconditionally granting financial assistance, social workers associated the use of sanctions with unpleasant confrontations. For their part, participants argued that they had been exposed to threats or sanctions, even if these had not always been expressed openly but implied in the way in which information about participation in the activation measures had been presented.

The 2002 survey in Sweden indicates that most social services offices used sanctions of different kinds but that the use of sanctions varied among localities (Salonen and Ulmestig 2004). Some municipalities used sanctions – but not as the first option – when a claimant did not follow procedures or refused to participate in activation measures. Instead, staff in these municipalities emphasized the use of sanctions relative to other approaches, e.g. dialogue or counselling. These municipalities evidently rarely completely cut off social assistance grants. However, a large number of municipalities embraced a stricter sanctioning policy, almost as a first choice and as a way to force the work issue. According to one case-worker, sanctions are '... my only method of control if the client really wants to work ... and if they are serious' (Thorén 2005). Moreover, some managers maintained that if claimants did not comply with the rules and regulations of the social service office and had their allowance reduced – or even completely withdrawn – they had other sources of income.

The significance of individual action plans

In general, the discretionary nature of social assistance in Norway and Sweden limited the transparency of administrative practices. More specifically, our studies indicate that administrative safeguards such as individual action plans played only a minor role in protecting the position of the claimant. Interviews with participants in Norwegian activation measures suggest that disappointments and vulnerability experienced in the interaction with front-line staff created distrust of the public authorities and stimulated a perception of social assistance offices as hostile social environments. Claimants had often experienced being approached as potential violators of the entitlement criteria. Repeated controls, checks, inspections and paternalism only made things worse. Moreover, the complexity of the rules and the use of discretion in individual case processing on the part of front-line staff meant that participants often experienced the decision-making process as imperceptible, opaque and incomprehensible. For many, these experiences overshadowed the possible benefits of individual action plans. Even though municipality representatives stated that they used individual action plans for all unemployed claimants, hardly any of the claimants knew anything about their individual action plan, let alone its contents. Other studies of individual action plans in Sweden have made similar findings. Despite political statements of greater user involvement, interviews by Thorén and Ulmestig demonstrate that social assistance recipients were seldom aware that they had an individual action plan or a clear idea that they had been involved in outlining it.

Participants as active agents

Unemployed citizens claiming social assistance have often been labelled 'passive recipients' in need of activation by others. By contrast, the Norwegian and Swedish studies of local activation processes demonstrate that claimants tried to make the best out of their situation and improve their life chances according to their needs and opportunities, as *they* perceived them. That participation in local labour market measures often led to disappointments or appeared useless or punitive and easily locked front-line staff and unemployed citizens into a vicious circle of mistrust. The choices that these actors made at one stage determined what opportunities were open for them at the next stages. Often earlier events and steps induced further steps in the same direction. In some cases a history of repeated conflicts made collaborating and developing dialogue difficult. For instance, if claimants perceived front-line staff mainly as gate-keepers to financial resources, staff found it difficult to convince them that they, the staff, were now really partners in a dialogue to plan the best possible individual activation measures (Halvorsen 2002).

In response to this situation, participants in activation processes developed counter-strategies to protect themselves from adverse consequences. From the Norwegian studies we learn the following:

- Participants tried as much as possible to limit contact and information exchange with front-line staff. Participants often delayed follow-up requirements and obligations or did not turn up for appointments.

- Participants in local activation programmes tried to do as little as possible while waiting for training courses to end ('we buy coffee and play chess'). They participated only as much as required to avoid cuts in social assistance payments.
- Participants attended and participated passively, using the time for other activities. For instance, some claimants with immigrant backgrounds chose to do their homework for their Norwegian language class during the working hours in activation measures, because they considered language training more important than work practice.

These individual counter-strategies at the same time represented active negotiation strategies aimed at influencing and changing the framing of local policies. Whether the local activation measures succeeded in improving participants' capabilities and labour market prospects depended on their relationships with front-line staff. We have already seen how the internal work organization within social services affected the likelihood of the two parties coming to a joint understanding. This likelihood was greatest in municipalities where social services offices made a clear-cut division between activation measures and the administration of cash benefits, where staff provided motivation grants, and where staff allowed individual adjustments.

Conclusions: implications for active citizenship

The analysis highlights three important implications for our understanding of active citizenship and individual approaches in a decentralized and separated system of activation: local regimes of active citizenship, new patterns of social control in social services and citizenship beyond client status.

Local regimes of active citizenship

What takes place in the context of local activation in Norway and Sweden is not unique, as several European welfare states have undergone comparable processes of decentralization and a widening of the agenda for local social services (e.g. Lødemel and Trickey 2001; Van Berkel and Hornemann Møller 2002). But what is striking in Norway and Sweden is the way in which the governments have kept and justified a dual model of welfare provision, thereby creating a separated and discretionary model of local activation.

Since the early 1990s unemployed citizens have been given more explicit obligations for participating in activation measures, and cash benefits have become increasingly conditional on compliance. Only limited institutional safeguards strengthen and protect the position of unemployed citizens in these welfare reforms. At the same time, unemployed citizens lack clear and explicit rights of participation in activation programmes, i.e. to influence the particular contents of the measures they are offered through negotiation and dialogue, or to appeal to administrative courts if they are dissatisfied with the activation measures required of them. Clearly, with few and weak legal or administrative safeguards for participants in local activation programmes, this preponderance of obligations relative to rights amounts to a one-sided process of individualization.

We initially asked whether identifying a clear status of active citizenship, involving a consistent set of rights and duties, is possible for unemployed people claiming social assistance. We have shown how activation policies, relative to their scope, profile, and priorities, vary among municipalities. Thus the institutional features of the Norwegian and Swedish systems of municipality activation have resulted in the development of local regimes of active citizenship, in which the rights and duties of unemployed citizens depend upon the discretionary profile and priorities of the municipality in question. We see this independence most clearly for citizens who greatly depend on means-tested social assistance for their livelihood over prolonged periods. If these citizens are essentially denied or excluded from the full benefits of active citizenship, then this inequity points to an important limitation in the high degree of universalism attributed to welfare provision in Sweden and Norway.

New patterns of control in social services

The task of social workers in Sweden and Norway has largely been to take care of groups of citizens who for some reason or another have needs that the national employment services or social insurance systems cannot cover. From their professional training, social workers have used methods aimed at enhancing and strengthening individual motivation, self-esteem, confidence and personal development.

However, their scope for doing so has been circumscribed by their role as gate-keepers to means-tested financial support. This role requires intensive and detailed control of the unemployed individual's personal circumstances and way of living, infringing on his or her scope for autonomy and self-determination. Clearly, the introduction of activation policies in the social services of Norwegian and Swedish municipalities has given front-line workers new instruments of control and renewed legitimacy to exercise this control, e.g. to prevent voluntary unemployment, fraud or misuse of public funds. This context translates the general work ethic into individual obligations for unemployed citizens claiming social assistance, in the form of stronger demands for their participation in local projects.

Another initial question was whether local activation programmes create possibilities for tailored solutions and encourage participants' voice, influence and choice. Our investigations of front-line staff activities indicate that the offers of activation measures tend to be standardized. Lack of resources and staff responsiveness does not encourage voice, influence and choice for unemployed citizens.

Although these issues are obviously complex and more research is necessary, a preliminary conclusion is that professional practices follow the patterns predicted by research on street-level bureaucracy. Front-line staff tends to standardize measures and activation processes so as to manage their workload, despite limited resources, and to meet at least some of their professional objectives. This standardization shows the limitations of their responsiveness and flexibility vis-à-vis variations in the preferences, interests and needs of unemployed citizens. Participants said that their chances of becoming involved in discussions of their future welfare were quite limited. They also complained that the front-line staff in the activation organizations sought to exert detailed control. These comments demonstrate how much the introduction of activation policies in Norwegian and Swedish municipalities has strengthened the discretionary and selective profile of local welfare systems.

Citizenship – beyond the claimant status?

We initially asked whether unemployed citizens were passive or active within the situational constraints that the local activation policies created. Open as well as hidden strategies of negotiations, adjustments and resistance on the part of claimants in their interaction with the staff meant that these claimants were *de facto* co-producers of the activation measures and their results (Williams *et al.* 1999). Moreover, claimants did not remain passive in the face of constraints or about the way in which front-line staff perceived, categorized and treated them. Instead claimants actively sought to define the situation in a way that was consistent with their self-image, preferences and priorities. Through their actions and non-actions, the claimants emerged as shapers of the conditions for action, e.g. in the ways they negotiated the conditions for receiving social assistance payments. Thus, we need to understand the outcome of the interaction between staff and claimants as the result of structured but open social processes.

Admittedly, interaction patterns are structured by unequal relations of power. Individual scope for negotiation depends considerably on the discretion of front-line workers. In a similar vein, the language skills, social networks and economic resources of claimants created both constraints and opportunities for their actions. Thus the individual approach to activation was largely an administered form of participation, with the stated aim that the participant became financially self-sufficient through paid employment. This aim gave space, albeit limited, for agency and choice on the part of unemployed citizens interacting with front-line staff.

Final comments

Norwegian and Swedish governments have, since 2000, expressed concern over the role of citizens in welfare services and formulated the aim of strengthening participation and user involvement. This goal presumably contributes not only to a democratic renewal but, even more important, also to the transformation of local welfare services (*Socialstyrelsen* 2000; St.meld. nr. 14, 2002–3). However, because our analysis of activation policies in Norway and Sweden reveals several institutional and organizational barriers to citizen participation, we must question the sincerity of the stated aim of citizen involvement.

Various institutional conditions not only differentiated the citizenship status of those involved but also limited the practical possibilities for engagement, e.g. in terms of citizens having a say or deliberating with staff. The wide scope for local and professional discretion exercised in a separated model of activation led to substantial uncertainty and unpredictability on the part of unemployed citizens claiming social assistance. In addition, few and weak institutional safeguards protect the potential and actual participants in local activation measures.

This institutional set-up has limited the possibilities for unemployed citizens to exercise active citizenship, and has made the legitimacy and accountability of the activation programmes disputable. Nonetheless, claimants were not generally inactive or passive; they developed different forms of strategies to go beyond their ascribed statuses as 'clients' or 'recipients'.

Norway and Sweden have so far opted for an individual approach to activation, with emphasis on strengthening individual responsibilities and obligations. They have only rarely developed mechanisms that aim to involve the individual on his or her own terms in a dialogue on how to handle unemployment.

Part III

The increased scope for participation and inclusion of marginal groups

7 Claiming participation rights

Social mobilization and citizenship in Denmark and Norway

Jørgen Anker and Rune Halvorsen

Introduction

According to the republican ideal of citizenship, citizens should actively participate in the public deliberation on the common affairs of society, beyond indirect forms of participation like voting. In practice, interest representation and other extra-parliamentary forms of participation often take place through social movements and a range of associations and organized groups. Although such collective action has involved a large proportion of the population in countries like the Nordic ones, some groups of citizens have tended to be absent: people who are in marginal positions, poor, out of work or socially excluded. According to conventional wisdom, marginalized or poor citizens lack the resources and competence to organize and act collectively.

Yet since the 1990s different groups of marginal citizens have organized in many welfare states, including the Nordic ones. Common to these groups is that they are challenging relations of power and dominance in the welfare state and demanding the right to be heard and involved in processes determining their welfare. For instance, we have witnessed social mobilization among people who for various reasons are out of work and claiming social benefits (social insurance or social assistance). These emerging groups are challenging public policies and legislation affecting their situation, e.g. the conditions for receiving benefits and the measures for helping them become self-sufficiently employed. These groups are also questioning not only what the government sees as legitimate changes in formal rights and practical interventions in the lives of citizens but also what society acknowledges as valuable contributions. The emergence of this social movement in the Nordic welfare states is a new phenomenon that requires improved understanding.

This chapter makes a comparative analysis of social mobilization among marginalized citizens in Denmark and Norway and, more specifically, explores to what extent we can understand their activities as efforts to achieve active citizenship according to a republican understanding (Chapter 3). We ask whether key actors in the social movements present an alternative interpretation of public welfare policy (e.g. Goffman 1974; Snow and Benford 1992; Johnston 1995). As we show that the Danish and Norwegian groups developed rather different action strategies, we ask how these differences relate to institutionalized policy traditions in the two countries. The comparison, therefore, allows us to more robustly conceptualize social movements among marginalized citizens and to focus on framing welfare policy issues as expressed in the interaction between public authorities and the social movements of marginal citizens.

National patterns of mobilization

We based the comparison on two separate national studies of mobilization among marginalized citizens (Halvorsen 2002; Anker 2004). In Denmark, through documentary analysis and snowball sampling (establishing contacts with relevant informants from earlier interviews), we identified 11 associations and networks claiming to represent social assistance recipients nationally or locally, and we interviewed 20 leaders and activists in 2001. The interviews revealed that six of these associations were then active, while the rest were inactive or had been dissolved. Some included only social assistance claimants and recipients, while others included other categories of beneficiaries of public provisions. The six active social movement organizations included two broader umbrella groups and many minor initiatives associated with these two larger groups. The largest group, the National Organization of Unemployed (*Landsorganisationen af Arbejdsledige*), with seven local branches, claimed more than 500 members and some collective members, including trade unions. In 2002, their revenue was DKK 170,000, two-thirds of which was contributions from other groups, trade unions and charities, with one-third from membership fees.

In Norway, likewise through documentary analysis and snowball sampling, we identified 25 groups, most of them local and active in the 1990s. This study had a broader focus than the Danish one, as it encompassed claimants' associations in areas such as social assistance, unemployment insurance, rehabilitation and vocational allowance and single parent allowance. All in all, we interviewed about 50 activists and other members. We collected the main part of the Norwegian data in 1996–99 and updated the data in 2005. Some organizing efforts had already folded before we started the data collection, while a national umbrella group, the Welfare Alliance (*Velferdsalliansen*), emerged in the late 1990s. As of 2005 this umbrella group had recruited 20 smaller groups and networks, and claimed to represent 45,000 people. In 2005, the Welfare Alliance received NOK 1,500,000 in annual financial support from the Norwegian Ministry of Social Affairs. The Alliance became a member of the European Anti-Poverty Network (based in Brussels) in 2005.

Both in Denmark and Norway, the groups tended to be locally organized, with participants recruited regionally, even though several initiatives – and the larger umbrella associations – took names indicating national ambitions. We interpret the figures cautiously, as uncovering the actual number of participants and groups is difficult. However, they indicate that membership in all of these grass-root organizations remained fairly limited when compared to what we know of claimants' unions and campaigns to achieve more generous social benefits in other countries (e.g. Fox Piven and Cloward 1977; Hvinden 1994; Lister 2004).

Moreover, membership tended to be low, relative to the potential number. For instance, in 2002 Denmark had 124,600 persons receiving social assistance, 293,900 persons received unemployment benefits and 68,000 persons receiving unemployment benefits participated in active labour market measures (Statistics Denmark 2004), while Norway had 128,800 social assistance recipients and 69,900 unemployment insurance recipients (Statistics Norway 2003; Aetat 2004). In other words, in both Denmark and Norway less than 0.1 per cent of the relevant benefit recipients were members. In addition, due to internal disagreements and co-ordination problems, many local initiatives were fairly short-lived, and most of them were informally organized, with loose structures. Many activists found recruiting new participants difficult and therefore gave recruitment low priority. National mobilizing activities emerged as dependent on a few persons, and the level of activity varied considerably.

The constituencies of both the Danish and Norwegian groups corresponded greatly to ideal-typical social democratic citizens. The key participants tended to be considered by others as people without any specific impairment (disability) – people who happened to be out of work but who ought to be financially self-sufficient through regular work. In both countries, activists were of working age, and about two-thirds were men (mostly 30–55 years of age) enrolled in temporary and short-term social benefit systems. Few people from ethnic minorities were involved in these associations, and core activists tended to define ethnic minorities as less worthy of public support and recognition than other recipients of public provisions. Some claimants' groups, fearing job competition, were also sceptical about immigration.

Strategies for achieving participation

Although these social movement organizations in Denmark and Norway shared many features and applied similar strategies to common problems, some clear differences existed between them, in the area of national political cultures and policy trajectories. This section discusses three broader issues, demonstrating some shared general ambitions, although the Danish and Norwegian organizations expressed them differently. The three issues concern their pursuit of recognition and redistribution policies, their challenges to the public framing of unemployment, and the different strategies for counter-mobilization.

In pursuit of recognition and redistribution

As in many other Western welfare states, Danish and Norwegian welfare policy underwent a period of retrenchment in the 1990s, with a substantial impact on working age people claiming social benefits. More than ever, these benefits were granted only on conditions set by others. In essence, citizens claiming cash benefits, especially social assistance, had to give up some of their citizenship rights in exchange for financial support (Chapters 4 and 6).

The political discourse on welfare reform often presented citizens claiming social benefits as mere 'passive recipients' who did not really try to become self-sufficient and who lacked the basic motivation or competence to contribute to society. Unemployment was perceived as a crucial barrier to social inclusion, thus creating a social problem. In particular, the public authorities viewed claimants of social benefits as an economic problem, because of the public expense and loss of tax revenue. Working age claimants were frequently referred to as 'idle', 'work-shy' and 'unreliable', or as 'scroungers' or 'benefit abusers' thereby presenting a moral problem.

The grass-root groups in Denmark and Norway challenged these stereotypes. They regarded the new policies not only as unreasonable demands but also as expressions of government paternalism, control and surveillance. In both countries, the groups called public welfare policy unjust, inhuman or unreasonable, and demanded recognition as autonomous actors with a right to control or have influence over their own lives while receiving benefits. Participants were concerned with opportunities for individual autonomy and respect and the issue of whether they would be able to build a life worth living while being unemployed. They demanded respect. Their requests clearly related to demands for the status of full members of society, capable of participating on a par with other citizens and not needing paternalistic help controlled by others. This social mobilization was largely for *recognition* of marginalized citizens as valuable social contributors.

The issues that the groups raised, however, did not deal exclusively with questions of recognition or 'identity politics', i.e. questions of identity and human dignity. They also presented claims related to socio-economic issues of *redistribution*, e.g. access to paid work and income, an adequate standard of living and health, and effective anti-poverty measures. Their mobilization efforts included claims for recasting the conditions for receiving social benefits and improved opportunities for political participation in democratic decision-making. They thereby sought to achieve more equality in the distribution of resources and opportunities for participation.

In these ways the claims of all the movements shared inter-related political-economic and cultural-valuation dimensions. Pejorative cultural attributions affected their access to resources, help and assistance, and prevented participatory parity. Economic and political disadvantage was associated with being maligned or disparaged in stereotypic cultural representations in the public sphere and in everyday life. Both economic disadvantage and cultural devaluation impeded equal participation in the making of society, in the public sphere and in daily life. The work for recognition and the work for redistribution were so intertwined as to be inseparable (Fraser 1995; Lister 2004).

For instance, the Danish national organization aimed at improving unemployed people's quality of life and at removing the requirement for people to participate in active labour market measures as a condition for receiving cash benefits. They argued for voluntary, not mandatory, participation in education, vocational training and job training. They demanded a more generous system of providing economic security for people out of work and more transparency and predictability in the allocation of social benefits.

The Norwegian Welfare Alliance campaigned to get the government to abolish poverty, improve the quality of life for its member groups, ensure user participation and provide its members with financial and practical support. The Alliance wanted maximum labour market participation to come about through people receiving opportunities for education and participation in employment-qualifying activities based on individual skills, interests and desires, not through the use of financial sanctions. The Alliance proposed that, in the short-term, the government would create a national minimum standard for social assistance payments and increase the daily allowance for unemployed citizens and, in the long-term, that it would create a guaranteed minimum income for all citizens.

For the beneficiaries of public provisions to be acknowledged as active, responsible and full citizens, the government and the rest of society had to allow greater scope for diversity. This issue was more one of achieving 'equal worth' than one of 'sameness'. The claims for a stronger cultural valuation of welfare beneficiaries implied changes in the political economy of welfare. Overcoming the stigma of their status demanded the reconstruction of the division between paid and unpaid work, moving in the direction of a broader notion of what constituted socially valuable activity; not only paid work but also unpaid care and voluntary social, cultural and organizational work had to be included. This issue was important in both Denmark and Norway. Yet, as the next section will show, these groups expressed ambivalence over the cultural valuation of 'paid work' as a criterion for access to full citizenship.

Challenges to the public framing of unemployment

Both countries experienced a new or reinforced emphasis on participation in active labour market measures as a condition for receiving cash benefits (Chapters 4–6). An unintended consequence of this emphasis was that more claimants interacted with others in similar situations. These interactions created or improved opportunities for claimants to create their own social networks and groups. In several cases, dissatisfaction with proposed measures, being summoned to information meetings and interviews by public authorities, and cuts in cash benefits became the breeding ground for social mobilization. Changes in policy measures were felt particularly strongly by people who had already received benefits. These groups experienced the new demands and cuts in social rights as worsening their situation.

The groups' opposition to the dominant work orientation in public policy was considerably more outspoken and confrontational in Denmark. The two Danish groups with the highest media profile wanted the obligation to participate in activation abolished and sanctions for non-compliance removed. They reframed activation measures as representing 'slavery', 'imprisonment' and 'coercion'. Their arguments resembled proposals for a basic 'citizen income' (Atkinson 1995; Offe 1996). Participants aimed at extending the definition of work, as well as extending the goal of social inclusion beyond the labour market. Others maintained that participants in activation measures should hold the same collective rights as workers in the regular labour market, such as a minimum wage and the rights to holidays.

In short, many participants challenged the cultural norms that defined fulfilment of citizenship obligations as participation in paid employment and compliance with activation requirements. One local group of Danish social assistance recipients developed and administered its own labour market training project. However, other activists strongly condemned the project, accusing them of betraying the overall cause of the social movement and being co-opted by the authorities, because they were receiving financial support and advocating the dominant policy.

In Norway, the groups expressed more demonstrative support for the dominant work orientation. Key participants sought to reduce existing status differences without challenging the underlying cultural assumptions that led to the demeaning of unemployed citizens. They protested against the conditions for being provided help and assistance, not against the official rationale or the objectives of public welfare policy. One of the groups campaigned for the development of new kinds of job opportunities for its participants, especially the development of new business ideas. They contrasted these forms of job opportunities with the public authorities' active labour market measures, which they said encouraged 'unsolidaristic behaviour' and 'learning how to jump in the job queue'. These activists considered it a success if individual members found paid work, even if this success meant that the group lost activists and that turnover increased. Few participants questioned that finding paid work was the ultimate goal or stated that they did not comply with employment service requirements. Refusals to comply actually received strong condemnation from other participants, who argued that if they did not do everything they could to obtain paid work, they had only themselves to blame.

These contrasts relate to differences in the historical policy configurations of these two countries. Danish central authorities have more explicitly than their Norwegian counterparts stated that participation in active measures might serve secondary objectives. Particularly in the 1980s, Denmark came closer than Norway to providing the working age population with a *de facto* minimum income guarantee. In Denmark this approach was the result of pragmatic and incremental adaptations to a relatively high level of unemployment (since the 1970s) rather than the result of an explicit or principal choice (Bay and Pedersen 2003). Denmark had a high overall employment rate, especially as the increase in women's labour participation and full kindergarten coverage happened earlier than in Norway. At the same time, Denmark had extensive exit opportunities through early retirement plans, different leave plans, transitional allowance for the unemployed above 50 and a disability benefit for non-medical reasons. The government aimed over time to reduce unemployment by lowering the labour supply and redistributing the burdens of unemployment through job rotation and work sharing (Halvorsen and Jensen 2004).

The Danish government essentially recognized that gainful employment is not a realistic goal for all income security beneficiaries (Danish Ministry of Social Affairs 2000). For this group of unemployed citizens, the government defined participation in activation measures as a goal in itself and as a way of promoting social inclusion. The government has viewed participation as an opportunity for participants to create a daily rhythm similar to that of labour market participants and to avoid social isolation (Torfing 2000). Activation measures for social assistance recipients have also included possibilities for participating in alternative measures such as cultural and organizational activities and charitable work (Goul Andersen 2002).

Given Denmark's more liberal welfare policy, that the Danish movement was more militant and confrontational than its Norwegian counterpart, may appear paradoxical. However, the more drastic shift in the Danish social benefit system, compared to the policies of the 1970s and 1980s, may account for the more outspoken disagreement over ideology, values and policy objectives. The work orientation – especially the stricter version of this approach, based on explicit obligations and sanctioning of non-compliance – had not been deeply ingrained in the shared assumptions of the Danish welfare culture. Danish activists therefore were able to frame their claims not only in opposition to the implementation and enforcement of 'the active line' of the 1990s but also in terms of older assumptions and values that had been widely held in Danish society.

In Norway, active labour market measures traditionally had a narrower goal, i.e. a means of assisting unemployed people in finding paid work. Underlying this goal was the concern that creating any secondary objectives for those with lesser chances of achieving gainful employment would undermine the political priority of achieving maximum labour market participation. The official commitment to the 'work line' – meaning that all possibilities to assist a person to become financially self-sufficient had to be exhausted before providing more long-term public income maintenance – dated back to the early post-war years and had never been officially given up

(Hvinden 1994). Admittedly, the Norwegian work line had suffered some policy erosion in the 1970s and 1980s, e.g. allowing some people to receive social assistance as their main source of livelihood over extended periods as a quasi-minimum income.

The registered unemployment remained exceptionally low in Norway during most of the 1970s and 1980s. As a political issue, it only had a salient position on the political agenda for short periods in the early 1980s and early 1990s. Unemployment was largely viewed as a short-term, transitional and individual problem, not an enduring structural or mass problem, thereby promoting the understanding that most people would be able to find work if they made sufficient efforts and that they were to blame if they did not succeed. In terms of the concept adopted by Offe (1984) and Esping-Andersen (1990), possibilities for 'decommodification' (choosing to receive social benefits instead of working) – in terms of both practical opportunities and political legitimacy – appeared to have been better in Denmark than in Norway, at least until the substantial welfare reforms of the 1990s.

Three strategies for counter-mobilization

The Danish and Norwegian groups used somewhat different strategies in their struggles for recognition and redistribution. To differentiate their positioning relative to public authorities, we distinguish between three ideal-type framings of the group activities: self-help groups, trade unions and citizens' rights campaigns (Weber 1949).

Framing as a self-help group

These groups emphasized improving the financial and social position of the individual. They sought to create arenas for improved autonomy, freedom from surveillance, shelter against unwanted intrusive inspection or paternalistic help, exchange of experiences, and assistance from peers. The group could ideally provide services that participants controlled and administered themselves. By emphasizing direct participant involvement, these groups stressed the development of local groups, through which they promoted smaller reforms that represented ideas about direct democracy and participation in the welfare state. In certain cases the groups had participation from professional helpers or outside supporters, but such alliances tended to be controversial as these were held to threaten their autonomy. Such an organizational model was a moderate version of the self-help group.

Framing as trade union

As the purpose of this type of group was to defend and improve the social rights of its members, activities related more to achieving public policy changes. The idea was to organize all social benefit claimants into one union whose large membership would give it legitimacy. This approach resembles the legitimization strategy that Tilly (1998) called being seen as 'worthy, united, numerous and committed'. The focus was on achieving a dialogue with the public authorities.

Participants sought to influence policy-making processes through formal channels and by following the working methods of well-established groups. They submitted written comments and responded to government proposals, presented and calculated the costs of alternative solutions, participated in parliamentary hearings, sought strategic alliances with more established groups and represented their members in the mass media. They strove to be centrally organized and emphasized clear-cut communication lines for a united front. They were also tempted to play the game of more established groups by imitating their structure and procedures (Scott 1992). In several respects, the establishment of a trade union emerged as the model for their strategy.

Framing as citizens' rights campaign

This model for collective action defined its own importance and objective as wider in scope with regard to basic citizens' rights than did the trade union model (Fox Piven and Cloward 1977; Lister 2004). These groups pursued the goal of what they saw as decent living conditions for all, whether gainfully employed or not. Participants sought to achieve public attention for their message and to seek alliances with outside supporters. They adopted more unruly tactics, symbolic protests and identity political statements, including attempts at achieving media coverage. For instance, they sought to frame activation measures as meaningless and involuntary activities, not goal-oriented, instrumental strategies for obtaining jobs. They gave less significance to achieving a dialogue with the government or having a large number of members.

Among these, the third model of collective action emerged as more developed in Denmark. The two Danish groups with the highest profile in the media protested against the obligation to participate in activation measures but refused to formulate an alternative. Some argued that their aim was to destroy the system from within, undermining the foundation of the official 'active line'. Others argued that continuous small acts of resistance could change the public administration, an approach reminiscent of what Mathiesen (1977) called 'disruption without alternative'. They refrained from making alliances with political parties and refused to become involved in activities that could lead to disciplining or co-optation. The participants focused on the cases they assumed could raise public debate, become controversial or reveal inconsistencies in public policy.

Equally important in this context is the adoption of legalistic tactics: Danish social benefit claimants filed lawsuits against the public authorities, increasingly using the legal system against the public authorities (Østre Landsret 2002; Vestre Landsret 2004). The groups launched test cases to question whether new activation obligations were consistent with the constitution and whether the government could instruct the municipalities to issue employment contracts for activation measure participation. The groups also complained about weak opportunities for appealing decisions about social benefits.

In contrast, the Norwegian groups emerged as more concerned about their legitimacy and the need to justify themselves to the public authorities and the mass media. Participants stressed that they were useful citizens who saved the government expense, presented realistic alternatives and agreed with the official objective of maximum labour market participation. This framing as a combination of self-help group and trade union emerged as the most prevalent mode of Norwegian mobilization. The citizens' rights campaign frame played only a limited role, with no legal strategy.

We can interpret these differing strategies as different 'phases' of social mobilization or 'the cycle of protest' (Tarrow 1994: 153). Some Norwegian groups used more confrontational and expressive strategies in the early stages, but, as mobilizing a large number of claimants was difficult, they shifted to strategies requiring fewer participants. The groups adapted to what they believed other social benefit claimants, politicians and employees in the welfare bureaucracy expected of them. Because the claimant status was to be temporary, they ensured their legitimacy by developing activities and services that could be seen as promoting job finding and reducing dependency on public assistance. To some extent – and also in Denmark – we discovered adjustments based on earlier experiences. Expectations of success via the trade union model had been higher in the early stages of mobilization. By 2001, however, only a few activists still believed in the possibility of uniting all unemployed people in one union. In the end, all these adjustments resulted not in reliance on the self-help model but rather a shift towards the citizens' rights model.

The welfare policy context of social mobilization

The previous analyses demonstrate that different strategies and ways of framing either reflect or relate to national institutional differences in the opportunities for articulating claims against the welfare state. Therefore, we now compare these differences in greater detail, focusing on national welfare policy systems and responses from the establishment and mass media.

National welfare policy systems

The Danish welfare state has a constitutional duty to provide for a person who is unable to support himself or herself and his or her family. The applicable rights and conditions for receiving social assistance are specified in greater detail in Danish legislation than in the Norwegian legislation. Although social assistance is means-tested, the law determines the levels of benefits according to family status, housing expenses, etc. Local authorities have discretionary power to reduce or possibly withdraw social assistance if the recipients do not participate in activation measures. A decision from the Danish Supreme Court in 2005 stated that social assistance could be curtailed if the recipient refuses to participate in activation. Nevertheless whether withdrawal of social assistance conflicts with the constitution remains a contested issue (Ketscher 2002).

An increasing legal orientation in the Danish welfare regime is also evident. More citizens are pursuing their social rights in court, whether in connection to reimbursement of expenses to health services and education abroad or to the conditions for receipt of social benefits (Danish Supreme Court 2003). If the government Ombudsman supports the complaint, the plaintiff usually gets a free trial. In other cases, trade unions and other large interest groups have taken cases to court on behalf of their members. In Denmark, therefore, we see a growing tendency to frame social policy conflicts as judicial issues.

The Norwegian welfare state has given strong emphasis to the role of professional and administrative discretion. The welfare regime has been open to paternalistic notions of help ('help to self-help'). The beneficiaries of social assistance have had fewer clear-cut rights than beneficiaries of social insurance, and social assistance has been less based on fixed and transparent rates. Norway has to a greater extent kept social assistance as a discretionary system of income support controlled by the municipalities (Chapter 4). Local control led to large variations among the municipalities in the level of assistance payments. Social insurance benefits have largely been rule-based, despite an element of discretion for some benefits, e.g. for disability. Staff both in national insurance offices and social services departments have had a duty not only to administer the rules for income maintenance benefits but also to provide appropriate treatment (e.g. job-training or education) to help claimants and recipients to (re)enter the labour market if possible.

These differences are greatly important to any general understanding of the participatory strategies of the groups under discussion. The Danish welfare policy system appears to allow more opportunities for contestation and legal complaints, thereby possibly leading to the more oppositional identity and approach of the Danish associations. However, when compared to Norway, the Danish welfare policy system has also been under stronger influence from alternative forms of politics. The underground culture in Denmark has been the most multifaceted in Scandinavia since the 1970s (Jamison *et al.* 1990). Beyond the established political system, a number of extra-parliamentary activities have existed, often connected to expressive and symbolic protest actions and alternative 'life politics' (Giddens 1991). These included autonomous villages ('Christiania', 'Thylejren', 'Tvind'), militant squatters ('bz'ere', 'the autonomous') and unorthodox political groupings ('the Consciously Work-Shy').

Relatively generous systems of social benefits served as a material basis for these experiments during the long period of high unemployment. Related to this tradition of alternative politics, a debate on a basic 'citizen income' took place in Denmark in the 1970s (Meyer *et al.* 1978). Although the proposal never gained broader political support, different actors still occasionally raise the issue in relation to different policy measures.

These national differences suggest that Denmark has been more receptive to or tolerant of voices opposing the dominant work orientation. In Norway, by contrast, the question of whether benefit claimants without any specific impairment or disability even had a moral right to have a collective voice was the underlying issue. These contrasts may in part clarify why making a case out of non-participation in the labour market has been possible in Denmark but not in Norway, and why the Danish groups emerged more clearly as expressions of a broader counter-culture.

Responses from the establishment and the mass media

Despite the obstacles they met in their efforts to mobilize social benefit claimants, both Danish and Norwegian groups brought attention to their perceptions of unmet needs and wants, shortcomings, wrong treatment and neglect on the part of the respective welfare states. Through appearances in the mass media, both the groups and individual participants made unsolved issues visible in the public sphere, thereby putting new needs and demands on the welfare policy agenda. The groups produced and advocated for alternative interpretations and redefinitions of social problems and provided new examples and illustrative material to the mass media. This approach emerged as their most clear-cut achievement.

A general problem with which the groups struggled related to lack of recognition from the establishment. Social benefit claimants were not represented in the corporative structures of the welfare state in either country. The institutionalized tripartite structure of public authorities, employers' federations and trade unions had no established ways of including the voices of unemployed people, unless unemployed trade union members could influence union policies.

The public authorities acted ambivalently towards these groups, to some extent accepting them as self-help groups. To promote more 'active citizenship', governments also provided supportive structures to encourage and extend the scope of voluntary work and self-help initiatives in the social policy area. Therefore, when the groups acted as self-help organizations – especially on the local level and with support from local authorities – they had the best chance of receiving financial support for their activities. When they framed themselves as trade unions or citizens' rights campaigns, they did not necessarily receive government recognition or support. However, the Norwegian Welfare Alliance found that EU expectations of the involvement of marginal citizens in social policy deliberations in member states helped improve their opportunities for participation from 2003.

In both countries, the established labour movement was reluctant to even recognize these attempts to form new platforms of political agency. However, in Denmark the groups gradually achieved informal co-operation and support from unions of both social workers and blue-collar workers. One of the larger unions (*Specialarbejderforbundet*) declared that municipal activation measures were distorting competition and replaced regular employment (*Fagbladet* 17 March 2004). A few local trade unions even tried to organize social assistance recipients.

In Norway, only the union of social workers (*Fellesorganisasjonen*) appeared to develop a sense of shared interests with claimants groups (*Dagbladet* 25 February 1998, *Fontene* no. 7, 1998). In this context that Norwegian social workers acted both as gate-keepers to resources and as helpers in the local social services offices appears paradoxical (Chapter 6). The Norwegian labour movement has been an explicit representative of wage labour as the crucial signifier of identity, respect and honour, and a strong advocate for the association between social rights and labour market participation. The virtue of wage labour has been the main basis for its claim for societal participation and influence.

Therefore, while the movement could see itself as representing temporarily unemployed members, it would have greater difficulty with people who appeared permanently unemployed and who might even question whether wage labour was something all citizens should aspire to achieve. Certainly the leadership of the labour movement worried that these groups represented people who either rejected the official work orientation or were unwilling to seek paid work. Conversely, the groups criticized trade unions for excluding or neglecting the voice and interests of unemployed citizens. For these two movements, their identity political claims and preferred principles for distribution of resources were completely at odds.

Conclusions: the significance of marginalized citizens' movements

We initially asked whether we can view the activities of these groups of social benefit claimants as efforts to achieve active citizenship according to a republican understanding. With some reservations we can answer *yes*: the groups we studied in Denmark and Norway offered members and other associates greater scope for participation. The key activists especially gained new opportunities for giving voice to and pursuing the interests and views of their constituencies within the public sphere, including through the media, and in some cases through consultation meetings and hearings with authorities. In a more limited way, ordinary members, some of whom were the most socially excluded, also achieved new possibilities for social participation, exchanging experiences and receiving support from peers.

What we have shown here is that even though working age claimants without any specific impairment have limited economic resources, they have been able to use their cultural resources to influence their own life chances. They have developed different strategies for challenging existing rules of welfare provision, public measures to foster social inclusion and public perceptions of the 'active citizen'.

First, the groups used different cultural tools, e.g. strategies for justifications, to achieve recognition and redistribution of resources and power. So far, the Danish and Norwegian groups had not achieved any substantial changes in the public policy. Yet even though the groups were not in a position to change or moderate the national policy, they nevertheless were able to achieve smaller victories in court and to protest and document unmet needs and shortcomings of national welfare states. They also became recognized as parties in negotiations with the political system, with the right to receive information and express their opinions, speak for the people they represented and keep this population visible in the public sphere. Although substantial or tangible results may vary and change over time, the symbolic dimension of participation (even for permanent groups with high legitimacy) can sometimes be the more important contribution.

Second, for the most active participants, their social mobilization efforts gave them the opportunity not only to receive but also to use their own experiences and expertise to help other claimants. These more passive participants received assistance, advice and information about social rights and other ways of solving their problems. In this way, participants in these groups started acting as subjects seeking influence over their own lives, not only as objects of other people's concern, help and control. Although the groups did not have a large number of active participants, a social goal of having all participants equally active, or active in the same way, was not realistic. Even large established political parties and interest groups have had increasing problems in recruiting members and mobilizing their passive members.

Third, for social movements, the symbolic positioning of their group and the population they claim to represent — along with acts that attract public attention — are increasingly crucial. Several groups successfully handled this new situation and sought a high media profile, especially in the local press. This behaviour emerges as an important form of political activity in an information society, where the media increasingly influences the policy agenda. Public communication is taking place in the form of advertisements, symbolic actions and media dramatization. The changing institutional order entails an intensifying of symbol production, including the self-presentation and symbolic positioning of these groups in relation to each other and to more established groups such as trade unions (Melucci 1996).

The main limitation was the substantial obstacles that these groups met in their efforts to attract members. As a result, the actual number of members and other associates amounted to a small proportion of the potential membership, and many groups became fairly short-lived or had to change their strategy from seeking to be 'self-help groups' or 'claimant unions' to become 'citizens' rights campaigns'. Even so, the groups created increased awareness of the situation of the poor and marginalized segments of the population and helped change the public agenda on these issues in both Denmark and Norway.

Nordic welfare states have generally either equated political subjectivity to the individual's status in the labour market or made this equation crucial in determining the qualities of 'responsible' and 'capable' citizens. Yet, as we have shown, new organized groups of social claimants have challenged stereotyped understandings of active participation, stressing their rights to decent treatment, respect and recognition of their resources and capabilities.

All in all, we can regard the emergence of a social movement among social benefit claimants as an element in the development of new forms of politics and thus part of ongoing structural changes in post-industrial society. As citizens develop the capacity for acting (and expecting opportunities to act) as subjects in their own lives, they increasingly demand that the state be responsive to their self-defined needs and give them opportunities for exercising agency. This attitude includes giving more choice to the beneficiaries of public provisions and helping services as part of overall demands for a participation-led welfare state. If the welfare state appears repressive, unresponsive or indifferent, it risks losing its legitimacy (Beck 1992; Eder 2001).

At the same time, we can also regard the emergence of a social movement among social benefit claimants as part of the general debate over participatory or deliberative democracy. The participants of these groups sought to define and carve out for themselves an autonomous space in which to pursue issues of life politics outside the confines of political parties and institutions of representational democracy. They expressed ambitions for self-governed participation and opportunities for handling their own situations. Through such activities, these citizens reacted against being reduced to passive help recipients or consumers of public services, and claimed the possibility to actively pursue their own life goals. Despite their marginal position in the labour market, these groups kept the republican ideal of citizenship alive and even extended its implementation in practice.

8 Capabilities and participation

Russian women immigrants in North Norway

Ann Therese Lotherington and Kjersti Fjørtoft

Introduction

Citizenship, which provides membership in a political society, describes not only the legal status of citizens in a nation-state but also their social belonging in a particular political community. In social and political theory, understandings of citizenship closely relate to questions of both democracy and justice. Citizens' political participation maintains democracy, and political decisions are legitimate by virtue of their being the outcome of free public reasoning among equals (Cohen 1999). This chapter examines access to full citizenship for Russian women immigrants in Norway through the lens of theoretical and normative considerations that derive from both old and new definitions of democracy.

To prevent massive immigration, Norwegian immigration policies are becoming stricter – and stricter still for people coming from the non-European Economic Area (EEA), which includes Russia. We focus on Russian immigrant women in Norway not only because their situation is illustrative but also because they are victims of both gender stereotyping and family reunification legislative exceptions. The combination of these factors makes their situation, in terms of democracy and active citizenship participation, even more compelling. We ask how their particular position challenges traditional notions of citizenship and justice, and how Norwegian immigration and integration policies either hamper or foster their citizenship-related activities.

A democratic ideal of equal citizenship

Before turning to the story of Russian immigrant women, however, we need to first discuss the general problem of how to create a situation of fair deliberation among equals, especially given recent criticism of traditional concepts of citizenship. Several feminist thinkers argue that a concept of citizenship derived from norms, rights and duties governing the relationship between state and individual, and between individuals in the public sphere of society, is not only too limited but also misleading. Activities within the private sphere – such as the family, social associations or voluntary organizations – have not yet received full recognition as social contributions (see e.g. Pateman 1989; Phillips 1991; Yuval-Davis 1997; Young 2000; Lister 2003). We have yet to evaluate relations, customs and structures of power within the private sphere against principles of justice. We therefore have to reconsider traditional assumptions regarding what it means to take the idea of equal worth seriously.

Given this criticism, the concept of citizenship needs reinterpretation in light of how the public and the private spheres are constructed and interrelated. On the one hand, relations and conditions viewed as private can be politically relevant and informing of struggles of citizenship in the public sphere. On the other hand, activities in the political arena are certainly important for the private sphere. Equal citizenship thus requires a concept of justice applied not only to the public social structure but also to areas often considered informal, private and apolitical.

These critical considerations concern what is required for realizing a democratic ideal of equal citizenship. The notion of deliberative democracy dictates the need for governing common life by the public deliberation of all members. The general idea is that a political decision is democratic if it is based on a process of reaching reasoned agreement among free and equal citizens (Bohman 1999). Based on this analytical recognition, the focal point of our discussion is a participation that does not limit itself to representative democracy but that extends to societal participation at large.

A deliberative model must also meet the challenges of pluralism and diversity, both of which are real challenges in modern democratic societies. We need to rethink participation in situations where people have different political and cultural values, loyalties and identities. Given these needs, we believe that models of deliberative democracy must identify democracy as a process of discussion, debate and criticism – a process that aims at solving collective problems. All should be entitled to take part in the discourses (Benhabib 2002).

We will use these theoretical considerations to show that public policies have serious consequences for the development of full citizenship for Norwegian immigrants in general and Russian immigrant women in particular, because these policies tend to reinforce a strong divide between a public and a private sphere. We will also question whether the particulars of the government immigration legislation – the underlying aim of which is to educate all immigrants for full and equal citizenship in Norway – really meet government goals or actually undermine and negate them.

Capabilities as a foundation for civic participation

When discussing the preconditions for equal citizenship we draw on Martha Nussbaum's capabilities approach (Nussbaum 1992, 2000). Nussbaum argues that when we discuss justice and equality, simply talking about fair distribution of rights and economic resources is insufficient. We must also focus on how factors such as traditions, religion, family life, educational possibilities, and social and political conditions affect peoples' abilities to function and participate in society, be able to make own choices of how to live their lives in society and make full use of their citizenship rights.

Nussbaum's capabilities approach posits certain universal norms of human capabilities that need to become political goals for all nations (Nussbaum 2000). Her intention is to justify the legitimacy of certain values that she considers universal, values aimed at protecting everyone, irrespective of culture, nationality, religion or gender. Nussbaum suggests that when we ask how people are faring in a nation, looking at the presence or absence of resources is not enough, because individuals differ in their needs for resources and their abilities to use them. In addition, the needs and experiences of people form the basis for a list of normative principles that, Nussbaum argues, all humans and all states must accept. Nussbaum suggests that speaking about common human needs, experiences, functions and problems remains possible (Nussbaum 1992). In addition to being social beings, each of us is an independent entity, living her or his own life, not anyone else's.

Nussbaum has developed a list of ten human capabilities, which we can thematically present as follows: longevity and bodily integrity; emotional, social and mental development; the ability to form a conception of what is good; the ability to live with the natural environment; and individual control over one's political and material environments. By positioning the individual at the centre, she transcends traditional divisions between public and private spheres. In essence, the capabilities approach offers some instructions for how people should act in society, particularly towards one another. It neither defines the 'good life' nor forces people to live according to that definition. Rather, it gives people the opportunity to formulate ideas about their own 'good life' and suggests that they must have the resources necessary for doing so. Nussbaum strongly believes that how public authorities meet these demands should be decided by public deliberation but that how people use their abilities must be an individual responsibility.

With the capabilities approach as both background and basis for rethinking democracy, we now return to the situation of Russian immigrant women in Norway.

Residence permit, dependency and equal participation

Our study comes out of 'Women Crossing Borders', a joint research project between the University of Tromsø and Norut Social Science Research Ltd. in Tromsø, 2002–5. The women we studied live in North Norway, which includes the three northernmost counties: Nordland, Tromsø and Finnmark. With only 10 per cent of the Norwegian population (i.e. 450,000 people), it is home to over 33 per cent of Russian immigrants to Norway. The net immigration of Russians to Norway from 1992 to 2002 was about 5,900, of whom 2,000 reside in North Norway (Statistics Norway 2006; Norut NIBR Finnmark). Our method was a mixture of qualitative interviews with Russian women immigrants, formal and informal meetings with public authorities, available statistics, public policy documents, and former research.

Compared to other European countries, Norway has a strict immigration policy, developed to prevent massive immigration. This policy is legitimized by the universal welfare system (Brochmann 1997). Because the welfare system includes all who reside in Norwegian territory, the immigration rules exclude the majority of potential immigrants. However, to those who gain residence permits, irrespective of reason, public policy appears generous. The policy's supreme goal is for everybody to have equal possibilities, rights and obligations for social participation. The guiding principle is that, given several ways of being Norwegian, everybody should have the right to bring her or his own values and traditions into the community. The Norwegian government stresses the importance of active participation, from the belief that every available social human resource should be activated and that participation increases the individual's opportunity to influence her or his own situation.

Russian immigration to Norway has increased steadily since the fall of the Soviet Union in 1991, and as many as 70 per cent of these immigrants are women. The reason for this gendered immigration is to be found in the Norwegian immigration rules. For a non-EEA citizen to gain residence in Norway, she or he has to be a refugee or asylum seeker, be an expert or receive an invitation to Norway via a special job, be a student, or come for family reunification.

The majority of Russian women move to Norway because of marriage to a Norwegian citizen, thereby obtaining a residence permit on the basis of family reunification. In 2002, 141 marriages between a Norwegian man and a Russian woman took place in North Norway. In the northernmost county, Finnmark, these marriages constituted 11 per cent of all marriages in 2002. By comparison, very few Russian men married Norwegian women and became residents through family reunification. The 2002 numbers for the country as a whole show that only five Russian men married Norwegian women, compared to 435 Russian women who married Norwegian men (Statistics Norway 2006).

Russian (woman)–Norwegian (man) marriages are becoming quite common. One Russian woman said in 2003: 'Almost everybody has a personal relationship to Russians nowadays. ... Most Norwegians will end up having a Russian in the family – or working with one'. (All following quotes are from Russian women from 2003, unless otherwise indicated.)

Marriage illustrates the intertwined and constructed character of the relationship between the private and the public spheres. On the one hand, the decision to marry and create a family is private, with the family as an institution constituting a certain sphere of legal privacy. On the other hand, marriage is a legal contract, providing a gateway for Russian women to participate with full rights in Norwegian society. In the case of a Russian woman and a Norwegian man, a couple cannot decide to cohabit instead of marry, because without the marriage contract, the woman has no citizenship rights – not even the right to stay in the country beyond the number of months a tourist visa allows. (Despite some exceptions, only a few Russian women in Norway have residence permits on such terms, as a later discussion will explain.) In other words, a private matter, a desire to share one's life with another person, is made publicly relevant by the Norwegian immigration rules.

Most importantly, Russian women who gain residence permits via family reunification do so only temporarily. In the case of divorce or the husband's death, they lose their permit and have to leave the country. They are not even allowed independent residence until they have lived at least 3 years in the country. The intent of this policy (called the 'three-year rule') is to prevent pro forma marriages, a subject we shall return to later.

The marriage contract becomes explicitly public in character because the Norwegian immigration authorities require proof of the couple actually living under one roof. Every year, as long as the residence permit is based on marriage, the couple has to fill out a form and have two witnesses sign it. Some informants consider this practice an intrusion in their private lives. One said: 'It was very humiliating in our situation, as we had been married for eight years before we moved here. Of course, we went over to some neighbours, and got them to sign'. Others find it unproblematic but ridiculous, as fraudulence is so easy. One woman said that anyone '. . . can sign, you know, people on the street, right? It's based on trust – and that's good – but it can be misused'.

The Norwegian government views the marriage contract as a public regulatory instrument but the relationship itself as private. The Norwegian authorities consider women who gain residence permits via family reunification as under the care of their husbands and therefore not in need of public support. The husband, who is considered the breadwinner, is responsible for her well-being. Informants, for instance, have explained that even though they applied for work permits, the long time it took before they were formally accepted by the labour market made them financially dependent upon their husbands. However, others have emphasized that their husbands helped a lot with filling out forms, writing applications and doing all the necessary paperwork. These authorities evidently did not help the women with any of these activities.

The requirement that everyone should have equal opportunity to express interests and concerns, and to respond to and criticize one another's arguments, cannot be realized without freedom from domination (Young 2000: 23). Most societies contain structures and patterns that create deliberative inequalities between the citizens, meaning asymmetry in people's opportunities to make use of their freedom and to participate in the public sphere (Bohman 2000: 107 ff).

The significance of marriage for Norwegian immigration policies makes the marriage contract such an unequal structure for Russian women immigrants. The rules surrounding the marriage contract construct Russian women as dependent, and as dependents they cannot be equal citizens. Even if the husband has no intention of dominating the wife, being a dependent puts her in a relationship of domination. As her residential status is considered a private matter, she cannot relate to the public sphere as a free and independent person. Consequently, her ability to participate as citizen in the Norwegian society is poor, if not greatly impaired. How to create a situation of fair deliberation, where Russian women immigrants can become equal citizens, is thus a highly relevant question for Norwegian public policies.

Limited access to citizenship education

The government takes an active role in the development of all immigrants' abilities to make use of their rights and fulfil their obligations as Norwegian citizens. The government is responsible for removing barriers against participation and for combating racism and discrimination. Such goals imply a responsibility for securing increased respect and tolerance, and for ensuring the equal distribution of public services throughout the population, irrespective of national background (St.meld.nr. 49, 2003–4).

Therefore, the government developed a set of legal instruments, as a form of civic education, to lay the groundwork for the integration of immigrants into Norwegian society. The 'Introduction Act' became effective 1 September 2004, and the law for adult immigrants on 'Education in Norwegian language and society/culture' went into effect on 1 January 2005. Both laws have considerable impact on immigrants' abilities to take part in social and political life and in the paid labour market. These laws follow the general rationale of the capabilities approach, stating that every human being should be able to participate effectively in political choices that govern her or his life (Nussbaum 2000: 78–80). These capabilities cannot be functional for people without sufficient education, language training and equal distribution of political rights.

However, the target group for the Introduction Act was immigrants with a need for basic qualifications – mainly newly arrived refugees and people allowed residence on a humanitarian basis or based on application for asylum. Those in the target group are both entitled and obliged to participate in an introductory program providing basic language skills, necessary insights into Norwegian society, and preparations for participation in the labour market or the educational system. Participants gain economic compensation corresponding to the existing rates of social security support. The Act rests on the government's general ambition to provide every individual, irrespective of background and status, equal possibilities, rights and obligations for participating in society and for making use of their resources. However, the Act specifically singles out those who come to Norway on the basis of family reunification as not needing this offer. A Russian woman married to a Norwegian man has no right to participate in the programme, because her spouse is supposed to give her what she needs with regard to financial support, language education and knowledge of her new country of residence.

Asking whether Norwegian immigration policies ignore these women because they came as wives and mothers is relevant. Although activities and practices related to women's functions as mothers and wives have traditionally not qualified any woman for citizenship, the exclusion of these Russian women and other women immigrants has come under heavy criticism (Ot.prop. nr 28 (2002–3)). The Gender Equality Ombudsman, The Ministry of Children and Family Affairs, the Contact Committee for Immigrants and the Authorities and the Ministry of Foreign Affairs have all, for different reasons, argued for an expansion of the target group.

As a result, the Norwegian government introduced a supplementary act on 'Education in Norwegian language and society/culture', making it compulsory for all adult immigrants to take part in some form of citizen education (Ot.prop. nr. 50 (2003–4)). But this programme is not as extensive as the original Introduction Act, because it reduces training hours from 2,000 to 300, and provides no economic support. Moreover, taking part in the programme has now become a condition for getting a residence permit: the law says that no one can gain permanent residence in Norway before completing the training courses. The rationale for the law is that immigrants need to acquire a basic knowledge of Norwegian language and society as quickly as possible so that they can both protect their rights and fulfil their duties as Norwegian citizens. The government considers the law as an important tool for active participation in society, and thus for the immigrants to feel comfortable in the Norwegian society.

We endorse the Norwegian government's will to provide all residents with equal rights, and we agree that language skills and societal knowledge are crucial to the development of full citizenship. We must, however, ask whether undergoing such training is enough for securing equal participation, and we therefore question other parts of the Norwegian immigration policy.

Bodily integrity and the 'three-year-rule'

One of the capabilities that Nussbaum believes should be a goal for public policy is bodily integrity, which she defines as being able to move from place to place and '... having the bodily boundaries treated as sovereign, i.e. being able to be secure against assault, including sexual assault, child sexual abuse, domestic violence; having opportunities for sexual satisfaction and for choice in matter of reproduction' (Nussbaum 2000: 78). This definition is important for analyzing the public regulation of the Norwegian 'three-year-rule', which mandates that one has to be married to a Norwegian citizen for at least 3 years to gain individual residential status through family reunification. Because Russian immigrant wives are dependents during these 3 years, they will be expelled from the country if they leave their husbands. There is one general exception from this rule: battered and abused women who bring charges and can prove the crime can independently obtain a residence permit earlier.

During this 3-year period the Russian women have limited rights of mobility. First, they are allowed to visit Russia for no longer than 90 days, or they forfeit their permits. This limit reduces the woman's ability to keep in touch with friends and family in Russia. Second, the government requires that the couple, in addition to showing good intentions with the relationship over years, literally live under the same roof. This requirement effectively prevents them from long-distance commuting for work or education. A more serious consequence of the 'three-year-rule' in practice is that it may foster violent relationships, despite the exception from the rule.

Not surprisingly, criticism of this rule has entered Norwegian public debate. The women's shelter movement has argued that this rule is a means for men to fully control their wives and has stated that it is

> ... quite evident that some men speculate in the situation for the women who come here on family reunion, and due to the 'three-year-rule' they have complete power and control over the women. If she doesn't fall into line with his demands, he threatens her with governmental expel.
>
> (Smaadal *et al.* 2002: 18)

This movement also claims that the rule puts women in an even more unfavourable position, as they have to prove an abuse case, and that what it takes for women to obtain a residence permit based on this rule remains unclear. In practice few cases are actually reported to the police. In the newspaper 'Sør Varanger avis', which covers a community with a high percentage of Russian immigrants in North Norway, a lawyer named Rønning reports that only a few Russian women are willing to bring charges against their husbands on grounds of abuse. The process of getting a residence permit is so complicated that many choose to stay in an abusive marriage for the full 3 years (Sør Varanger avis, 31 August 2000).

Language, the key to mental and social development

The capabilities approach pinpoints mental and social development as essential needs for all human beings. Nussbaum emphasizes the importance of the capability for using one's senses, imagination and thoughts – and to do so in a truly human way, informed by adequate education and knowledge. Doing so involves being able to use one's mind in ways protected by guarantees of freedom of expression, with respect to both political and artistic speech, and freedom of religious exercise. A necessary part of mental development is education and the opportunity for using the education in a productive way (Nussbaum 2000: 78–80).

A substantial part of the Russian population in Norway has higher university education, i.e. the equivalent of a master's degree. These Russians have even higher levels of education than the Norwegian population (Statistics Norway 2006). For most immigrants, however, no direct line exists from education in their home country to the everyday use of it in Norway, because of strict rules governing approval of education from non-Western countries.

The process of formally translating educational credits should ideally take place soon after arrival in the country, during the insecure period when immigrants like the Russian women are dependent on their husbands both for money and for information:

> I would very much like to use my university education here. But it was very difficult at first. I didn't know how to, or to whom I should apply to approve my education, what courses to take ... I got no information about it. At the end we found it on the Internet. I'm waiting for the approval now.

As a result many women delay starting the approval process and instead apply for unskilled work. Many Russian women therefore have the feeling of not being good enough, or that the devaluation of their Russian education likewise devalues the traditions and values they bring to Norwegian society. Consequently, official rules and procedures constitute bottlenecks for the improvement for citizen participation.

Nevertheless mental development is not only about education and the ability to participate in the labour market but also about being able to use imagination and self-expression (Nussbaum 2000: 79). For immigrants, this self-expression presupposes an opportunity to maintain and express themselves in their native language and culture. The Norwegian school system offers children of Russian origin education in Russian language as long as they have problems in mastering the Norwegian language, as proficiency in the mother's tongue is seen as a prerequisite for learning other languages. Yet, as soon as the child is capable of speaking Norwegian, this offer vanishes.

Similarly, children born to one Russian and one Norwegian parent do not even receive this educational offer, because the government does not view Russian as their mother tongue. Russian women have expressed several criticisms of this policy. Some state that the definition is too limited and they claim that a mother tongue is '... the language your mother speaks'. Other have called for extended education in Russian language and culture for their children and organized Russian associations for the purpose. In the city of Kirkenes, such an association (set up in 2003) fought the local authorities but lost. Thereafter, the association developed a children's club that educates children of Russian origin, and helps them to develop an active relationship to their Russian heritage.

From our perspective, campaigns for children's education are part of a broader strategy for improving the recognition of Russians in Norway.

These campaigns also build symbolic and cultural bridges to Russia. We therefore need to analyze these activities as related to citizenship activities, because they may have a considerable impact on the development of civil society (Lister 2003). What at first may appear as a mother's desire for her child's development may in the end contribute to the development of a common good. Education in Russian language and culture will possibly enable children to become confident bilinguals, able to provide important resources for societal development. In a similar vein, this collective action may help mothers to see themselves as political actors and effective citizens (Parry 1992).

Clearly, Norwegian immigration and integration policies contain elements both fostering and hampering Russian women immigrants' capability of participation. However, the ability to participate also depends on informal societal structures.

Citizen participation and the problems of prejudice

Nussbaum argues that, to sustain and fulfil all the other capabilities, capabilities of practical reason and affiliation are of special importance. These capabilities include the ability to form a conception of the good and to engage in critical reflections of one's life, to live with and have compassion for other people, and to have a social base for self-respect (Nussbaum 2000: 79). Having such capabilities implies a minimum of protection against discrimination based on race, sex, sexuality, religion, cast, ethnicity and nationality, as part of Norwegian policy towards immigrants suggests. However, all good intentions notwithstanding, public policies cannot control the development of stereotypes and prejudices.

To frame a conception of the good, one must be able to engage in social relations and discourses with mutual recognition with other people. It is important for immigrants to bring their own values and norms to this process and be able to participate in the Norwegian society without having to assimilate. The question may not be who the Russian women are or where they came from but what and who they may become, how they are represented and how those identities bear upon how they may represent themselves (Hall 1996: 4). Because the media are so influential, how the media portray Russian women strongly influences their options in using their history, language and culture in the process of becoming and representing themselves on their own terms.

One result of the opening of the border between Russia and Norway was the proliferation of sexual services and crime, activities that the media gave high priority. When Leontieva and Sarsenov analyzed the presentation of Russian women in Swedish and Norwegian newspapers, they found that female Russian immigrants had become the target of a rhetoric that always represents them as prostitutes, mail-order brides or family members dependent on a Western male citizen. The newspapers even represented marriages as connected with selling and buying sex (Leontieva and Sarsenov 2003).

The media focus has been a strain for Russian women. Some say that they have changed the way they dress; others say they do not speak Russian in public. Still others stress that they have not come to Norway as 'fortune hunters' in search for a better life.

> It's depressing and very negative. It seems as if they believe that all Russian women who come to Norway are prostitutes, or thieves, or I don't know what. It's only negative. It feels bad. Earlier I used to speak Russian in the shop, but now I don't speak Russian with my girl when we're in the shop, and I don't want to go to the restaurants with Russian friends. It doesn't feel safe. I have to think first. Shall I open my mouth and ask? No, it doesn't feel good. Earlier I was happy about being Russian. We have such a good country. But now, when I live in Norway, I'm a bit embarrassed by being a Russian. I have to hide the fact that I'm Russian. No, it's not good.

Hence, the media have contributed in maintaining symbolic and cultural differences by constructing Russian women as distinct from Scandinavian women, i.e. 'the other'. Although many Russian women immigrants struggle to disprove these media-established stereotypes, clearly rooted in 'anti-other' social and cultural patterns, many others withdraw from social and political activities (Kramvig and Stien 2002a, 2002b).

According to the capabilities approach, such patterns of stereotyping will have damaging consequences for people's self respect, eventually affecting their likelihood of engaging in political deliberation or controlling their own environment – preconditions for effective participation in the political choices that govern their lives (Nussbaum 2000: 80).

Political deliberation and voice

To what extent can these Russian women use the right of free speech in the deliberation processes, and do other deliberation parties consider them equal participants? When we asked our informants what they felt about participation in Norwegian society and whether they could influence their own life situations, some reported good control, while others did not feel that they had much control at all.

As for normal political participation, the informants reported that they voted or that they most likely would vote if they had the right. Beyond that, only a few showed an interest in active political participation. Some expressed a limited interest, and others were so fed up with politics from the time of *perestroika* in Russia that they had limited faith in politicians.

Regarding influence via informal discussions or expressions of opinions in newspaper columns, some expressed great interest in writing for local newspapers but, anticipating access only to the letters-from-readers sections, ending up not writing. Others felt that their voices were being heard in the local communities, e.g. their comments on primary health care or the school system were considered. Yet, quite often, they believed, their comments were neglected because they used their Russian experiences. One informant said:

> I would very much like to come up with my opinions if it wasn't for the usual reply: 'No, that's a cultural difference . . .' Often when I have comments or remarks, it becomes such a little break, and then: 'But may be it is a cultural difference that Russia is like that . . .' Then I understand I made a mistake again!

Others report that they do not criticize, that they do not want to interfere. They feel that they should adapt to the system they have chosen to move to:

> My daughter is happy at school. In Russia it's more learning and discipline. In Norway it's about play and being happy. But I observe his daughter. She is clever. So if it works, they may well play . . . No, I do not want to interfere.

These experiences suggest how justice is not only a matter of redistribution of rights, and social and economical goods but also a question of recognition. Nancy Fraser (2003) has developed conceptual tools that enable us to grasp these dual aspects of justice. She emphasizes the importance of distinguishing between two different claims of justice that correspond with two types of injustice. The first is related to redistribution of resources and wealth; the second is related to recognition. Claims within the redistribution paradigm aim at removing injustice rooted in the socio-economic structure of society. The recognition paradigm targets injustice rooted in social patterns of representation, interpretation and communication. This kind of injustice is often less visible than socio-economic inequality because it is maintained in the private sphere and only cultural and symbolic change can remove it.

Fraser argues that redistribution and recognition are mutually interconnected irreducible paradigms of justice (Fraser 2003). For instance, being a member of a stereotyped group will have consequences for one's standing in both the redistribution paradigm and the recognition paradigm. An approach to justice that pays attention to how the whole spectrum of capabilities interacts might perhaps improve our understanding of people's ability, or lack thereof, to function on equal terms in both of these types of justice.

Conclusion

In general, equal citizenship and justice are matters of respect for every individual's dignity. Justice requires social arrangements that permit all adult members of a society to interact on equal terms. The distribution of material resources and rights must ensure people's independence and 'voice'. Cultural values must express equal respect for all participants and ensure equal opportunity for achieving social esteem, as a form of parity of participation (Fraser 2003: 36).

But democratic participation also requires institutions and spaces where deliberation can take place, free from discrimination or stereotypical ideas and attitudes. Full realization of ideals related to deliberative democracy requires creation of public practices, dialogues and spaces surrounding controversial normative questions, in which all affected can take part (Benhabib 2002). We argue that new initiatives to promote full and equal citizenship must be based on such a notion of participation, including the right to criticize. Only when public participation is guided by normative principles such as equality, inclusion and mutual respect can the right to criticize truly be realized.

From Nussbaum to Fraser, we see the complexity of justice and the interrelationships of different aspects of human lives. From a theoretical and normative position, all of Nussbaum's capabilities are essential if people are to have equal opportunity to realize themselves as participating members of a society.

All in all, this chapter has shown that Russian women's citizenship in Norway is formed by a series of interrelated factors, with some tending to limit their access to full citizenship and equal participation in Norwegian society. Possibilities for public and equal participation are restricted by the marriage contract, which constitutes their rights of residence and thus has wide-ranging influence over their status in Norway.

Contrary to political declarations, the practical outcome of public policies enforces the unequal relationship between men and women, as institutional bottlenecks tend to reinforce the financial dependency of Russian women on their husbands. Political programmes also make women dependent upon their husbands, as they make the husband the gate-keeper and provider of information about Norwegian society at large. Public regulations, such as the three-year rule, constitute an important institutional example of how a public social contract between the welfare state and each individual citizen is downgraded and even put aside by a private contract.

These factors limit the possibilities for Russian women immigrants to develop capabilities on their own. We argue that institutional bottlenecks of this kind reduce access to public institutions and public participation. The *de facto* restrictions created by specific rules with the government's immigration policy belies – and, in this case, defeats – the primary principle and citizenship goals of the overall policy. Public policies in Norway need to be based on the recognition of these Russian women (and all other similarly situated immigrants) as independent equals, rather than as dependents. Recognized as individuals with the right to participate and the right to criticize, Russian women immigrants may experience the fulfilment of equal citizenship in Norway.

9   Europeanization 'from below'

The OMC process on social inclusion in the Swedish welfare state

Håkan Johansson

Introduction

The Europeanization of social policy has created a challenging, complex and fascinating situation for social non-governmental organizations (NGOs). The European Union (EU) has deployed a number of initiatives to encourage NGO participation in an emerging European polity. Social partners, voluntary organizations and citizen groups have gained key positions in new policy-making processes, such as the processes built on the open method of co-ordination (OMC), processes more inclusive to a variety of stakeholders and resting on the idea of reciprocal policy learning for every partner. The European Commission has encouraged the formation of EU-based networks and forums – e.g. in social inclusion policy and racism, xenophobia and age issues – aiming to encourage capacity building among national organizations and to help spread best practices. These initiatives have created new political opportunity structures at an EU level, thereby potentially challenging institutionalized patterns of policy-making in national contexts and pressuring national governments to introduce new forms of co-operation with organizations in the social field. Social NGOs now have the chance to take advantage of EU-related initiatives and transfer them to a national context, with the aim of strengthening their position (e.g. Della Porta *et al.* 1999; Ruzza 2004; Duffy and Jeliazkova 2005).

This chapter analyzes these issues from the perspective of the OMC process on social inclusion (e.g. Brandsen *et al.* 2005). It asks whether and, if so, how the OMC process for social inclusion has created new opportunities for social NGOs to take part in public deliberation and policy-making in Sweden. The chapter is based on analyses of Swedish National Action Plans on inclusion ('NAPs/incl'), interviews with officials from the Swedish Ministry of Health and Social Affairs and interviews with representatives from social NGOs.

Of particular interest are the opportunities created for social NGOs representing marginalized groups. If the OMC process has given them greater scope for participation and influence at the national level, this change may also indirectly affect the conditions for active citizenship for the groups they represent. Do we see the development of new patterns of

interaction between these social NGOs and the national government? How
has the Swedish government responded to opinions from the EU institutions such as the European Commission? Moreover, can the OMC process on
social inclusion threaten institutionalized policy-making models in Sweden?
The Swedish welfare state rests securely in a corporative tradition; i.e. social
policy reforms include consensus building between the government and
'social partners' (organizations of employers and employees) but to a lesser
extent between the government and social NGOs, citizens groups or
voluntary organizations (Lewin 1992; Rothstein 1992). Can the OMC process on social inclusion change or modify this tradition, and provide social
NGOs and citizens groups with greater possibilities for taking part in
public policy-making or discussions on the direction of social policy?

The emergence of a new political opportunity structure

The 'social dimension' of the EU has developed far beyond what was per-
ceivable some years ago and, since the late 1990s, EU institutions have
repeatedly emphasized the importance of social policies in strengthening
European integration (Kleinman 2002; Scharpf 2002). The European
Council expressed these ambitions at its March 2000 meeting in Lisbon,
and the resultant 'Lisbon strategy' included the ambition to not only
become '... the most competitive and dynamic knowledge-based economy
in the world, capable of sustaining economic growth with more and better
jobs and greater social cohesion', e.g. by '... modernising of the European
social model, investing in people and combating social exclusion' but also to
decisively affect the eradication of poverty in the EU (European Council
2000a). The Council President even explicitly mentioned the ambition of
significantly reducing the number of people at risk of poverty and social
exclusion by 2010.

From the perspective of 'political opportunity structure' theory (McAdam
1996; Koopmans 1999), the consequent OMC process on social inclusion
provided new opportunities for national social NGOs. These opportunities
result not only from the introduction of new policy-making procedures but
also from the acceptance of new policy ideas and beliefs at the EU level.

The Lisbon strategy was closely related to the adoption of OMC processes.
Even though they play a fairly minor role in EU policy-making at large,
they have gained great significance in policy fields closely related to national
welfare state characteristics, such as employment and social policies. However, to consider the OMC process as completely new is misleading, because
it largely constitutes the codification of practices developed previously in
the European Employment Strategy and within economic policies (Hodson
and Maher 2001; Mosher and Trubek 2003; Eberlein and Kerwer 2004).
Given the growing academic discussions on OMC processes, we need to
understand both the purpose and the practice of the process (De la Porte
and Pochet 2002; Borras and Jacobsson 2004).

The OMC process does not rely on legal rules. It is a post-regulatory method of governance resting upon general procedures and standards. Hence it differs from the supranational law-making generally recognized as the trademark of EU policy-making (Jacobsson and Schmid 2002). This difference does not imply that legally binding regulations, directives and the European Court of Justice have lost importance but rather that they have been complemented by new forms of governance procedures. The OMC process provides flexibility for all actors; while it accepts differences in national contexts, it co-ordinates them through a set of mechanisms and instruments, thereby making policy influence based upon the process highly complex and difficult to discern. Even though joint objectives are agreed upon at an EU level, national governments have wide discretion for how to implement these typically broad and general objectives. Clearly, the success of the OMC process depends upon the willingness of national governments to follow the general ideas and objectives agreed upon within EU institutions. As the OMC does not allow EU institutions to use formal sanctions against national governments, the OMC process is largely a voluntary method of policy-making.

To further explain, the OMC process is based upon an idea of iterative, reciprocal policy learning for every partner, using instruments such as guidelines, indicators, national action plans, peer reviews and best practices. At the Lisbon meeting, the European Council stated that the OMC was based on four major elements: (i) the setting of short-, medium- and long-term guidelines for the EU, with specific timetables for their achievements; (ii) the establishment of performance indicators and benchmarks tailored to each member state and sector, to allow comparison of best practices; (iii) the translation of targets from the European to the national level; and (iv) periodic monitoring, peer review and evaluation, emphasizing mutual learning (European Council 2000a). These elements gives us some insight into the functioning of the OMC process, in which the ambition is not only to spread best practices as a method for policy learning across the EU but also to create greater convergence in reaching EU goals, e.g. better jobs, greater social cohesion, less poverty.

The OMC on social inclusion provides opportunities for national social NGOs by presenting a number of policy objectives, issues and ideas for national governments to consider or even adjust to. The December 2000 Council meeting in Nice created a set of objectives for how member states were to fight social exclusion and poverty (Atkinson 2002). Member states agreed to complete biannual national action plans (NAPs) and to report on their strategies and actions for fighting social exclusion and poverty. Moreover, the Council encouraged all member states to fulfil the following four objectives (European Council 2000b):

1 To facilitate participation in employment and access by all to resources, rights, goods and services (i.e. to promote access to stable and quality

employment, to mobilize training policies, and to promote the reconciliation of work and family life).

2 To prevent the risk of social exclusion (i.e. to put into place policies that seek to prevent life crises, indebtedness, exclusion from school and becoming homeless).

3 To help the most vulnerable (i.e. to promote the social integration of those who face persistent poverty).

4 To mobilize all relevant bodies (i.e. to promote not only the participation and self-expression of people suffering exclusion but also the dialogue and partnership between all relevant bodies, public and private).

The lack of greater detail in these objectives naturally gave member states an opportunity and a responsibility to interpret them according to national standards. As for the fourth, which is of greatest relevance for our discussion, the European Council in Nice explained that mobilizing all partners meant to

> ... promote dialogue and partnership between all relevant bodies, public and private, for example: i) by involving the social partners, NGOs and social service providers, according to their respective areas of competence, in the fight against the various forms of exclusion, ii) by encouraging the social responsibility and active engagement of all citizens in the fight against social exclusion and iii) by fostering the social responsibility of business.
>
> (European Council 2000b)

The actual impact of these policy objectives is difficult to discern and it is unlikely that they have had any great impact, e.g. as the OMC process does not give the Commission the authority to make recommendations to member states. Nevertheless, despite these limitations the OMC process on social inclusion has put combating poverty on the political agenda across European member states, introducing detailed targets for poverty reduction and emphasizing that policy-making in this field ought to include all relevant stakeholders. These very acts encourage member states to develop improved common knowledge about how to combat poverty as a social problem of common concern for all European countries. The results have been wide-ranging discussions engaging both politicians and academics, including what indicators to use for measuring social exclusion and poverty, and the development of common databases (Atkinson *et al.* 2002).

Since the Lisbon and Nice meetings, the OMC on social inclusion has developed even further. In late 2005 the Commission presented the plan of streamlined OMC processes of social inclusion and social protection, as part of a revised Lisbon strategy (European Commission 2005). The following discussion will analyze the period *before* this streamlining began, specifically the OMC process on social inclusion in Sweden. We can divide the Swedish experience into four different phases, starting before the introduction of the process itself, stretching over the completion of two NAPs (NAP 2001, 2003), and entailing the institutional innovation of a new platform for participation and consultation with stakeholders. The following analysis covers the broader process in Sweden and will include quotes from some of the stakeholders.

Social NGOS exploring the OMC before the government

The first phase of the Swedish OMC process on social inclusion started well before any formal decisions came out of Brussels. In the spring and summer of 2000, representatives from Swedish social NGOs were exploring what opportunities this process would provide and how they could best take advantage of them nationally. Representatives from national social NGOs, who knew what had occurred at the EU level, provided Swedish social NGOs with information and experience on the detailed content and implications of the OMC process.

Several Swedish organizations were represented in EU-based networks and forums, such as the European anti-poverty network, the European Disability Forum and the Euro-Diaconia, and in 2000 the OMC process on social inclusion was a debated subject in these networks and forums. Individuals from other Swedish organizations had central positions in EU institutions, e.g. as representatives in the European Economic and Social Committee, an EU advisory body.

These contacts and positions enabled the NGO representatives to get started before the Swedish government, clarifying their strategies, developing their capacities, and directing their efforts to mobilize partners. As a way of strengthening NGO capacities, one representative from the national Swedish co-operative institute invited other social NGOs to form a national network on social exclusion. As a representative in the European Economic and Social Committee, this person had long experience in building national civil networks and conducting social economy activities. The planning took place in early autumn of 2000, with a threefold aim: (i) to explore the possibilities of the OMC process on social inclusion; (ii) to form a network capable of speaking to the Swedish government with one voice; and (iii) to become the one recognized actor for co-operating with the government in writing NAPs on social inclusion.

Even at this early stage, it was apparent that officials from the Ministry of Health and Social Affairs did not know much about the OMC process, nor did they show any great interest. Although the social NGOs invited representatives from the Ministry to discuss the EU initiatives, they were turned down. In contrast to the lack of Swedish government interest, these NGOs successfully mobilized a network giving the fourth objective high priority. It was called 'the Network Against Social Exclusion' (Network).

The Network consists of national social NGOs and voluntary organizations, representing marginal citizens with limited resources for full social participation in society. Some of these organizations provide services while others express a voice. Several member organizations are large, in terms of members and resources, and have a central position in Swedish social policy. Others are small, with few members and limited resources. The Network has aimed to establish itself as *one* collective actor for a spectrum of national organizations that previously worked individually with different agendas. To facilitate participation from an array of organizations, the Network remains informal, with no formal rights or obligations. Nonetheless, members of the Network hold key positions in their respective national organizations (general secretaries, chairpersons or senior advisers), a factor that has given the Network a high status among social NGOs.

The Network includes organizations belonging to the Swedish movement of people with impairments, religious organizations and communities, user organizations, client organizations, social economy organizations, immigrant organizations and ethnic associations. Although the Network attempted to include the workers union and the white-collars union, both declined the invitation.

NAP for and by the government

After these initial activities on the part of social NGOs, the Swedish OMC process entered a second phase: the Swedish government began to work on the first NAP on poverty and social exclusion at the start of 2001, and the Ministry of Health and Social Affairs and its unit for social services prepared the reports. Interviewed officials recalled how very pleased they were with the Network, which solved the problem of mobilizing all partners. However, despite several formal and informal meetings in spring of 2001, both partners described the relationship as conflict-ridden. The main issue was to what degree the Network would participate in the OMC process on social inclusion.

The Network wanted to be full partners in the formulation of the NAP, arguing that this kind of partnership was an explicit objective of the OMC process. The Network established different task forces to decide what issues to bring forward and how best to influence the OMC process. Ministry officials expressed uncertainty about performing the OMC process, including how to write a NAP, how to interpret the EU guidelines and what degree of autonomy a government enjoyed at a national level. Although their concern was hardly surprising at the very start of the process, government representatives stated that the expectations of Network participants were too high. The Swedish government defined the NAP as a document *for* the Swedish government and written *by* the Swedish government, as a state-of-the-art document. This position was later reflected in the final document, published in late spring 2001, mainly describing Swedish social policy and the Swedish social model.

With regard to the objective of promoting dialogue and partnership with all relevant bodies, the plan mentioned that a

> ... large number of user and voluntary organizations has formed a network in order to influence, contribute to and monitor the efforts to implement the Swedish Action Plan Against Poverty and Social Exclusion. Consideration is currently being given to ways and means of establishing a dialogue between the network and the Government.
>
> (NAP 2001: 25)

However, according to the Swedish government, the OMC process on social inclusion had limited significance for national policy-making. In the next NAP, the government explained that a national political reform process involved the identification of problems, investigations, political negotiations, budget considerations, a bill and, eventually, a parliamentary resolution enacting legislation. Yet for the Swedish government the

> ... context of the NAP against poverty and social exclusion was different, and the action plan was therefore more like a concise description of political strategy and action than a platform for new political reforms. This is why no new political initiatives were launched in the action plan and why it cannot claim to have determined the direction and scope of welfare policy.
>
> (NAP 2003: 15)

The Network challenged this position. It argued that the Swedish government presented an inadequate picture of the Swedish welfare state, by failing to describe Swedish social policy from the perspective of social NGOs and voluntary organizations, and thereby implying that social policy was operated only by the state and governmental actors. To demonstrate both its criticism and its willingness to be partners and participants, the Network produced a 20-page alternative action plan, discussing its view of EU objectives, and gave the plan to the Ministry of Health and Social Affairs in April 2001. By presenting an alternative plan, the Network substantiated its claim that the Swedish government did not fulfil the common EU objectives to which it had agreed.

The Network sought support from the European Commission. In its 2001 *Joint Report on Social Inclusion*, the Commission stated that a major challenge would be to develop effective mechanisms for the involvement of stakeholders, not only in outlining NAPs but also in implementing and monitoring them (European Commission 2001: 8). In written correspondence, the Commission reported that several member states had developed interdepartmental structures, such as co-ordinating committees or agencies, gathering representatives from different administrative bodies (and in some cases from NGOs), as a way of strengthening the administrative structure for fighting poverty and social exclusion. The Commission reported that Sweden presented its universal social policies, in combination with vigorous employment policies, as key measures for fighting poverty. The Commission stated that references

> ... are made in the NAP to the efforts which the Government and a large range of different bodies and interest groups at all levels have put in, although it is not possible to assess to what extent the participation of the bodies outside the normal administration has resulted in actual contributions to the NAP/incl.
>
> (European Commission 2001: 112)

This criticism became significant in Sweden, because the government disliked the official EU reprimand. The Network used the same report to pressure the Swedish government, to 'open' the OMC process on social inclusion. The Network also argued that its members had contacts with various EU-related networks and forums, which indirectly could put pressure on the Swedish government.

Different views on participation

The third phase of the Swedish OMC process on social inclusion started in spring 2003, when the Swedish government initiated the second round of preparing the NAP. This time the government adopted a slightly different stance on participation, expressing an aim to develop '... closer cooperation and partnerships at all social levels and a clear user perspective' (NAP 2003: 2). The government, said it had consulted with the Network and public authorities, keeping them informed throughout the NAP process. To substantiate this claim, the government attached two appendices to the NAP, one from the Network and one from the three biggest cities, which had been involved in developing local action plans as part of the European employment strategy and the Eurocities co-operation.

As to the objective of promoting dialogue and partnerships with stakeholders, the government expressed the ambition to strengthen partnerships between public and private actors, predominantly at the local level. The government claimed that the Network had an important role to play. It could raise awareness about the social inclusion process among the groups it represented, and it had the necessary local contacts for influencing efforts to combat economic and social vulnerability (NAP 2003: 42–3). To accomplish closer partnerships of this kind, the Swedish government expressed the intention of initiating a user committee in social vulnerability matters. The newly appointed Minister paid greater attention to issues of user involvement and participation than the former Minister and his proposal fit well with propositions from the European Commission, which had reported in the *Joint Inclusion Report* (2001) that some member states had already developed innovative administrative structures for enhancing the participation of social NGOs. According to the government, members from the Network would play a major role, as the committee was to

> ... act as a body for consultations between the public sector and voluntary and user's organisations for the purpose of mobilizing relevant bodies in the efforts to combat economic and social vulnerability. The committee will function both as a forum for consultations and information exchange in connection with implementation of the NAP and will be a model for, and give legitimacy to, consultation arrangements at the local and regional levels.
>
> (NAP 2003: 41)

The Network, according to interviews with members, continued to criticize the government throughout the spring of 2003 for not accepting it as a full partner in producing the next NAP. In its appendix to the NAP, the Network described itself as a forum for dialogue and exchange of experience among organizations with shared values in the fight against social exclusion. Moreover, the Network claimed to have experience in

> ... creating meeting-places and dialogue with users and many examples of good practice. It is necessary for representatives of central and local government to engage in direct dialogue with the most vulnerable. The Network can contribute to the establishment of this dialogue and ensure that it is conducted respectfully and on equal terms. We attach special importance to the fourth objective of the action plan, i.e. to mobilise all relevant bodies. We consider that this objective is an essential condition for achievement of the first three objectives.
>
> (NAP 2003: 48)

The Network claimed that it was still important to work for a transparent framework for consultations and co-ordination which '... actively engages authorities and voluntary organisations in the formulation and implementation of the action plan at the national and local levels' (NAP 2003: 49). In other words, despite their differences, the Network and the Swedish government started to express more similar ambitions.

Institutionalized participation

The fourth phase of the Swedish OMC process on social inclusion started in autumn 2003. The government decided to initiate a forum for information exchange and consultations with user organizations, i.e. a 'user committee on social and welfare issues', with the special aim of highlighting the perspective of poor and socially excluded people. Above all, the committee would strengthen user involvement and influence related to outlining and implementing the NAPs on poverty and social exclusion.

From the perspective of the Network, the establishment of this user committee represented substantial progress, because it gained access to a forum in which top politicians and public officials participated. The Minister chaired the committee, accompanied by his senior political adviser. The Director General of the National Board of Health and Welfare and higher officials from the Swedish association of local authorities also participated. However, the Network had the numerical majority. After some internal election procedures regarding gender, ethnicity and organizational positions, the Network put forward 11 people (later accepted by the Ministry of Health and Social Affairs) as its representatives. Although the delegation had no formal power to make decisions, the Swedish government still took some important steps in developing the participatory dimension of the OMC process.

Network members stated that they have generally been very pleased with the committee and the role of the Minister, who has shown personal interest in issues of user involvement. All the partners identified the committee as a possible model for how to implement the NAP locally and how to build local partnerships between public agencies and citizens' organizations. Moreover, all partners stated that the committee probably would not have been set up, had it not been for the OMC process.

However, the work of the committee illustrates some unresolved ambiguities. Instead of arguments and struggles over influence and participation ceasing, they began taking place within the committee. While the forum was formally presented as one of consultation and information exchange, Network members said that they had limited influence on the agenda. In spring 2004, the delegation held meetings, concentrating on topics of interest to the Minister. When the government invited external experts to meetings, Network members were not allowed to invite their own. In addition, the agenda for meetings was distributed only a few days in advance, restricting Network to limited preparation.

The government's behaviour in this context draws attention to the disadvantaged role of social NGOs in public policy-making. Some members of the committee even called it 'a hostage situation', in which they mainly functioned as 'experts' on the user perspective, answering questions from the Minister when asked. From its point of view, the government needed the committee to fulfil EU objectives. Other members of the committee believed that these problems merely resulted from the committee having just been established and not yet having found its procedure or form. They expressed a pragmatic approach, arguing that social NGOs had to accept some difficulties when working closely with public authorities, as a necessity for gaining additional influence. Moreover, some Network members criticized the Network itself for focusing only on establishing contacts with the government and failing to develop an agenda for further action.

Contrasting views on the NAPs from the government and social NGOs

Debates over visions and theories relating to the OMC process are ongoing. Some academics have stressed its participatory and deliberative qualities, in terms of facilitating a critical engagement of civil society actors, possibilities for voice and participation in public debate, and policy-making on the part of citizens or the organizations representing them (De la Porte and Nanz 2004). Others have emphasized that the abstract, theoretical and sometimes highly ideological promises of the OMC process sharply contrast with the process in practice – how national governments have handled it and what scope for effective voice, influence and participation it has given national social NGOs (Radaelli 2003; Jacobsson 2004). Key issues are the scope of the OMC process (as a political opportunity structure), its relative openness or closure, and its strength in a national context. This chapter shows that we can identify some ways in which the government and the Network strategically operated to 'open' or 'close' the process. Even though these examples come only from Sweden, they illustrate both the ambiguities and the tensions within the overall OMC process.

The OMC process on social inclusion has clearly contributed to new and enlarged opportunities for participation for social NGOs. The Swedish government has gradually adopted a more generous attitude towards the Network and its mobilizing objective. The best example is the introduction of the user committee as an institutionalization of participation and co-operation between the government and social NGOs. Therefore, we can conclude that this particular OMC process has opened new opportunities for social NGOs representing groups holding a marginal position in society to influence agenda-setting and public decision-making. Nonetheless, the Swedish government has used and still uses different strategies to limit or resist such NGO participation. The following three dynamics give us a framework for understanding the different positions and approaches of the government and the Network.

Reduced versus expansive approaches: one issue concerns the scope of the OMC process, especially whether to define it as a national or a European process. The Swedish government used different strategies to reduce the OMC scope within the Swedish national context, because it viewed the NAP process as external to Swedish social policy and therefore of limited importance. Accordingly, the government gave it low priority and peripheral status at the Ministry unit for social services.

The Network, for its part, worked strategically to expand the OMC process beyond government control and to define it as an EU-related issue. The Network believed that the process was and should be out of the hands of national governments, as they had signed the Amsterdam treaty and taken part in developing the Lisbon and Nice conclusions. The Network also used its contacts and affiliations with EU-related networks to push the OMC process beyond the complete control of the Swedish government. The conflict between the government and the Network was over the scope and ambition of the process: whether to understand it as one of limited importance for national policy-making or as one involving local, national and supranational actors.

Static versus dynamic approaches: another important issue concerns the nature of the NAPs – whether they are documents written by the government and for the government or joint products of the government and social NGOs. At first the Swedish government defined the NAP as a state-of-the-art document that did not describe future actions or welfare reform. Moreover, that only a few people at the Ministry were involved in writing the NAP meant that the Swedish government kept the NAP under very tight control and circumvented all social NGO claims for inclusion in policy-making.

The Network developed several strategies for involvement in discussing, writing and implementing the NAPs. Network members tried to prove their competence and experience by, for instance, producing an alternative action plan. They also challenged the government's view as they integrated the NAPs into their own activities, e.g. developing informational material based on the NAPs.

Passive versus active participation: although the OMC process on social inclusion builds on the objective of mobilizing all relevant bodies, in Sweden we see different views on the role of social NGOs. For instance, official documents described the user committee as a body for consultations between the public sector and voluntary organizations, serving as a forum for information exchange. However, even though committee membership was a significant improvement for the Network, we question how the Swedish government defined contributions from the social NGOs. The government mainly perceived them as 'consultants' on user issues, with a possible mandate to function as 'experts'.

But the Network argued for recognition as a full partner, with the right to give input on its own initiative, express criticism, and have a recognized mandate to speak for its members. Some committee members said that the committee largely functioned as a government instrument for fulfilling EU objectives without giving social NGOs real opportunities for influence and co-determination. But others disagreed, either for pragmatic reasons or because they did not want to be critical. These tensions and disagreements within the Network and the committee will probably become even more apparent if members start to discuss more detailed and practical issues.

At the risk of making a complex process appear too simple and unequivocal, Table 2 summarizes these positions.

Table 2 can serve as a basis for some analytical reflections on different approaches to the OMC process on social inclusion in Sweden. The emerging issues are in line with experiences from other European member states, despite some differences in the details (e.g. De la Porte and Nanz 2004; Jacobsson 2004; De la Porte and Pochet 2005).

Table 2 Contrasting views on the national action plans (NAPs)

	Government position	Network position
Scope of the OMC process: a limited or expansive understanding?	The OMC as an external process, of limited significance for Swedish policy-making	The OMC as a European and multi-level process, beyond the sole control of the national government
Nature of NAPs: static or dynamic approaches?	NAP of limited significance for Swedish welfare reform; a state-of-the-art document	NAP as a document of action and reform; a document for discussion, debate and education in society at large
What role for social NGOs: passive or active participation?	Social NGOs as informants, consultants or possibly experts on the user perspective	Social NGOs as full partners, with a right to critical voice

Conclusion

When making social policy, the Swedish welfare state has rarely included organizations representing poor, marginalized or excluded groups. Social partners (along with a few large social NGOs) have been selected to represent the greater society in discussions with the national ministries. One obvious reason is that poverty has not been a high-profile issue in Sweden. Although social redistribution and economic equality are important political aims, fighting poverty has hardly been identified as a separate issue requiring a specific arsenal of anti-poverty measures. Swedish social policy rather rests upon the assumption that poverty is a residual problem best combated through active employment-promoting policies combined with an encompassing system of social benefits. Given this history, and because the OMC process on social inclusion contains some controversial and challenging components for the Swedish welfare state, some of the government's controlling responses and strategies begin to make sense.

The OMC process has been a catalyst for encouraging new patterns of co-operation among social NGOs and for strengthening their position with the government. The EU expects member states to mobilize and involve even marginalized groups in the policy-making process, rather than defining them only as target groups for welfare state provisions and interventions.

This chapter finds that the OMC process on social inclusion has provided social NGOs with a reason to mobilize, develop a common agenda and act collectively. As we have seen, the Network's overarching ambition is to reach internal consensus and speak with one voice to the Swedish government. The Network is something very new in the organizational landscape of Swedish social NGOs. Although broader networks, umbrella organizations and informal constellations have existed earlier, this is the first all-embracing network, gathering social NGOs from a wide number of policy areas. It is also the first network that aims to become *one* powerful actor, too powerful for the government to ignore. In that respect, the OMC process not only reflects existing structures of co-operation among social NGOs but also appears to transform them.

The OMC process on social inclusion has emerged as an important component in the Network's overall engagement and negotiation with the government, because the Network is the one actor that has managed to establish closer, more reciprocal contacts with the Ministry. Given existing analyses of the corporative dimension of the Swedish welfare state, that the social partners did not participate in these discussions is remarkable.

These institutional innovations have been further encouraged by the relative redefinition of poverty policies in Sweden, especially as the OMC process on social inclusion strongly urges member states to reduce their poverty levels. In sharp contrast to its policy discourse, the Swedish government in 2001 adopted a parallel objective to reduce poverty. The Social Democratic government explicitly formulated the goal of cutting the number of people receiving social assistance by 50 per cent by 2004 (based on 1999 calculations) – the first time a Swedish government presented a national goal for social assistance.

Even though the Swedish government failed to accomplish its objective, it is striking that the objective was announced at the same time as the first round of NAPs. For instance, an important aspect of the OMC process is that each national government has to present its plans for and achievements on fighting poverty before its European colleagues and face their response. Possibly Swedish politicians did not want to be 'shamed and blamed' for not taking poverty issues seriously (Jacobsson 2004). This is not to claim a causal link between EU objectives and the Swedish government's actions; policy influence between the EU and member states occurs in much more complex and subtle ways. From a broader perspective, however, these political and discursive changes in Swedish politics might make it easier for marginalized groups (and the organizations representing them) to take part in the public deliberation on policy responses to their situation.

Given these considerations, and in contrast to some previous studies, we argue that the OMC process on social inclusion has had an impact on the Swedish welfare state (see e.g. Halleröd 2003). The OMC process has provided social NGOs representing marginalized groups in the Swedish welfare state with new opportunities to demand participation in making national policy relevant to their situation. Swedish organizations have used the OMC process to their advantage as a new structural setting to explore and develop. Moreover, these organizations have proven to be skilful, competent actors as they adopted the multi-level and multi-actor style of the EU polity. This relative success demonstrates the importance of applying an analytical perspective that focuses on activities 'from below' in EU policy-making, particularly in analyses of the relationships between the EU and national welfare states.

Part IV

Marketization of citizenship?

Choice, anti-discrimination and human rights

10 Contrasting legal concepts of active citizenship

Europe and the Nordic countries

Kirsten Ketscher

Introduction

The Nordic countries are characterized by the state's more active involvement in citizens' well-being than in most other European countries. The development of welfare rights has been a political project in which national parliaments and social democratic parties have been the driving forces, and until the early 2000s, control through courts and legal tribunals played a minor role. As this legal area has not been the object of systematic legal analysis, a legal framework for understanding citizens' rights in the welfare state has been missing.

Various factors are now challenging the dominant role of the Nordic national parliaments in the construction of welfare rights. The national concepts underlying the legal constructs of the Nordic states are becoming increasingly 'de-nationalized', not only from the influence of European Union (EU) regulations but also from the limiting effects in the welfare arena of the European Convention of Human Rights (ECHR) on the power of national parliaments. All the Nordic countries are part of the EU, either as full members (Denmark, Finland and Sweden) or as associated members through the European Economic Area (EEA) treaty (Iceland and Norway). Therefore, comparing and contrasting the Nordic national understandings of active citizenship with the values and initiatives of the EU is highly important.

This chapter explores the legal notions of active citizenship in the Nordic countries. It analyzes active citizenship as a legal relationship between the state and the citizen, starting with the fundamental values of the Nordic countries as they are expressed in national constitutions. The chapter then relates these fundamental Nordic values to those of the EU, arguing that the notion of self-support plays a key role in the Nordic understanding of active citizenship and social welfare rights. The discussion will focus on legal interpretations of this self-support principle (e.g. as expressed as activation policies) in the light of the human rights, represented by the European Court of Human Rights ('the Strasbourg court') and the European Court of Justice (ECJ). Finally, the chapter argues that the building of a socially balanced European market constitutes a counterpoint to the traditional welfare thinking in the Nordic countries. To illustrate the legal conflicts and problems in the Nordic legal welfare concept, the chapter will draw primarily from Danish legislation and legal practice.

Fundamental values in the Nordic welfare states

A constitutional framework generates fundamental values, written or unwritten. Although all the Nordic countries have written constitutions, the visibility of the welfare state is very different in their constitutions. The Danish constitution is the most archaic, and the Finnish is the most modern. Two features distinguish modern constitutions from old ones. Firstly, modern constitutions explicitly highlight the values on which they are based. Secondly, modern constitutions have a well-developed human rights list embracing the international conventions accepted by most Western states, especially those of gender equality. Sweden and Finland have modern constitutions with explicit values. Iceland, Norway and Denmark – in this order – have fewer and less explicit values. The foundation of constitutions can, however, embed values even if they are not visible in the text.

The Finnish and Swedish constitutions

The constitutions of Finland and Sweden have a well-developed list of human rights; the welfare state is considered an important part of the nation's foundation; and the protection of gender equality is explicit. The Finnish constitution (since 1999) has a chapter of basic rights and liberties and a full list of human rights, protects equality between women and men as part of a general non-discrimination clause, and uses gender-sensitive language (e.g. 'his' and 'her'). To a certain extent, the Swedish constitution (since 1975) is similar. Even though it is remarkably less modern in its outlook, it also guarantees equal rights of women and men, as well as the rights of ethnic, linguistic and religious minorities.

However, the Finnish constitution has a detailed section on the right to social benefits. The constitution guarantees the right to basic money and care for those 'who cannot obtain the means necessary for a life of dignity'. Even though the Swedish constitution includes this right to some extent, because individuals' economic and cultural welfare is considered a fundamental aim, it does not express this right as clearly in relation to the welfare state. The legal language of the Swedish constitution is also less gender-sensitive, using 'he' and 'his' when referring to citizens as individuals.

The Danish, Icelandic and Norwegian constitutions

The older Nordic constitutions date from the nineteenth century and start by defining the powers of the king, parliament, courts and the applicable procedural rules. Although these constitutions are characterized by few explicit values, values can still be embedded in the basis of the constitution without being visible in the text.

For instance, the Norwegian constitution, which dates from 1814, does not state any basic values: the list of human rights is very sparse, and equal rights between women and men are not mentioned. Social protection is not mentioned either, even though at a later stage legal scholars have used some of its provisions articles to argue for the protection of social benefit rights within its scope of prohibition of retroactive laws (Article 97; Kjønstad 1997).

The Danish constitution dates from 1849, with amendments in 1953. As a non-modern constitution, it does not state any explicit general values, does not protect human dignity or equality between women and men, and does not refer to newer human rights concepts. The welfare state is barely visible, with the few regulations of social provisions primarily concerning provision for the poor.

Even though the Icelandic constitution is from 1944, it adopts an old style, expressing few fundamental values. However, it recognizes equality between the sexes both as a general right and as a specific provision (Article 65), albeit without gender-sensitive language. The welfare state makes itself slightly known, as the constitution guarantees the '. . . necessary assistance in case of sickness, invalidity, old age, unemployment and similar circumstances'.

The principle of self-support as a common ground

Despite these differences between the Nordic constitutions, a fundamental value in all Nordic countries is that the individual has the obligation to support herself or himself. This value applies to both care support and financial support (Ketscher 2001). The legal notion of active citizenship is above all connected to situations where an individual for various reasons is not able to earn an income because of social or personal circumstances (e.g. unemployment, health or family problems). Nevertheless public cash support is subsidiary to the importance of self-support. The welfare state is under no obligation to support a person who can provide for herself or himself. The citizen has a duty not to be a burden on the social benefit system or on society in general. This socially understood obligation expresses a basic aspect of active citizenship within the framework of the self-support principle in the Nordic countries.

A key legal question is what activity public authorities can require from an individual person who is not able to support herself or himself, in exchange for the support provided as part of 'society's' obligations towards persons in this situation. The labour market does not provide jobs for all persons who need work as a source of access to money. Public authorities must provide work – or the skills that enable people to find work – to make them self-supporting. This obligation is recognized and expressed in practically all Nordic constitutions, usually in the phrase 'the right to work'. For instance, Nordic constitutions state:

> ... efforts should be made to afford work to every able-bodied citizen on terms that will secure his existence.
>
> (Danish constitution, Section 75, 1)

> ... the public authorities shall promote employment and work towards guaranteeing for everyone the right to work
>
> (Finnish constitution, Section 18)

> ... it is the responsibility of the authorities of the state to create conditions enabling every person capable of work to earn a living by his work.
>
> (Norwegian constitution, Article 110, 1)

> ... it shall be incumbent upon the public administration to secure the right to work.
>
> (Swedish constitution, Article 2)

In a Nordic context the provision of paid work takes precedence over social assistance as a means of helping citizens to obtain a livelihood (Chapter 4). The legal possibility for the state to create work can be found in several versions, e.g. as 'social clauses' in collective agreements, government subsidies for employers (targeted at individuals who are not able to find work under normal conditions), or public training programmes for upgrading individuals' skills. Measures such as these improve the possibility for citizens to be active and at least partly self-supporting. All are well-known legal constructions illustrating the ways in which the state fulfils its obligations to secure its citizens' 'right to work' and thereby enable them to become active citizens. Paid work and the labour contract form the normal legal frame for a person's self-supporting activity.

Human rights protection and Nordic values

International human rights conventions represent a common legal language across borders. Fundamental rights and values are considered universal and made visible in conventions to form a common legal platform for the signatory parties (national states). For our discussion, four conventions are central: two from the Council of Europe – the European Convention of Human Rights (ECHR 1950) and the European Social Charter (ESC 1969) (Mikkola 2000) – and two from the United Nations: the Convention on Elimination of all forms of Discrimination Against Women (the Women's Convention (CEDAW 1979)) and the Convention on the Rights of the Child (CRC 1989).

These conventions in different ways deal with the human rights problems created by active citizenship and related principles of self-support. However, only the ECHR contains effective legal enforcement (the Strasbourg Court) for individual complaints. The CEDAW committee has an individual complaint protocol for issues involving the Women's Convention. The two other conventions have monitoring committees that follow state practice and that issue general interpretative recommendations.

All five Nordic states have integrated the ECHR into domestic legislation. The Strasbourg Court is the authoritative interpreter and can enforce the nations' observance of the human rights covered by the convention. Dating back to 1950, the ECHR is already marked by its age and therefore less dynamic than later UN instruments. Therefore, we need to interpret the ECHR with reference to UN conventions if they cover the same field. The CEDAW and the CRC supplement the interpreting arsenal of the ECHR. The question is whether particular conditions related to Nordic principles of self-support and activation might infringe upon the rights guaranteed by the ECHR. The relevant provisions are ECHR Article 4, prohibiting slavery and forced labour, and Article 8, guaranteeing the right to respect for private and family life. Nevertheless problems relating to the principles of self-support generate not only general human rights problems but also those specifically endangering the rights of women and children, as specifically protected by the CEDAW and the CRC.

The first issue is that the anti-discrimination clause in the Women's Convention, Article 1, defines discrimination against women as

> ... any distinction, exclusion or restriction made on the basis of sex which has the effect or purpose of impairing or nullifying the recognition, enjoyment or exercise by women, irrespective of their marital status, on a basis of equality of men and women, of human rights and fundamental freedoms in the political, economic, social, cultural, civil or any other field.
>
> (CEDAW, Article 1)

According to Article 3, states are obliged to take all appropriate measures, especially in the social and economic field, to guarantee equality with men. Article 5 stresses that in family matters 'the interest of the children is the primordial consideration in all cases'. Article 11 ensures women and men equal rights to social benefits: 'The right to social security, particularly in cases of retirement, unemployment, sickness, invalidity and old age and other incapacity to work, as well as the right to paid leave' (CEDAW, Article 11e).

The second issue is that the CRC ensures in Article 9 that a child must not be separated from the parents against its will unless necessary for the best interests of the child. According to Article 18, the state shall render appropriate assistance to the parents in their responsibility towards the child. Furthermore, the child has the right to benefit from social protection ('social security') (Article 26) and, in the exercise of this right, the state is obliged to include the circumstances of the people, usually the parents, responsible for supporting the child.

The third issue is that the right to adequate social assistance is ensured by the ESC, Article 13; according to ESC Article 16, the family has a right to social, legal and economic protection to ensure '. . . the full development of the family as a fundamental unit of society'.

Therefore, national legal constructions must integrate all these legal considerations with the state's international obligations, and all constitutional values must be understood in an integrated context with these international legal sources. Such integration is especially relevant for the non-modern constitutions, where these fundamental values are either unclear or invisible.

Nordic active citizenship in a European context

In all the Nordic countries, the principle of self-support has become increasingly important in a number of areas, among them the different forms of activation policies. These have created a new platform from which the welfare state can create reciprocity between state and citizen, or even make participation in active measures a condition for the right to social assistance. However, from a legal point of view, some of these activation efforts are highly questionable. Like a legal employment contract, the concept of activation presupposes some kind of equal exchange, and activation regulation often borrows its legal idiom from contract law. The authority 'negotiates' activation 'contracts' and the authority 'agrees' with the citizen about the kind of activity that can be demanded from him or her (Andersen 2004).

For instance, the Danish government has described the relationships between municipal authorities and newly arrived refugees and immigrants as 'binding contracts', mutually binding for the local authority and the alien, to be followed up regularly (National Action Plan against social exclusion 2003: 26). However, legally speaking, this relationship is not a reciprocal contract but rather a one-sided decision on the part of the municipality administration. The relationship between the municipality and the citizen cannot be compared to a relationship between an employer and an employee: the municipality does not have the competence and legal tools of an employer, nor does the citizen have the rights (e.g. for negotiating pay) connected to an ordinary labour contract. Moreover, activation measures can bring the citizen into a special form of labour contract on other conditions, than for ordinary workers in the same workplace. This hybrid labour contract muddles the obligations of private employers. Current legal practice illustrates the legal grey zone between labour contract as part of labour law and social assistance as part of social welfare law. In addition, these new activation policies stand in sharp contrast to international legal regulation.

One issue is that, in relation to EU regulation, we need to consider whether activation measures entail a distortion of competition, since many activation programmes are state-subsidized enterprises that probably would not survive under regular market conditions. In other words, to provide work according to national legislation might violate EU regulations on competition and prohibitions against nationality discrimination. This dilemma has appeared in Danish court decisions, which have concluded on unclear grounds that these public enterprises are not anti-competitive, as the courts more generally have accepted that workers taking part in these enterprises were not able to find work under normal conditions (e.g. VLD Vestre Landsrets 3. afdeling B-1495-03, 10 November 2004).

A second issue is that activation policies also express new ways of socially integrating individuals. In the Nordic societies, taking part in the labour market has generally been defined as having almost a democratic quality, in accordance with the fundamental values of democracy and the right to be seen, heard and recognized as an individual. To be in the labour market becomes both a democratic right and a democratic obligation. In contrast, 'passive' social assistance creates sub-groups (e.g. immigrants, young people with adjustment problems), or leads to living on the margins or outside of ordinary civil and democratic society (Clasen and van Oorschot 2002). When identity and self-esteem are created and maintained by inclusion in the labour market in the broadest sense, exclusion from the labour market for reasons of disability, age, unemployment, etc. could therefore violate human dignity.

The new legal issue concerns the conditions under which the state can include the individual in activation measures as part of a collective democratic project, against the will of the individual. This question is basically a human rights question about what activities and under what conditions the state can demand that a citizen is activated in exchange for social assistance. ECHR Article 4 prohibits slavery and forced labour, stating in Section 2 that 'No one shall be required to perform forced or compulsory labour'.

A Danish Supreme Court decision (U.2006.770H) has interpreted the meaning of this aspect of activation as follows. The case concerned a man who for a number of years had received unemployment benefit, after which he received social assistance. Attempts to activate him did not succeed, as he found the job offers meaningless, disciplinary and degrading. Finally, he was offered a job as an assistant in a municipal library and he was informed that if he did not accept the position, his social assistance would be cut off. He replied that he considered this activation forced labour and threatened to turn up for work in a striped prison suit, with his feet and hands in chains. The library then notified the municipality that it was not willing to accept him. The social assistance was withdrawn, leaving the man without any economic means of support. The legal question was whether this outcome was in keeping with the Danish constitution, Section 75, 2, and ECHR Article 4. Legally, the case was not designed in a way allowing a clear interpretation of the constitution and the convention. The man lost the case on the grounds that the work and activity were part of a government provision for making him self-supporting.

The Strasbourg Court has not yet made any decisions relating directly to the question of what activities and on what conditions the state can demand that a citizen is activated in exchange for social assistance. These issues are also new in an ECHR context. Nevertheless, the court has expressed an opinion as to what constitutes 'compulsory labour'. In Van der Mussele v. Belgium appl. 8919/80, the question was whether a lawyer could refuse to defend a person free of charge as part of his legal training. Details aside, the court decided that two cumulative conditions had to be fulfilled for an activity to be compulsory labour: not only must the labour be performed by the person against his or her will, but either the obligation to carry it out must be 'unjust' or 'oppressive' or its performance must constitute 'an avoidable hardship' (i.e. be 'needlessly distressing' or 'somewhat harassing') (para. 37).

The third issue in regard to EU regulation relates to public authorities making participation in agency-defined activities a condition for receiving social assistance. A failure to meet this condition will have consequences for the right to social assistance (Chapters 4–6). In all Nordic countries social assistance ceases if the recipient refuses a job offer or activating measure without reasonable grounds, or if he or she repeatedly fails to make an appearance when being activated. As long as the job offer remains open, the financial assistance for that person cannot be resumed. In Danish law this condition (Act on Active Social Policy, Section 41, 1998) is fairly new, created without any legislative considerations as to how some people are going to survive without social assistance. The failure to be active may contribute to people's marginalization and exclusion from normal societal life from lack of economic means of participation in everyday life. From a legal perspective, some of these demands have questionable relationships to human rights (e.g. see ECHR) and could possibly infringe on the right to family life (Article 8; Ketscher 2002: 251 ff).

For example, Danish law states that a joint responsibility for activity applies for spouses (Act on Active Social Policy, Section 13). A person who depends on social assistance and whose spouse does not fulfil the demands for activity is not eligible for social assistance because of the mutual obligation for spouses to support each other. Moreover, children may risk being without financial support if a parent is inactive. On the other hand, if the couple is not married, they are not covered by the mutual obligation to provide for each other and therefore do not have joint responsibility in activation situations (constitutional provision, Section 75, 2 states that 'no other person is responsible for his or their maintenance').

We can assume that this joint responsibility has gendered effects, as probably more men than women will be in situations where they are tempted to refuse an activation offer. If the wife is herself a recipient of social assistance, then she will have to divorce, separate or live apart from her spouse to ensure support for herself and her children. Pro forma arrangements are strictly controlled by the authorities. If the woman does not actually live apart from her husband, she is in danger of criminalizing herself (i.e. committing social welfare fraud). But the children have a legal right to parental support. If the parents cannot support them because of inactivity, the state must support the children anyway (CRC, Article 26). In extreme situations, the state must assume care of the children, thereby separating them from their parents.

This Danish example demonstrates how certain policies aimed at promoting certain sets of citizenship activities might ultimately split families to ensure their physical or financial survival. However, as a family living together is a human right, the question is whether the reason for this separation fulfils the condition of ECHR Article 8 to be 'necessary in a democratic society'. Because sanctions are never to be disproportionate to the social goal, states should look to less stringent ways of solving the problem. The state must be able to prove that taking the conditions of only one spouse into account is not enough. As for the children, they have an independent right to state support. Cutting parents' social assistance for labour inactivity victimizes children. To remove children from parents whose social assistance has been withdrawn also seems disproportionate. Although the Strasbourg Court has not yet tried any case embodying these problems, this Danish legal construction most likely seriously conflicts with ECHR Article 8.

EU citizenship, mobility and immobility

Even though the contours of a European citizenship are not completely clear, the new legal concept of European citizenship has created a legal platform for strengthening and creating new rights on the part of European citizens (Tuori 2004). Contrary to the situation in the Nordic countries, the EU makes the market the primary force and makes rights connected to the market the crucial ones.

The draft proposal for a European Constitution (Article 2) clearly marks the fundamental shape of the union as a market or '... an area of freedom, security and justice without internal frontiers, and a single market where competition is free and undistorted'. Although the tools and legal remedies are centred on making this market work, it is not expanding, unrestricted and free. On the contrary, it is meant to be a controlled and regulated 'social market' (constitutional draft proposal, Article 3, 2). The aim of the social market is to '... combat social exclusion and discrimination, and ... promote social justice and protection, equality between women and men, solidarity between generations and protection of children's rights' (Article 3, Section 29). These initiatives challenge Nordic citizenship in several ways.

Although the Nordic welfare states and the EU have a common legal base in areas covered by the EU and EEA treaties, they operate on the basis of two different legal concepts that in some areas are incompatible. The basic difference is the national versus the non-national starting point.

The foundation of national welfare states is to protect and promote national values. Even though these values are common European values, the aim remains to promote them in a national setting. The most valuable right of the citizen within this national context, therefore, is national citizenship. In contrast, the objective of the EU is to remove barriers between the member states and the associated states (EEA). This EU objective collides with a very established Nordic legal tradition, where the relationship between the state and the citizen has excluded closer relationships with foreign states. To put it bluntly, the Nordic welfare states reward immobility. Most social benefit and welfare legislation is based on residential status within the state except for shorter stays, e.g. holidays outside the country. An example from the Danish Supreme Court (U 2001.1258 H) illustrates this point in the following paragraph.

A visually disabled student received rehabilitation benefits because of his handicap. He had studied for and received his bachelor's degree at a Danish university. For his masters degree he wished to study at a Swedish university in Lund for 2 years. His reason for so doing was that the courses and the curriculum were better adapted for his impairment, and he could finish his education faster. Furthermore, a stay at a foreign university could improve his job opportunities, allowing him equal treatment with other students, who are entitled to use their study allowance abroad. The case went all the way to the Supreme Court, which denied the student the right to take his benefit with him. The legal justification was that the Act on Active Social Policy, Section 5, states that a citizen must reside in the country to be within the personal scope of the benefit. As only shorter stays abroad were acceptable, 2 years was too long for the exception to apply.

This decision exemplifies the interpretative prominence of national values. Neither equal treatment considerations nor the EU mobility concept were accepted in the legal argumentations. The court stated that the legal text had no specific exceptions covering this case and that the provision concerning demand for residence must be understood in harmony with its original explanation (which dated back to 1933).

The decision, however incorrect, illustrates the barriers to integrating modern EU interpretations into a legal concept of rights originating from the national welfare state. The fundamental value of the EU is mobility and the four freedoms: free movement of goods (Nice Treaty, Title I) and free movement of persons, services and capital (Title III). These form the basis for the EU. The means of carrying out the values formulated in the preamble are to '... ensure the economic and social progress of their countries by common action to eliminate the barriers which divide Europe' and '... removal of existing obstacles calls for concerted action in order to guarantee steady expansion, balanced trade and fair competition'.

EU citizenship also mirrors these values in the Nice Treaty, Article 18, 1, according to which '... every citizen of the Union shall have the right to move and reside freely within the territory of the Member States'. Most Nordic citizens (except for those in Iceland and Norway) therefore enjoy two citizenships: national and European. Nevertheless European citizenship is a fairly new invention (introduced by the Maastricht Treaty of 1993), the legal contents of which are still not very well defined or under development. From EU-sceptical states (Denmark, Sweden and the UK), the enthusiasm has been limited; e.g. the Danish government showed its reservations following the Danish referendum of 1992, which turned down the Maastricht Treaty.

Nevertheless, the question of European citizenship has been tried before the ECJ in a number of cases. One of the leading cases is the Martínez Sala case (C85/96), in which the question was whether an unemployed Spanish woman with Spanish citizenship residing in Germany was entitled to child benefits. She was a legal resident in Germany. Her petition was refused by a German court on the grounds that she did not have a formal permit to stay in Germany and had for a long time been without work, therefore placing herself outside the scope of EU Regulations 1612/68 (on freedom of movement for workers within the Community) and 1408/71 (on the application of social security systems to employed persons, self-employed persons and members of their families moving within the EU).

In paragraphs 61–63, the ECJ concluded that, as a national of a member state lawfully residing in the territory of another member state, she was within the personal scope of the provisions of the Maastricht Treaty on European citizenship. This status gave her the right (laid down in Article 6 of the treaty) not to suffer discrimination on grounds of nationality within the material scope of application of the treaty. Therefore, the German state could not refuse to grant her a benefit that it provides to all persons lawfully resident in the territory on the grounds that the claimant did not possess a document that nationals of that same state are not required to have and the issuance of which may be delayed or refused by the authorities. EU citizenship thus created a new right for a national of another member state who had made use of her right to move freely.

In a similar vein, the ECJ has taken other decisions to enforce mobility as a fundamental principle for European citizenship. In the D'Hoop case (C-224-98), the court stated that member states could not place their own nationals at a disadvantage simply because they have exercised their freedom to move (e.g. to pursue education in another member state): such unequal treatment was contrary to the principles of EU citizenship, i.e. the guarantee of the same treatment in law in the exercise of the citizen's freedom to move.

In both cases the ECJ set aside the demands for immobility within a national setting with reference to EU citizenship as a fundamental right for every citizen. The right to move is protected at the cost of the interest of the national state to retain its various benefits for permanent nationals. The ECJ defines such efforts as nationality discrimination in the context of European citizenship.

Common rights for poor and marginalized citizens

The question remains open whether the chosen methods for combating social exclusion can achieve results at a European level (Schoukens 2002). These ambitions nonetheless stand in contrast to traditional Nordic welfare thinking, which often considers the market as a danger, especially for poor and marginalized citizens. The Nordic national welfare state often concerns itself with protecting these groups from market forces, especially through welfare rights, e.g. restricting free choice in various welfare areas such as hospitals, schools and social services.

Furthermore, the EU Lisbon strategies address poverty problems, an issue that has not been a political priority in the Nordic welfare states. This lack of priority probably results from exaggerated self-esteem on the part of Nordic governments, fostering the belief that poverty has been eradicated in the Nordic countries. No Nordic state has established guaranteed minimum levels for subsistence payments or created any systematic approach to combating poverty.

A market-based constitutional framework for exercising active citizenship

In the emergent European market, the rights to buy, sell, consume, be a contract partner and 'own' are fundamental values. These rights are clearly spelled out in both the draft constitution treaty and the human rights list in the present EU Charter of Fundamental Rights. However, human rights in national constitutions are not defined in the context of the market or citizens' participation in the market. As we shall see, this difference is a challenge to more traditional understandings of citizens' rights.

First, freedom of assembly is a classical political right. Nevertheless in the EU draft for a new constitution '... the right of everyone to form and to join trade unions for the protection of his or her interests' is highlighted alongside with more traditional political and civic rights (Article 12), the freedom to conduct a business (Article 16) and the right to collective bargaining (Article 28). Title IV of the draft constitutional treaty on solidarity is an entire list of labour market rights, including those of social insurance and social assistance (Article 34).

Second, the right to own is protected in Article 17. In the classical constitutional tradition, this right is defined as the right to protection of the property an individual already possesses; therefore, its function is protecting privileges. But the 'right to own' is something different. Traditionally, women and children have been denied this right. Giving everyone an equal right to ownership is a crucial precondition for enabling citizens to perform in a market and can promote the inclusion of poor and marginalized groups.

Third, the draft constitution expresses some new rights. A high level of consumer protection is a relatively new human right. It mirrors the market by including the smallest market unity, the consumer, and consequently covers all citizens. Even though this right has a weaker legal shape than other rights, the right to consumer protection nonetheless reflects modern society. Article 3 protects the right to integrity, restricting the market by prohibiting making the human body and its parts a source of financial gain. The same idea underlies the prohibition against trafficking in human beings (Article 5) and the rights of people with disabilities to benefit from measures ensuring their social and occupational integration (Article 26).

The EU's list of fundamental rights is obviously more updated and more reflective of a modern market economy than those of most states. In addition, this list also challenges the more conservative structures of national constitutional rights. For instance, contrary to Nordic national constitutions, equality between women and men is considered the most prominent value and area of non-discrimination in the emerging EU legislation. It was added (Part I, Article 2) as part of the final changes to the draft constitution in June 2004, just as gender equality is included in Part III, Article 2, underlining the importance of women as a crucial part of the economy.

Combining European and national legal concepts of active citizenship

Active citizenship in the EU takes a primary place in the market – especially in the labour market. Preconditions for enjoying one's rights as a European citizen are that one earns an income, takes part in the market as a customer and consumer, and obtains the best choices by making use of the scope for European mobility. This concept of active citizenship is not the Nordic one, where mobility is not an objective for active citizenship. The active Nordic citizen – in a legal sense – tends to be a marginalized citizen, however he or she is dressed up as a contract partner.

The EU Commission noted this problem in 2003:

> One increasingly popular measure has been to get the personal involvement of the unemployed by conditioning the entitlement of the benefit to the signature of a contract in which the person involved is committed to undertake certain activities. ... However, such an approach has to be carefully monitored in order to avoid that the reduction or suppression of benefits set off a pathway to poverty and social exclusion.
>
> (EU Commission 2003: 8)

Even though it is not clear exactly how the EU's list of fundamental rights applies to cases where citizens comply with such conditions, the quotation demonstrates a more nuanced conception of rights and considerations than is usually evidenced at the national level. The new activation policies in the Nordic countries are closely related to the tax-financed systems of social benefits in the Nordic welfare states. The preservation of these systems depends upon public confidence that social assistance benefits are not used by people who are 'idle and wish to be a burden upon society', as bluntly expressed in the former more outspoken Danish Act on social assistance legislation (Ketscher 2002).

In the EU the ideological – and therefore the legal – objective is to create cohesion though strengthening the rights of marginalized groups in the labour market by making the four freedoms more generally accessible. This objective includes encouraging (and forcing) member states to accept mobility as a right for their own citizens in relation to other member states, as well as becoming aware of the duties member states have towards EU citizens.

At the time of completing this article (2004) national values and constitutions might in themselves be barriers to this development. The EU-sceptical Nordic states (all except Finland) have not been convinced of the excellence of the EU's legal and political design. This scepticism is a serious problem for ensuring EU citizens' rights, because the Nordic courts are rather unwilling to meet their obligation to submit 'doubtful' cases to the ECJ. The Nordic courts are practically never in doubt about their national income security and social welfare legislation and its compatibility with EU treaty and legislation. Often their decisions demonstrate a very poor legal quality in relation to the interpretation of EU regulations, and these decisions stand as a silent judicial resistance to EU law. All in all, the resilience of governments and courts in the Nordic nation-states may effectively impede and delay Nordic citizens' enjoyment of active European citizenship.

11 Membership and migration

Market citizenship or European citizenship?

Øyvind Stokke

Introduction

The social dimension of the European Union (EU) raises a normative conflict over the principles that should govern non-citizens' access to national
systems of social protection. A European Community (EC) law on the free
movement of workers has developed since the 1960s. The politicians who
sought to create a common European market were concerned that national
systems of social protection might hamper the mobility of workers across
borders, e.g. because such movement could lead to a loss of benefit rights
(Van der Mei 2003: 62–3). In the early 1970s the European Council adopted two regulations aimed at promoting freedom of movement by co-ordinating national systems of social benefits (called 'social security' in the EU).
Regulations Nos. 1408/71 and 574/72 essentially established the principle
that the country in which the person had worked was responsible for his or
her acquired rights to social benefits.

By contrast, non-contributory social benefits have often been seen as an
expression of solidarity with other members of the same national community. We may link this idea to the broader political norm that all members
of a given community deserve equal treatment, irrespective of contribution.
Allowing citizens to export such benefits would run counter to both the
financial grounds and moral justification of the principle that solidarity
benefits are for those belonging to the same national community.

This normative conflict has now come to a head, with debates around
intra-European mobility and exportability of social benefits at the top of the
European agenda. Important decisions suggest a new direction for the
granting of public benefits within the EU: an increased emphasis on fundamental rights (Menéndéz 2003; TCE 2004, Part II).

In the spring of 2004, to simplify the rules of co-ordination of social
benefits and to improve social protection for European citizens, the European Parliament and Council adopted Regulation No. 883/2004 (which
will apply only after an amended implementing regulation is adopted and
entered into force). Still, it remains significant that Article 2 of Regulation
No. 883/2004 appears to significantly extend the personal scope of Regulation

No. 1408/71. A possible scenario is that future rules of social benefits co-ordination will cover not only workers (employees or self-employed) and their families but also all EU citizens who are or have been insured in any member state. The new regulatory regime, however, will not apply to social assistance systems.

The purpose of this chapter is to explore the normative conflict between free movement and residence in greater detail, in particular in the light of the trend towards broader coverage of the co-ordination rules. The argument from normative political theory is that principles of income security should be decided by the members of the political community, guided by the free and democratic action of society upon itself. One implication of this principle is that the host state (of residence) should be responsible for awarding social benefits to all persons residing in its territory. The chapter asks whether the EU is moving towards fulfilment of this norm and thereby introducing a new principle of equality within the European polity.

What is the European system for co-ordinating social benefits?

While European welfare states are increasingly confronted with international migration and the mobility of capital, services and goods across national boundaries, social welfare has traditionally been organized at the national level. Member states have had great sovereignty for deciding on national economic and social policies, reflecting the prevailing principle of subsidiarity for welfare provisions in Europe. But this principle has been increasingly challenged by the plan for establishing a single European market.

As early as the 1960s, a growing number of so-called 'guest workers' migrated from Italy to the industrialized north (Van der Mei 2003: 22–7), increasing the need for reaching agreements on how non-nationals should be treated and which country should be responsible for their social benefits. In response, several countries initiated social welfare regulations presupposing a qualification period for non-nationals, to be completed within the state territory; otherwise, they were not entitled to insurance benefits. From the perspective of the EC, such residence clauses constituted an obvious obstacle to the desired economic integration and the free movement of workers. These clauses effectively restricted social protection to attachment to the nation-state territory, constituting an implicit nationality requirement. Largely in opposition to these clauses, the European Council adopted a complementary regulatory framework (Council Regulations 1408/71 and 574/72). These regulations constituted a system of legal rules co-ordinating the social benefits rights of migrant workers and their family members who moved from one member state to another.

The basis for the European system for co-ordinating national social benefits is the principle of free movement of workers. According to Article 39 of the treaty establishing the EC (TEC 2002), '... freedom of movement shall entail the abolition of any discrimination based on nationality between workers of the Member States as regards employment, remuneration and other conditions of work and employment'. Article 39 explicitly formulates a particular principle of equality that implies the principle of free movement of workers. The co-ordination rules are intended not only to secure but also to promote free movement. Thus Article 42 of the TEC states: 'The Council shall ... adopt such measures in the field of social security as are necessary to provide freedom of movement for workers; to this end, it shall make arrangements to secure for migrant workers and their dependents' (TEC 2002).

Key measures are: (i) aggregation of periods qualifying for social protection under the laws of several countries; and (ii) payment of benefits to persons resident in the territories of member states. These measures include the possibility of exporting benefits for persons resident in a member state other than that in which the institution for payments is located (Art. 10 of Regulation no. 1408/71).

In this way the EC has sought to ensure that migrant workers do not lose their acquired rights when residing and working in another member state or when finally returning to their country of origin. In addition, the European Court of Justice (ECJ), responsible for interpreting and enforcing EC law, has not only viewed national residence clauses with suspicion but also actively extended the exportability of benefits for migrant workers (Van der Mei 2003: 151–4).

As to which state is responsible for awarding social benefits, Regulation 1408/71 largely follows the principle of *lex loci laboris*, i.e. that the benefit system of the country where the person works is responsible. As Christensen and Malmstedt (2000: 76) point out, this principle is not only technically legal but also moral, because it makes work and contributions the legitimate ground for awarding social benefits.

Given the goal of promoting free movement of workers, focusing on rights acquired through employment was natural. First, the emphasis on contribution enabled those rights to be detached from other bases of social obligations and to be claimed outside the national context. Second, the social benefit systems of the original member states were largely based on the Bismarckian contributory insurance model. However, from the start, Regulation 1408/71 also covered some benefits that, under national legislation, were not work-related but residence-related, e.g. child allowance. Some of the hardest conflicts over exportability concerned those latter kinds of benefits.

ECJ case law has extended the scope of the exportability provisions, and amendments to (and modifications of) Regulation No. 1408/71 have done the same (Van der Mei 2003: 150–65). These are the two reasons that European social welfare principally came to mean exportability of rights earned through employment and contributions.

Solidarity benefits and exportability

The principle of *lex loci laboris* conflicts with another legitimate normative ground for awarding benefits. In EU member states, we also find cash benefits not based on employment and contributions or aimed at horizontal redistribution across the individual's life. These non-contributory provisions express solidarity among members of the national community, aiming at vertical redistribution of resources, and usually financed by general taxes. Entitlement to these benefits is based on long-term residence within the territory of the state, that is, the principle of *domicile* as a condition of eligibility. Typical examples of such 'solidarity benefits' (Christensen and Malmstedt (2000: 71)) are non-contributory benefits like family benefits and universal minimum pensions, as well as some special cash benefits in the area between classical social insurance benefits and social assistance, e.g. benefits related to disability. For instance, according to Norwegian National Insurance Law, child benefits are not linked to parental employment or income status but are awarded on a flat rate to all children residing in Norway.

Solidarity benefits clearly express the norm of securing a fair standard of living for all persons. They symbolize the idea that human dignity should be the standard for the distribution of social goods. Usually the solidarity in question is presumed to be 'bounded', that is, limited to 'those who belong', the members of the national community. An important question is whether the scope of the residence principle may be extended, in the sense that the (host) state should be responsible for a fair provision of social benefits even to non-nationals residing in it – within the frame of basic principles of equal treatment and non-discrimination.

The ECJ has often been confronted with the question of residence-based benefits: could residence requirements for provisions such as, say, child benefits, be disallowed, thus enabling migrant workers to export these benefits out of the state of employment? Broadly speaking, the ECJ has tended to answer 'yes' to such questions (Mabbett and Bolderson 2002: 195). For instance, in the *Pinna* case, the ECJ dealt with rules that reserved the fairly generous French child benefit to children residing in France (Case 41/84). The ECJ found that the residence requirement was an obstacle to the free movement of workers, and that it represented a case of indirect discrimination against foreign workers. It made France – the country of work – responsible for awarding benefits even to children resident in another member state, and at the same rate as if they were residing in France. The idea underlying this principle is that migrant workers should not be 'deprived' of the higher child allowances provided for in that country, as such deprivation would amount to an obstacle to the free movement of workers.

This case illustrates a conflict between two different principles of equality: the ECJ's decision was based on the principle of equal treatment of *workers* with the same number of children within the state territory, while the French rules were aimed at equal treatment of *children* residing within the same territory (Christensen and Malmstedt 2000: 96). Thus, the ECJ linked the principle of equal treatment to the role played by the claimant in the process of economic integration. This linkage may relate to the concept of the 'market citizen' or labour as a production factor along with capital, goods and services, in contrast to the concept of a citizen whose social rights stem from membership in a democratic community.

The free movement of workers also receives priority from Regulation 883/2004. An EU Council press release stated that

> ... the draft text substantially reduces the list of special non-contributory cash benefits, in particular social allowances and disability benefits, that are not exportable ... It is expected that this improvement will further reduce the obstacles to the free movement of persons within the European Union.
>
> (Council of the European Union, press release 163,
> no. 9507/04, 2/6/2004)

This statement clearly gives limited weight to the moral justification and the social aims of national solidarity benefits. The clearest examples of solidarity benefits occur among non-contributory cash benefits aimed at supplementing social insurance benefits (based on work and contributions) and giving protection against various risks. These benefits, which tend to be oriented towards the needs of the claimant, may include universal minimum pensions, disability-related benefits and family benefits. Tax financed, they have in many countries been established as clear rights for citizens and therefore are based less on discretionary assessments (Ferrera 2005). The benefits may thus be termed 'hybrid', as they bear some resemblance both to social insurance benefits and classic social assistance (Christensen and Malmstedt 2000: 81–4; Van der Mei 2003: 122–5).

Traditionally, the normative ground for being granted solidarity benefits has been attachment or 'belonging' to the community (Christensen and Malmstedt 2000: 74). Yet the trend in both case law and the amended EU legislation has been to diminish the role of residence or territorial attachment as the basis for receiving social benefits. For instance, as discussed by Christensen and Malmstedt (2000: 77–9), *Pinna I* is one of a series of judgements that reject the principle of solidarity based on residence as a legitimate ground (or limit) for granting social benefits. Even though other ECJ decisions have acknowledged the principle of residence, the long-term ECJ trend is to give it less weight.

A normative opening of residence as basis for social protection

The preamble to Regulation No 883/2004 states that 'In the Community there is in principle no justification for making social security rights dependent on the place of residence of the person concerned'. Although this preamble adds that special cases allow exemptions, the implication of the stated

principle is worth discussing. This principle clearly challenges the normative basis for viewing national welfare states as communities of solidarity.
However, here the term 'national' needs reading beyond a cultural-linguistic
or ethnic sense, and we need to distinguish between a community of solidarity and a national community of belonging.

The national community of belonging is defined by nationality laws and
consists of people sharing the same nationality. By contrast, the welfare
state, as an expression of a community of solidarity, was the result of a historical compromise in the struggle between capital and wage-labour at the
turn of the nineteenth century (Zimmermann and Wagner 2004: 7–9):
social risks could no longer be handled satisfactorily within local or municipality settings. With the coming of modern industrial society and more
effective means of transport, people became more mobile, rarely experien-
cing a life-long attachment to one local area. Therefore, the state became the
appropriate frame for the risk protection, rights and duties of citizens,
thereby becoming the more relevant (albeit the more abstract and distant)
community of mutual responsibility and solidarity (Marshall 1965).

European economic and political integration calls for a similar broadening
of the scope of risk protection, not from local territories to the state but
from the national level to a transnational one. The current co-ordination of
social benefit systems is the first step in this process. The end point could be
a situation where persons moving within the EU/EEA area are members of a
wider community of solidarity, without needing to become full members of
the national communities of the territories in which they are residing at a
particular moment. Such a situation would establish a more universal principle of residence as the basis for membership in the community of solidarity. Full membership in this community would become a political confirmation
of the principle of equality and non-discrimination as a condition for
autonomy and democratic self-determination.

National responsibilities for administering systems for social protection
and for granting benefits would not prevent the rules of eligibility from
incorporating a more inclusive welfare policy consistent with the principle
of non-discrimination. Similarly, the historical embedding of the welfare
state within the nation-state does not necessarily restrict welfare provisions
to nationals. Nevertheless, after decades with a lack of explicit discussion of
questions of membership in welfare state theory, processes of Europeanization and globalization now force the political community to rethink these
questions. As Zimmermann and Wagner point out (2004: 9), contemporary
dilemmas are not completely new, as the national welfare state of today is
the starting point, not the end point, of ongoing processes.

Membership and justice

Michael Walzer is the political philosopher honoured for reopening the
question of substantial membership. He stresses the political character of

communal membership, arguing that the term 'membership' is preferable to 'citizenship', because access to welfare provisions is almost never connected to nationality requirements (Walzer 1983). The collective right to choose distributive criteria of membership expresses the deepest meaning of self-determination. Membership in some human community is the primary good we 'distribute' to each another. What we do with regard to member-ship structures all our other distributive choices, so it represents its own sphere of justice. What constitutes membership as a social good is not only our collective self-understanding and our work but also our relationships with strangers – our contacts, connections and alliances beyond our borders.

For example, the Norwegian welfare state has a double normative foun-dation. First, it highly values the obligation to work and the blessings of work. Second, it strongly supports the universal norm of equality of treat-ment. Besides providing for refugees and asylum seekers entering its terri-tory, Norwegian welfare obligations extend beyond the national borders to the Nordic and European communities.

Still, as a primary good for distribution, membership is incompatible with a situation where long-term residents do not gain full membership rights. In the context of labour migrants or 'guest workers', Walzer argues that host societies either must find other ways to get their work done or extend full citizenship to strangers invited to fill the gap that labour shortages create. Anything short of this, in his view, is tyranny: 'These guests experience the state as a pervasive and frightening power that shapes their lives and regulates their every move – and never asks for their opinion' (Walzer 1983: 59). Membership questions are therefore highly significant for theories of democracy and justice. 'The members must be prepared to accept, as their own equals in a world of shared obligations, the men and women they admit ...' (ibid.). The basic principle of democratic equality must, accord-ing to Walzer, be observed.

Walzer, however, tends to conflate the principles of cultural integration with those of political integration. He compares national admission policies to clubs or neighbourhoods, arguing for the need for closure on the basis of the value of cultural distinctiveness. But this argument ignores human rights as a dimension of truly public institutions. While clubs express the freedom of association and may base their membership criteria on strong evaluations and local traditions, 'democratic people constitute themselves as sovereign because they uphold certain principles of human rights and because the terms of their association interpret as well as flesh out these rights' (Benhabib 2001: 5). To base practices of civil, social and political integration on identity politics is to ignore the core normative elements of political integration in liberal democracies. These are conceptions of funda-mental human rights, constitutional traditions, and democratic practices of participation, election and representation.

Habermas has put forward similar arguments. In several different contexts he has argued that it is precisely to these normative elements that citizens and other residents have to show respect and loyalty, not to any particular kind of cultural tradition (Habermas 1996: 264ff). When citizens demonstrate this respect and loyalty, they constitute a community of democratic interpretation and articulation. But self-understanding and common traditions, rather than being static entities, are defined and redefined as we acquire new knowledge, and are faced with new 'others'. Thus the communitarian strain in Walzer's approach seems at odds with a post-national Europe with porous borders and economic and political integration. Moreover, membership based on the rhetoric of belonging and nationality is far from the reality of administrative allocation of social benefits, as national social benefit legislation seldom refers explicitly to nationality (Mabbett and Bolderson 2002: 192).

If we continue to approach membership as a question of distribution, John Rawls' theory of justice offers a more liberal-egalitarian alternative. Nevertheless can liberal contractualism offer any standard for the evaluation of basic normative principles governing migrants' access to welfare provisions? Rawls' concern is to develop a principle of justice within the frames of a well-ordered society without either immigration or emigration: 'I shall be satisfied if it is possible to formulate a reasonable conception of justice for the basic structure of society conceived for the time being as a closed system isolated from other societies' (Rawls 1971: 7). Concentrating on domestic distribution, he does not speak to the implications of distribution across borders. However, the changing significance of sovereignty, as well as integration in the legal, economic and political dimensions, raises the question of whether Rawls' principles of justice can apply outside a closed system.

Rawls asks what principles of justice citizens of a political community would agree on if they found themselves behind a 'veil of ignorance', knowing nothing about their own social starting positions, natural talents, class, sex and historical contingencies (Rawls 1971: 118). As these properties are morally irrelevant, any distribution based on them must be deemed unfair. From this hypothetical position, citizens would choose two principles: equal liberty for all, and a difference principle allowing for social and economic inequalities as long as these were to the advantage of the worst off and attached to open positions. In addition, the first principle has priority because basic liberties cannot be limited for the sake of economic gain.

Some scholars have explored this position in greater detail, in particular for the EU as a political community. From a complex view of social institutions, Føllesdal develops an argument for equal shares among Europeans, an argument that nonetheless comes close to Rawls' (Føllesdal 1997: 154ff). According to this view, social institutions should guarantee an equal share of political power, opportunities, life income and wealth for at least three reasons. First, social institutions have a pervasive impact on our life prospects, creating and distributing opportunities for action. Second, they generate legal powers constituted by the rules of rights. Third, these powers are goods created or constituted by the joint participation of all upholding these institutions.

For instance, rights are benefits of co-operation, made possible by the citizens' general compliance with laws and norms within a state. Thus, citizens should have equal claims on how social institutions regulate the distribution of goods. 'This grounds a claim on social institutions, that they should engender equal shares of these benefits – unless unequal shares of certain goods may benefit all …' (Føllesdal 1997: 156). This contractual argument implies claims to equal shares among Europeans under legal and economic integration. Given the increasing importance of the four economic freedoms (the free movement of persons, goods, services, and capital), conferring rights directly on individuals and weakening national sovereignty, this argument gains stronger weight.

This argument may be interpreted as supporting distributive justice over time, i.e. the need for balancing market-making against considerations of membership and solidarity. But it does not answer the question of when justice requires European citizens to set up and maintain social institutions. We are left with an argument for equal shares, based on the principle of subsidiarity – recognizing that equally just ways of maintaining a public order exist. Thus, the contractual argument does not provide any criteria for determining 'the limits to permissible variations concerning domestic institutions, within which populations should be free to determine their fates by participatory procedures. It appears that we must temper individuals' claim to equality with their claims to sovereignty' (Føllesdal 1997: 161).

The argument for equal shares seems to allow a necessary refinement of the normative conflict in European social security law. As discussed earlier, the co-ordination rules constitute a social institution, based on the rights to free movement and non-discrimination, upheld by the joint participation of citizens within the EU/EEA area. When moving to another member state, Europeans benefit from the right to equal treatment as a legal norm, however, national variations, enacted democratically, must be accepted. The principle of solidarity based on residence reflects a claim to equal shares *within* the egalitarian welfare state, and therefore is not less legitimate than claims at the European level.

The relevant sense of 'equal' share is, after all, difficult to determine, due to substantial differences in living conditions, public provisions, wage levels and systems for funding pensions across Europe. The ways in which to construct a benefit in national legislation, the conditions for entitlement, the social aim of the benefit, the need for means-testing – these are all political questions that should be subject to public deliberation in political relevant forums, according to procedures that include all affected parties. Therefore, the conflict between the economic principle of free movement and the principle of equal treatment based on residence cannot find an appropriate solution through the efforts of lawyers and ECJ judges.

From a Rawlsian perspective, then, co-operation under social institutions and weakened national sovereignty allows for an argument in favour of equal shares at the European level. Among the goods to be shared is the right to equal treatment. This liberty cannot be limited for economic reasons, e.g. to protect the financial sources of welfare provisions, because basic liberties should not be restricted except for the overall protection of liberty.

The problem, however, is that the Rawlsian argument does not resolve the conflict between equality and sovereignty. The argument is based on a conception of the EU as merely a problem-solving organization. This *instrumental* view of the EU makes its legitimacy dependent on its ability to solve the problems of the member states under the pressure of a globalized capitalism, thereby viewing citizenship in very narrow economic terms. In contrast, and according to a *communicative* logic, we should analyze the EU as a rights-based political union, because the integration process has proceeded well beyond a treaty-based inter-governmentalism. When European decisions directly affect the citizens of member states, then mutual recognition of rights and standards of deliberative democracy are called for. We will return to this argument for 'justification by deliberation' later.

Questioning the legitimacy of *lex loci laboris*

As previously discussed, there has been a trend within the ECJ's interpretation of the co-ordination rules to extend the scope of the principle of *lex loci laboris* (i.e. that a person is subject to the social benefit system in the country where he or she works). One of the clearest examples is the *Ten Holder* judgment from 1986 (Christensen and Malmstedt 2000: 77–8). The plaintiff, a Dutch woman named Ten Holder, returning to Holland after residing and working in Germany, had fallen ill with back trouble. Shortly before her German work-related illness benefit expired, she applied for a Dutch residence-based disability pension. Given the principle of *lex loci laboris*, one could expect that German law was applicable to Ten Holder as long as she was employed in Germany.

The Commission argued that the country of work was responsible as long as she was entitled to *Krankengeld* ('illness money'), referring to the close connection between the illness benefit and previous employment. The ECJ, apparently choosing to establish the principle of *lex loci laboris* as an authoritative principle, went even further. It ruled that Ten Holder was covered by the legislation of the latest country of work as long as she did not take up any work in the new country of residence. Besides depriving Ten Holder of the disability benefit to which she was entitled under Dutch law, this judgement replaced the Dutch residence principle by a norm stating that employment and contributions are the only legitimate bases for benefit eligibility (Case 302/84).

Yet the legitimacy of this principle as a norm for determining applicable legislation is being increasingly questioned. A growing number of persons do not belong to any contributory systems, either because of unemployment and low-waged work in unregulated areas, or because the labour force is posted in another member state (Mabbett and Bolderson 2002: 197). Today, migration patterns are less clear and symmetric than in the 'guest-worker era', as migration by non-workers, pensioners and students is increasing. More generally,

> . . . a social security co-ordination system based, fundamentally, on economic citizenship sits increasingly uneasily alongside wider efforts to expand the social dimension of European citizenship. All these factors suggest that less reliance on exportability and more host state responsibility in European social security law could be desirable.
>
> (ibid.)

Mabbett and Bolderson mention the example of non-workers who are not seeking work in other countries. According to Council Directive EEC 90/365, non-workers can be required by the host state to show that they have adequate means of support before the state grants them a residence permit. One reason for the ECJ to promote and defend exportability is therefore to enhance citizens' effective freedom of choice of residence. In the important *Snares* case, the claimant argued that precisely the non-exportability of a non-contributory disability allowance contravened the principle of free movement. Yet the Court found exportability to be neither a necessary nor a sufficient condition for securing the claimant's means of support – and thus the right of residence in another member state. The reason was the great variations among the welfare states across Europe, variations making it impossible to calculate an appropriate minimum income in another member state (Case C-20/96).

From market citizenship to European citizenship?

The welfare state is not only an arrangement of collective insurance based on contributions. As '[it] aims at the creation of autonomous citizens and at turning formal rights into real capabilities . . . it should also be seen as an instance of increased justice' (Eriksen 1996: 4). Political means keep some basic needs out of market competition. However, European integration has since the beginning been marked by an imbalance between market-making and market redressing, rendering the two more or less contradictory objectives (Menéndéz 2003: 2). The first treaties were explicit in their economic ambitions: integration was to come about solely through economic means, something that the centrality of the four economic freedoms emphasizes. The role of the ECJ was to ensure that legislation and actions on the national level did not undermine European market-making. Questions of redistribution and solidarity were left to national welfare provisions, over which national governments demanded full sovereignty.

It is quite clear that the EU does not simply consist of market-making. In the 1990s, the Commission formulated an agenda for the future personal scope of Regulation No. 1408/71 on the co-ordination of national social benefit systems. The adoption of three residence directives in 1990 and the introduction of the provisions on European citizenship in the Maastricht Treaty strengthened the idea of extending this regulation to all individuals residing in member states – including non-workers and third-country nationals (nationals of states not belonging to the EU). As to transforming the EU from an economic community to a political union granting citizenship rights, the Commission found that Regulation No. 1408/71 had become outdated (Sindbjerg Martinsen 2003: 14, 21). With this extension of the regulatory and personal scope

> ... the Commission went far beyond the strict wording of the Treaty's Article 42, literally aiming to provide freedom of movement for workers by co-coordinating their social security rights. According to the Commission, the Regulation 1408 had become an instrument of social policy, and not merely an instrument of promoting free movement.
> (Sindbjerg Martinsen 2003: 21)

These references to political integration and European citizenship are significant because they allow a movement towards positive integration. Such movement might reduce the gap between organized solidarity within a national community and the fundamental norms and rights instituted through the EU legal order. Replacing 'employed persons' with 'nationals of a member state, stateless persons and refugees residing in a member state' seems to imply that all European citizens will have the right to aggregation and exportability of their acquired social benefit rights when moving to another member state.

This extension appears to confirm and sanction a development towards a democratic 'Citizens' Europe', altering the balance between free movement and equality. The principle of equality would no longer be reduced to an instrument for promoting free movement of workers but gain the status of a normative principle in its own right. What remains legitimate in the regulation is that citizens who choose to move to another member state should be treated equally with the nationals of that state and that they should not lose any rights they acquired during residence in other member states.

From the perspective of a Citizens' Europe, the co-ordination of national social security and the rulings of the ECJ strengthen the significance of fundamental rights in the social field. The EU right to non-discrimination on grounds of national origin affects not only legal status but also substantive entitlements for persons moving within it (Meehan 1997: 75). Therefore, the principle of equal treatment is strengthened at the level of national welfare states that are now operating as parts of a European framework of common legal rights.

The contradiction here is that democratic sovereignty is currently tied to a particular national community, making distributional justice end at the borders of its territory, while the human rights enshrined both in national constitutions and the Charter of Fundamental Rights (EU 2000) make universal moral claims. Even though these claims often suffer from weak enforcement, due to the lack of regional or international institutions monitoring them, European integration will strengthen their enforcement, conferring rights to non-discrimination and equal treatment directly on European citizens.

To the extent that constitutional rights embody fundamental moral values like freedom, equality and dignity, we could say that the state's moral obligations are transformed into fundamental legal rights with direct effect. For example, the development of a legal instrument co-ordinating national social benefit law on the basis of the fundamental right to non-discrimination will give member states the opportunity to fulfil their moral obligations towards non-citizens, in the spirit of Article 25 of the UN Declaration of Human Rights:

> Everyone has the right to a standard of living adequate for the health and well-being of himself and his family, including food, clothing, housing and medical care and necessary social services, and the right to security in the event of unemployment, sickness, disability, widowhood, old age or other lack of livelihood ...
>
> (Glendon 1994: 36ff)

The normative tension between nationally confined democracy and universal rights is also reflected in a double empirical incongruence between democratic decision-making and transnational processes like migration, capital mobility and intensified trade (Zürn 1998, 1999). 'Output incongruence' exists to the extent that a state's jurisdiction is too restricted compared to the spatial reach of the social transactions and problems it is meant to regulate. On the other hand, 'if there is no "input congruence", then a group affected by a decision but not participating in its making can be considered as being subject to foreign determination rather than self-determination' (ibid.: 16). This problem of spatial incongruence has implications insofar as 'certain functional tasks of political and legal integration once solely in the purview of states are no longer subject to democratic control and accountability' (Bohman 2004: 337–8).

Fundamental rights to non-discrimination, as interpreted in European courts, therefore represent a gain in democratic legitimacy on the part of the welfare state, but the lack of a European democratic citizenry weakens the legitimacy of European law-making. The goal of a democratic union – providing its citizens with a public autonomy to decide what rights they mutually should grant each other – should therefore guide EU decision-makers and judges.

Conclusion

As a union of nation-states, the EU cannot – and should not – become a supranational welfare state, but positive social measures need adoption at the European level, showing that 'economic integration has resulted in the forging of a community of economic risk' (Menéndéz 2005: 4). So far, such measures have resulted from the regulatory politics that characterize a purely problem-solving conception of the EU. Risk regulation nevertheless has redistributive consequences that affect citizens' rights and collective identity widely. Consequently, it raises fundamental questions that institutions of deliberative conflict resolution should handle (Eriksen 2004: 19–20).

The notion of justice inherent in the concept of deliberative conflict resolution is based not on mutual advantage but on the mutual recognition of the parties' public and private autonomy. It thus speaks to the rights-based conception of the EU. 'In a deontological Kantian perspective, norms are valid when they can be justified from every affected party's perspective, viz. when everybody's interests and values are taken into consideration and given a due hearing' (ibid: 20). We can only test the quality of arguments in a free and public debate involving all affected parties. We cannot know whether certain rights, including the reasons supporting them, satisfy certain normative criteria of rightness or deserve respect unless they are submitted to such a test. Only those norms that affected parties have approved in a free, open debate are valid.

From this perspective, transnational systems of rights like European social benefit law suggest the creation of a political community beyond the national welfare state. More specifically, the making of a social Europe depends on the EU's ability to include its citizens in public deliberation. Given economic globalization, only transnational political institutions can produce the kind of *normative* legitimacy necessary for the citizens to accept the decisions as legitimate in *empirical* terms. Like the original nationalization of welfare, the Europeanization of welfare must take place under the guiding light of the principle of democracy.

Nevertheless if 'political Europe' is to be a 'social Europe', a community of solidarity, then constitution makers and citizens should agree on the emerging polity as a community of responsibility based on European social citizenship. The real challenge for such an institution is to formulate a European principle of residence, while avoiding freeloading and welfare tourism and respecting national patterns of social solidarity. Forty years of co-ordination of social benefits and supranational law-making in the social field shows that the nation-state is not the only possible framework for organized social solidarity. Weighing and balancing economic and social objectives is already common practice in the ECJ; it has already moved from automatically confirming the four market freedoms to balancing them against other legitimate considerations.

We therefore see that integration as a market-making and functional problem-solving tool is no longer a resource for further integration (Eriksen *et al.* 2002: 3). Instead, we need inclusive processes of deliberation and will-formation in an emerging European public sphere. One could hardly imagine a better catalyst for such a democratizing process than Europeans discussing how to deal with questions of membership and principles of distributive justice in the new Europe, and what appropriate levels of responsibility for social protection are. Just as democratic and social citizenship went together within the development of the nation-state, so they should in an emerging European polity.

12 Double discrimination

Human rights and immigrant women
in Denmark within the context of the
Nordic legal tradition

Stine Jørgensen

Introduction

The 1979 United Nations Convention on the Elimination of all forms of Discrimination Against Women (the Women's Convention) presents a new way of framing legal problems in Denmark. According to the Women's Convention, women have the right to be included in society and to be active citizens on equal terms with men. This understanding of active citizenship differs from the traditional Nordic understanding, one generally confined to activities in the labour market and a subject to which this chapter will later return.

Nevertheless the Women's Convention also stresses the ways in which traditions and cultural practices discriminate against women. This emphasis is critical in the Nordic context, where not much attention has been given to gender equality for immigrants, especially immigrant women. Instead, the general Nordic focus has been on racial and religious discrimination, which has a rather collectivistic character, with the emphasis on the position of a minority group in relation to the majority population. By contrast, the Women's Convention focuses on the woman as an individual person within the group and within society at large, making the woman's rights more important than the rights of the group.

This women's perspective poses a challenge for the Danish welfare state, because it reveals that what appear to be sex-neutral law and practices can have negative consequences for ethnic minority women, most of whom are immigrants. In sharp contrast to public ambitions to give immigrant women the opportunity to be an active part of society, these Danish laws and practices instead place these women in an even further marginalized and passive social position, creating a form of *double discrimination*. Simply put, double discrimination here means discriminating against an individual because of *both* gender and ethnicity, not merely because of one or the other.

This chapter will look at the Women's Convention and its perspectives in the context of the Nordic legalistic tradition and recent legislative decisions in some of the Nordic countries. As Denmark and all the Nordic countries are parties to the Women's Convention, this chapter will also examine

Danish social assistance legislation in the light of the country's obligations as a signatory, with some contrasting examples from other Nordic countries. The major question is whether women's rights in Denmark are being ignored or lost under the framework of 'human rights'.

Given the legal, historical and theoretical complexities of these issues, this chapter will begin with several sections of necessary background material.

The Women's Convention and the principle of gender equality

Modern legal challenges relating to the social inclusion of women arise from the principle of equality between men and women. The right to non-discrimination on the ground of gender is a widely recognized element of any set of fundamental rights and is based on a shared idea about the equal dignity and liberty of persons. This principle is reflected in all human rights documents (see e.g. the European Convention on Human Rights, Article 14, the International Covenant on Civil and Political Rights, Article 3, and the Convention on the Rights of the Child, Article 2).

The UN Assembly adopted the Women's Convention in 1979. As of June 2006, 183 countries – 90 per cent of the members of the UN – have been party to the convention, including all the Nordic countries and all member states of the European Union (EU). It is one of the most comprehensive charters of human rights, at the core of human rights instruments. (The other core human rights documents are the International Covenant on Civil and Political rights, the International Covenant on Economic, Social and Cultural rights, the Convention on the Rights of the Child, the Convention against Torture and other Cruel, Inhuman or Degrading Treatment or Punishment and the International Convention on the Elimination of all forms of Racial Discrimination.) While the Women's Convention does not establish new rights for women, it makes clear that despite various human rights instruments, extensive discrimination against women continues to exist (Charlesworth and Chikin 2000).

The committee on the Convention on Elimination of all forms of Discrimination Against Women (CEDAW) examines country reports to monitor how well the states are meeting their obligations under the Convention. CEDAW also interprets the contents of the provisions in the convention, based on the broad insight into women's lives it obtains through these reports. These interpretations are known as General Recommendations, which are important tools for the further development of women's rights. In 1999 an Optional Protocol was adopted, extending the competence of the CEDAW committee with an individual complaint procedure.

The Women's Convention concerns all forms of discrimination against women. Such discrimination includes:

> ... any distinction, exclusion or restriction made on the basis of sex which has the effect or purpose of impairing or nullifying the recognition,

enjoyment or exercise by women, irrespective of their marital status, on a basis of equality of men and women, of human rights and fundamental freedoms in the political, economic, social, cultural, civil or any other field.

(The Women's Convention, Article 1)

Discrimination includes both direct and indirect discrimination, within all fields of life. Discrimination within the family is of special importance, because the subordination of women in the family has an impact on all other spheres of women's lives. Of major importance is the work on the elimination of violence against women, because violence prevents women from taking an active part in society (General Recommendation no. 19). The Convention requires member states to take all appropriate measures to eliminate discrimination against women, regardless who performed the discriminatory act (Article 2e), thereby making any discriminatory act by private persons within the family illegal. In essence, no space where discriminatory treatment is legal can exist within states that are parties to the convention.

The Women's Convention has developed the legal norm of non-discrimination from the woman's perspective. One major issue is the ways in which women's rights are often restricted on the grounds of culture, tradition and religion. These arguments are often framed within the context of religious freedom, a claim that generally has had strong influence in legal discourse (Raday 2003). Nevertheless the preamble to the Women's Convention stresses that '... a change in the traditional role of men as well as the role of women in society and in the family is needed to achieve full equality of men and women'. Article 5, among others, urges the member states to work for the abolition of '... prejudices and customary and all other practices which are based on the idea of the inferiority or the superiority of either of the sexes or on stereotyped roles for men and women'.

CEDAW has pointed to the ways in which traditional practices like forced marriages, family violence and female circumcision are used to justify gender-based violence and to keep women in subordinate roles. The Women's Convention confronts traditional role patterns and stereotyped perceptions of women so common to many traditional cultures and religions. In this way, the Women's Convention has moved beyond traditional human rights instruments by confronting the pervasive, systematic nature of all forms of discrimination that women suffer.

The legal status of the Women's Convention in the Nordic countries

Gender equality is a cornerstone in all of the Nordic countries, although only Finland has constitutional protection of gender equality (Finnish Constitution, Article 6), and only Finland (Sops 67–68/1986) and Norway

(LOV-2005-06-17-62) have incorporated the Women's Convention into domestic legislation. In Denmark, the constitution does not protect gender equality and the first legal expression of a general principle on equality between men and women occurred in 2000 (Act No. 388 of 30 May 2000 on Equality Between Women and Men). As mentioned previously, all of the Nordic countries have ratified the Women's Convention, binding their parliaments and courts to conform to its principles. By ratifying the convention, these states have agreed to

> ... embody the principle of equality of men and women in their national constitutions or other appropriate legislation if not yet incorporated therein and to ensure, through law and other appropriate means, the practical realization of this principle.
>
> (The Women's Convention, Article 2a)

The positivistic legal tradition in the Nordic countries makes the national parliaments the primary centre of all legislation. These bodies have not paid much attention to the issues of immigrant women. For instance, child marriages made abroad (allowed by the laws of a particular country) were accepted in Sweden until as late as 1 January 2004, due to the Swedish legal concept of the nation-state. Given the Convention on the Rights of the Child, as well as the Women's Convention, such marriages are now illegal (DS 2002:54). Slowly, globalization and Europeanization (where, for example, EU regulations have legal power for its member states) are challenging the traditionally nationally oriented laws of the Nordic countries.

Even though the Nordic countries are parties to the Women's Convention, the fact that Denmark, Iceland and Sweden have not formally 'recognized' it in national legislation presents a problem. Although the lack of formal recognition does not exempt these countries from the obligations they accepted by signing, formal legislation has great importance for both the visibility and national awareness of the Women's Convention and the rights therein (Ketscher 2003). In these countries, the lack of formal recognition has essentially rendered the Women's Convention invisible in the legal culture. This is why CEDAW expressed its concerns in 2002 and 2003 about the country reports from Denmark, Iceland and Norway, and recommended that they incorporate the Women's Convention into domestic legislation.

In 2001, a Danish government committee on the Incorporation of Human Rights Conventions recommended not incorporating the Women's Convention into Danish legislation. Its argument was that the Women's Convention was a 'special' convention, because it focuses only on women. Yet the committee also noted that women constitute half of the world's population and stressed that the improvement of women's rights is greatly important not only to women but to society at large (Danish government 2001: 290). Other conventions (i.e. the Convention against Torture and the Convention against Racial Discrimination) received higher priority in Denmark. Again, the lack of formal recognition of the Women's Convention has made it invisible in Danish law. With regard to the rights of immigrant women, very little attention is paid to how traditional stereotyped images of the female sex – based on historical, cultural and religious norms – are contributing to the exclusion of these women from mainstream society.

In Norway the discussion was not if but how to legally incorporate the Women's Convention (Høringsnotat 2003). The convention is incorporated in the Act on Equality, not in the Act on Human Rights. This represents a new way of incorporating conventions into domestic legislation (Act No. 30 of May 1999). One argument against the incorporation of the Women's Convention into the Act on Equality is the isolation of the principle of gender equality protected in the convention (Hellum 2004).

Therefore, even though opposing gender discrimination is a fundamental and important principle within all of the Nordic countries, the Women's Convention has typically had low priority and remains neither a common nor a well-known legal document in the Nordic countries. This situation has negative consequences relative to gender equality, for example the neglect of the problem of double discrimination against many immigrant women.

Gender equality and the EU

The right to gender equality is also a fundamental principle within the EU. Originally gender equality was rooted in the market orientation of the EU, but today gender equality is mainstreamed within the EU, and equal treatment of men and women must be implemented within all parts of the EU, as well as in domestic legislation. (See EC Treaty Article 3 (2) for greater detail.) As a part of the mainstreaming strategy, the Women's Convention is directly mentioned in the preamble of all new European Council directives on social issues. In this way, the Women's Convention not only forms a part of a basic understanding of the directives but also – and more accurately – becomes a part of domestic legislation in EU member states. Thus, during the implementation of EU directives within national legislation, member states are bound by the Women's Convention. It therefore forms a part of national legislation, even though four of the Nordic countries have not incorporated it into domestic legislation. From a legal perspective, a correct implementation of the EU directives demands the ensuring of equality between men and women. Such an implicit demand also challenges the traditional positivistic legal position of the Nordic countries.

EU Directive 2000/43/EC on the equal treatment of people, irrespective of racial or ethnic origin, is just one example of the mainstreaming strategy in the EU. The preamble to the Directive in Section 14 states that

> In implementing the principle of equal treatment irrespective of racial or ethnic origin, the Community should, in accordance with Article

3(2) of the EC Treaty, aim to eliminate inequalities, and to promote equality between men and women, especially since women are often victims of multiple discrimination.

(CEU 2000a, Preamble)

The interrelationship between gender and ethnicity is further underlined in Article 17 of the directive, which establishes an obligation for member states to inform the European Parliament and the Council on the impact of the directive at the national level. This information must include facts on the impact of the measures that the state has taken. This obligation should lead to an increased focus in member states on the interrelationship between gender and ethnicity. Moreover, with assistance from the creativity of the European Court of Justice, the Women's Convention has become an even more important document in the EU. It has promoted a focus on gender and ethnicity that will likely eventually support the rights of immigrant women.

The Nordic governments have implemented the Council Directive 2000/43/EC – together with a second Council Directive establishing a general framework for equal treatment in employment and occupation (CEU 2000b). The latter directive includes a focus on discrimination on the grounds of religion. Norway was not legally obliged to implement the directives under the EEA Agreement (Jakhelln and Aune 2006), but the Norwegian government has introduced legislation related to the directives in the 2005 Work Environment Act (LOV-2005-06-17-62) and the 2005 Discrimination Act (LOV-2005-06-03-33).

Denmark has implemented the directives with only a reference to the Convention on the Elimination of all Forms of Racial Discrimination (Act No. 253/2004). This piece of legislation does not focus at all on the way the directives have integrated the gender dimension into this question and makes no reference to the Women's Convention, despite the interrelation between gender and ethnicity underlined in both directives.

Sweden has implemented both Directives (Act 2003: 308). In the implementation phase, the Swedish parliament also missed the inter-relationship (in the directives) between gender and ethnicity. The Swedish bill states that the EC directives do not include gender discrimination (Proposition 2002/03: 65, part 6.2), and the gender dimension was thus excluded from this legislation.

Clearly, by neglecting the gender perspective in the directives, neither Denmark nor Sweden has correctly implemented them. Above all, both countries failed to recognize the legal problem of double discrimination: that an individual may be discriminated against because of both gender *and* ethnicity, not simply one or the other. This traditional way of treating dis-crimination fails to take into account the discrimination that women face within their minority group.

Explorations of double discrimination

The way a legal problem is presented determines the claims it makes. The traditional approach to a case concerning immigrant issues is the general human rights approach, which opposes discrimination on the grounds of race, religion or ethnicity. As previously argued, this approach has a rather collectivistic character, since it is not centred on the individual. Consequently, no legal attention has been paid to the discriminating and subordinating practices existing *within* a minority group itself. Instead, practices such as forced marriages and female genital mutilation have been discussed as problems relating to the rights of a minority group due to cultural practices (Raday 2003).

This chapter suggests that the principle of gender equality challenges this traditional way of framing legal issues. It does so by focusing not only on the rights of the individual but also on the ways in which certain traditional minority practices contribute to a further exclusion and marginalization of women. Exploring this issue through a highly controversial legal problem, the right to wear a religious head garment at work, will further clarify this point.

The right to wear a religious garment on the job concerns a claim to manifest a religious affiliation. The right to non-discrimination on the grounds of race, ethnicity or religion poses the legal framing of this problem. But the wearing of a religious headscarf is mainly a problem for women. The legal solving of the problem must therefore also include this gender perspective. In Norway a case concerning a woman's right to wear a religious headscarf on the job as a chambermaid in a hotel was settled by the Norwegian Board of Equality (between men and women) in accordance with the provisions of the Act on Gender Equality (Klagenemnda for likestilling 2001, now Likestillings – og diskrimineringsnemda). As already mentioned, the EU has focused on the intersection between gender and ethnicity, e.g. by including the gender perspective in EU Directive 2000/43/EC on the equal treatment of people, irrespective of racial or ethnic origin. Moreover, the European Court of Human Rights has implemented the gender perspective in a case concerning a woman's right to wear an Islamic headscarf (Leyla Sahin v. Turkey, judgement of 10 November 2005).

The women's perspective focuses on the individual woman, thus recognizing the woman as a holder of rights herself, not mainly as part of a religious or ethnic group. In addition, the focus on both gender and ethnicity directs legal attention towards the impact of religious and cultural practices on gender relations.

Immigrant women and Danish welfare policy

The legal tradition in Denmark has mainly been occupied with the concept of discrimination on the grounds of race, religion and ethnicity, essentially ignoring the gender perspective. This Danish approach has a rather collectivistic character, focusing on immigrants as one group and then contrasting it with the majority. The general picture is one of 'them' against 'us'. In the worst case, this approach only contributes to a further social exclusion of the minority group. Especially for minority women, the traditional human rights approach has negative consequences, because the concept of respect for the culture or religion is invariably invoked at the expense of women's rights. The following sections will analyze how different social benefit systems contribute to the double discrimination against immigrant women.

Great differences in the levels of integration and social participation exist among immigrant women in Denmark. Some have learned how to use the rights provided by the welfare state, e.g. educational training. But the group of immigrant women on which this chapter concentrates is characterized by a very low level of integration. They typically come from non-urbanized areas in Somalia, Turkey, Pakistan or other developing countries, and they tend to have a Muslim background. Within this group of immigrants, men as well as women have a very low employment rate. The employment rate for Somali men is 23 per cent and for Somali women, 9 per cent. Iraqi men have an employment rate of 29 per cent, with 12 per cent for Iraqi women, and the numbers for Turkish men are 63 per cent, with 41 per cent for women (Danish National Institute of Social Research 2003a). Both women and men from these countries greatly rely on the state for financial support.

Many of the families adhere to traditional ethnic role patterns, according to which women and girls are not considered the equals of men and boys. Therefore, many women and girls live isolated in their homes. Young girls in particular are subject to powerful family control.

In this way, stereotyped images of women are perpetuated and maintained within these minority groups. The women are likewise marginalized in Danish society. As a result, we still see a significant number of immigrants continuing to identify themselves with the culture and traditions of their country of origin, despite being born in Denmark. Forced marriage is but one of the resultant social problems.

The barriers that immigrant women and men face – not only to social inclusion but in particular to the labour market – are quite different. A 2003 survey by the Danish National Institute of Social Research on young immigrants between 18 and 25 on social assistance in Copenhagen finds a major difference between the obstacles men and women face with regard to the Danish labour market. The report lists the obstacles for men as problems with the Danish language and having a criminal record, whereas 50 per cent of the young women cited children and traditional role patterns (in addition to the language barrier) as the main obstacles (Danish National Institute of Social Research 2003b). In sum, we have a group of immigrant women who not only remain unintegrated into mainstream society but also – and more importantly – face discrimination from both mainstream society and the minority group itself. Unfortunately the Danish administrative system is not prepared to handle all the concomitant problems.

Danish social assistance and the Women's Convention

A fundamental value for the Danish welfare state is activation and participation in the labour market, for both men and women (Chapter 4). The entitlement to basic social assistance in Denmark is provided in the Act on Active Social Policy and the Act on the Integration of Aliens. These laws make clear that an individual can receive social assistance only if he or she (and his or her spouse) does not have a reasonable job, an activation offer, or other measures promoting employment (Consolidated Acts Nos. 709 and 1035). This self-support principle is supplemented by the legal obligation of mutual support between spouses and the legal obligation of support attached to parenthood, concerning children below 18 years of age. According to the Act on the Integration of Aliens, self-support obtained through labour market participation is the central goal.

However, according to the Women's Convention, women are to be regarded as full and active members of every part of society – including, the right to education and the right to work (Articles 11 and 12). Of major importance with regard to the rights of women in society is the focus of the Women's Convention's on the impact of cultural and traditional factors on gender relations. Article 5 establishes that, for gender equality to come about, stereotypical images of men and women supporting a traditional division of labour between the sexes must be modified; family care and responsibilities rest upon both men and women.

Yet the Women's Convention is not mentioned in the explanatory notes to the Danish Act on Social Policy or the Integration Act. Still, Danish administrative systems are bound to conform to the document and must include the gender perspective in all of their decisions. Given a common traditional division of labour between the sexes within immigrant families, sex-neutral laws and practices inadvertently support these stereotyped role patterns.

Gender equality and financial benefits

Within certain groups of immigrants we see a large dependence upon social benefits. The following discussion will analyze how various parts of Danish social benefits legislation contribute to the inclusion and/or exclusion of immigrant women in relation to 'mainstream' Danish society, above all in relation to the Act on Social Policy and the Act on the Integration of Aliens. The Integration Act applies to 'aliens' (refugees and immigrants) within the first 3 years of residence. The object of the Act is '. . . to ensure that every newly arrived aliens are given the possibility of using their abilities and resources to become involved and contributing citizens of society' (Consolidated Integration Act No. 839, para. 1, sect. 1).

The Integration Act essentially views every new immigrant as a potential member of the labour market. It emphasizes that every immigrant should have the opportunity to use his or her resources to play an active role in society on equal terms with other citizens. This perspective on newly arrived immigrants departs from the traditional approach, which viewed aliens as burdensome and costly. Section 2 of the Act also declares that one objective is to impart '... to the individual alien an understanding of the fundamental values and norms of Danish society'. To reach these goals, local authorities must offer every newly arrived immigrant an introduction programme (para. 16). The programme includes Danish courses (under the Act on Danish Courses for Adult Aliens) and activation, consisting of Danish language classes and courses in Danish culture and society (Act No. 375, 28 May 2003). These courses must explain the fundamental structure of Danish society. A basic knowledge of Danish language and Danish culture is a precondition for making use of the rights that the laws ensure. Danish language skills are also necessary for learning about one's rights within the Danish welfare state.

Therefore, as the ability to speak the language of the country of residence is a precondition for both social integration and labour market integration, it must be characterized as a fundamental right. Equality between men and women is also a fundamental value in this regard. According to the Women's Convention, women must be included in all spheres of society (and especially the labour market), i.e. women must be ensured equal access to and equal opportunities in political, economic, public and private life.

The situation of some immigrant women in Denmark poses a great challenge to local authorities. The women's lack of skills and poor knowledge of the Danish language make them very difficult to place in the labour market, and attempting to activate all immigrants would make a heavy demand on the local councils. The explanatory note (Part 2.1.5) of the Integration Act states that before making a job training offer to immigrants who are not entitled to the integration allowance, the local council must find out if the immigrant is serious about finding work. Because this examination must be gender sensitive, it must take account of the ways in which some ethnic traditions and cultural practices restrict the inclusion of ethnic minority women in the labour market. Assuming that immigrant women are less serious about or less interested in getting work than immigrant men – an assumption an interviewer might make from traditional role patterns in that particular culture – would be in contravention with the principle of gender equality. In other words, the general principle of gender equality must necessarily restrict the discretionary power of the authorities.

However, many newly arriving immigrants are coming to Denmark for family reunification, and the newly arrived spouse can receive a residence permit only on the condition that the spouse in Denmark undertakes to maintain her or him. The newly arrived immigrant is thus not entitled to a financial benefit because the spouse has agreed to support her (or him). Consequently, this immigrant does not have to work.

Nevertheless every municipality must offer new adult immigrants a course in the Danish language, in accordance with the Act on Danish Courses for Adult Aliens. The Act emphasizes the local council's duty to inform every new immigrants of this offer (para. 8). An interesting question is how the local council can meet this obligation. First, this information must be communicated in the language of each immigrant; informing the spouse alone of this offer is not sufficient. From a gender perspective, and in relation to the problems that immigrant women face, the local council must make sure that the immigrant knows the content of the offer and the consequences of a refusal.

Today, to help new immigrants find jobs, local municipalities also can offer job training measures and job training with a wage supplement to those not receiving an introduction allowance (Integration Act, No. 839, Articles 23b – 23c). The argument for such a change in the Integration Act was that new immigrants constitute a large labour force reserve, which Danish society needs. As already mentioned, these immigrants do not receive an integration allowance but are supported by their spouses. Therefore, they are not a burden on the social benefit system. However, the right to continuous state support is only one of many rights. From a long-term perspective, the immigrant will (as will all citizens) use the rights that the Danish welfare state provides, e.g. old-age pension and health services. Because these services need financing, everybody must (in principle) contribute. The Danish welfare state cannot afford individuals who live on spousal support (e.g. housewives). Following this argument, we must also view the Integration Act in the light of the overall political goal that everybody must work and contribute to the Danish welfare state to maintain it and to ensure its continuity.

In the late 1990s, the Act on Social Policy introduced an allowance for the head of a household (Consolidated Act No. 764, Article 13, Section 6). In Denmark, this section is generally called the 'headscarf section', because of its field of application. According to this section, the spouse of an individual receiving social assistance can choose not to fulfil her (or his) obligation to either work or accept activation. If she makes use of this option, she will lose her own social assistance. Instead, her active spouse will get a head-of-household allowance. Even though the section is gender neutral, the field of application is women and, in particular, immigrant women whose way of life differs radically from women in mainstream Danish society. Thus, Section 6 of Article 13 contributes to a further exclusion of immigrant women from the labour market. In a society based on a financial economy, the right to one's own money is a fundamental right. But the introduction of a head-of-household allowance violates a woman's right to her money, creating an increased dependence upon her husband.

In 2003 this section was extended (Act No. 417), allowing the municipality to decide that a person is not at the disposal of the labour market. The local council is now turning new immigrant women into housewives if it allows them to lose their personal allowance (which then goes to the spouse, as a head of household). Moreover, as long as an individual receives social assistance, the local council is obliged to have continuous contact with him or her (Act on Social Policy, Article 10). Therefore, when a local council decides to withdraw social assistance and instead provide a head-of-household allowance, it effectively excludes that individual from the Act on Social Policy and has no corresponding responsibilities towards the individual.

From a gender perspective, this extended Section 6 has very negative consequences, since it leaves women to their own devices. More likely than not, this section impairs immigrant women's attachment to society and further excludes them from society. The explanatory note to the Act does not even mention the principle of gender equality or the obligations in the Women's Convention, i.e. to work for the abolition of stereotypes and traditional gender roles. We therefore can argue that this section of the Danish Act on Social Policy helps to further exclude and marginalize immigrant women from mainstream society, not to mention violating the Women's Convention.

Gender equality and care-related benefits

The social structures of mainstream society, according to which both women and men support themselves in the labour market, mean that children spend much of their time in public day-care facilities. In Denmark, care-related benefits allow parents time off from work to care for children, i.e. parental leave. In general, participation in the labour market is a precondition for receiving parental leave or other forms of care-related benefits. The state generally provides these benefits, aimed at balancing family life and working life, as a compensation for the loss of income from the labour market.

In the summer of 2002, a care-related benefit was introduced by the Act on the Public Social Services (Act No. 398). This care-related benefit entitles an individual to take care of his or her own minor children at home for 6 months. What is interesting about this Act is that it does not allow participation in the labour market during this period. On the contrary, lack of labour market participation is a requirement for qualifying for this benefit. Moreover, the benefit is so low that recipients cannot survive on it alone. However, the Act does not suggest how the recipient is to support herself or himself. By implication, the recipient must have a spouse or a cohabitant who can support her or him.

Act No. 398 therefore reinforces the stereotype of a housewife, with the woman at home taking care of the household and the man supporting the family in the labour market. No pension rights attach to this care-related benefit. Participating in this benefit system is naturally appealing to some women, especially those with little or no labour market affiliation – and, as we have seen, immigrant women are highly over-represented within this group. At the same time, however, the benefit tends to weaken the recipient's relationship to the labour market, thereby not fulfilling the standards of gender equality in the Women's Convention (Article 1). The benefit instead supports a traditional division of labour between the sexes, but a large number of local municipalities have chosen not to make use of this section of the Act, particularly those communities with a large number of immigrant citizens. The reason is that these women are already performing the care-related functions for free. These municipalities see no reason to pay a care-related benefit to someone who is doing the job anyway.

These examples from Danish social benefit legislation show how these laws contribute to the exclusion of immigrant women from mainstream society. In several different respects, existing legislation supports a traditional division of labour between men and women within the family. Clearly, these regulations perpetuate traditional stereotyped images and are likely to violate the Women's Convention. It is obvious that the Danish Parliament has not been attentive to the interrelationship between gender and ethnicity as put forward in the Women's Convention, thereby making the integration of the immigrant women into the Danish society even more difficult.

Conclusions

Equality between men and women is a fundamental right within the Nordic countries, as well as in the EU as a whole. Nevertheless, the Women's Convention has played only a marginal role in the Nordic legal tradition. The lack of formal recognition of this document offers one general explanation, with the main consequence of weak attention to the interrelationship between gender and ethnicity. The Danish examples make clear not only that immigrant women often live isolated, marginalized lives, excluded from mainstream society, but also that the Danish legal tradition and social laws support and perpetuate this double discrimination. More generally, only the integration of the gender perspective into Nordic legislation can help give immigrant women equality and include them in the Nordic societies.

13 From disabling barriers to participation

The opportunities created by the EU equality strategy

Richard Whittle and Rune Halvorsen

Introduction

This chapter explores the extent to which people with impairments have gained new opportunities for active citizenship as a result of the European Union's (EU) equality strategy in the context of disability. Emerging at the EU level during the mid 1990s, this strategy has since so evolved that it now dominates EU disability policy and has led to a number of key advances. The most significant of these advances comes from what we call the core components of this strategy, namely 'anti-discrimination' and 'design for all'. The first component pursues the prohibition of discrimination on grounds of disability; the second, the principle of accessibility to goods and services for all.

As with the strategy as a whole, the rationale behind these components is to remove the physical, organizational and attitudinal barriers that people with impairments regularly encounter. In other words, the strategy is to enhance the societal participation of this population group and, in so doing, to provide a valuable contribution to EU-led activities aimed at activating their citizenship.

The anti-discrimination and design-for-all components are, however, essentially concerned with removing barriers to market participation and thereby limited in their scope of application to the economic context – prioritizing the removal of barriers to people with impairments, whether as workers or as consumers. This observation is not intended to deny the existence of equally important barriers in the social and political contexts, or the relevance of the equality strategy to them. It merely highlights the EU-level priority of the economic context – what in European terms is called the 'internal market' – and the competence that EU institutions have to ensure the proper functioning of this market.

Because EU institutions can most readily demand changes to national laws and policies in relation to the internal market, the 'anti-discrimination' and 'design for all' components enjoy a prominent place in the equality strategy. Specifically, these components benefit from clear legal bases (in the European Community (EC) Treaty) that enable EU institutions to adopt measures requiring changes to existing laws and policies at the national level, or introducing entirely new ones. These changes can lead to concrete improvements to the rights and interests of people with impairments. Therefore, the mere existence of these core components and the potential their legal bases provide offer new and valuable opportunity structures for this population group and their associated non-governmental organizations (NGOs) at local, national and EU levels.

By 'opportunity structures', we mean the institutional, political and legal environments that might evolve from these core components: structures that can encourage or discourage individual and collective action by affecting actors' expectations for success or failure (Koopmans and Statham 2000; Tarrow 2003). From this perspective, individuals and groups can draw on resources from the social contexts in which they operate. These resources may include improved access to material resources (i.e. redistribution) and better possibilities of being heard (e.g. access to participation), and acquire recognition from political and administrative elites (Fraser 1995). These structures can encourage individual and collective agency because the actors now believe that they have more to win by taking action and that their likelihood of success is greater. Crucially, however, the ability to realize the potential of these components depends on whether people with impairments and their associated interest groups understand the nature of the components and are able to fully take advantage of the opportunities they offer.

The second part of this chapter explores the ways in which these core components are likely to be used within different national contexts – in particular the impact of different systems of social protection, different socio-political legacies, and different patterns of relationships among public authorities, social partners, and NGOs in member states. For practical reasons, therefore, we have limited our studies to six countries: four Nordic countries (Denmark, Finland, Norway and Sweden), France and the United Kingdom. (Even though Norway is not a member of the EU, the Norwegian government has aligned itself with the EU's disability equality strategy.) Nevertheless, we need first to locate the core components of the disability equality strategy within a contextual framework. The following three sections outline the development of EU disability law and policy and highlight the distinguishing features of these core components and the opportunities they present.

The starting point: national control of disability policy

As of 2006 most 'disability policy' within the EU has been regulated at the national level, with the dominant part the provision of income security for people with impairments who are out of work. This provision is typically supplemented with cash compensations for extra costs (e.g. special diets, transportation) and services assisting people with impairments. In addition, many member states promote the employment of this population group through rehabilitation, vocational training and job placement services. Some have even supplemented these activities with publicly subsidized jobs or the creation of employment quotas favouring people with impairments. We refer to these largely tax-financed and redistributive measures as the 'traditional' elements of disability policy.

These traditional elements have been complemented with various forms of 'social regulation' (Majone 1993), the area in which we can locate the core components of the EU's disability equality strategy. Social regulation comprises government efforts to influence not only the functioning of markets but also the behaviour of non-governmental actors, to promote social objectives either through legislation, financial incentives, persuasion or a combination thereof. For example, in many European countries, early regulatory measures included legal provisions imposing particular duties on employers in relation to employees and job seekers with impairments (e.g. strengthened job security).

Nevertheless, national governments have been unwilling to transfer control of their redistributive social policies to the EU arena. While the EU institutions have recently sought to co-ordinate elements of the social protection systems of the member states (Chapter 11), national control over such social policies has remained largely intact. Member states therefore continue to view the traditional elements of disability policy as falling outside EU competence.

Nonetheless, EU engagement in disability issues from the late 1990s reflects a wider, more multifaceted understanding of regulatory social policy, and of what can fruitfully be called disability policy. As already indicated, regulatory social policy is a natural part of, or at least compatible with, general market regulation, an area in which the EU can increasingly claim competence. Moreover, depending on the foundation and profile of each country's disability policy, the mid 1990s re-branding of EU disability policy has in many cases also introduced new ways of thinking about the physical and organizational barriers encountered by people with impairments and ways of removing these barriers. This seizing on this emerging category of disability policy has allowed the EU's disability equality strategy to evolve so successfully.

Therefore, while member states still retain competence over most disability policy, the balance of control has somewhat shifted in favour of the EU arena. In particular, EU emphasis on the equality strategy has opened new opportunities for EU policymakers, individuals and NGOs operating at local, national and EU-levels. Moreover, the core components to this strategy offer an especially significant potential for generating concrete positive changes for people with impairments.

The development of EU disability policy

EU-level activity has had an impact on national disability policies since the 1960s, following the inception of the European Social Fund in 1957 and its distribution of funding for employment-related priorities at the EU level and among the European regions. However, not until the mid 1970s, with the EU institutions adopting the first of four multi-annual action programmes on disability – the Initial and the First Action Programmes, Helios I and II (1974–96) – did an EU dimension to disability policy truly emerge.

Concerned solely with disability issues, these programmes constituted the first EU-level attempt to strategically harness disability as a policy agenda. In essence, they sought to facilitate an exchange of ideas and best practices among the member states on particular aspects of disability policy, and they aimed to achieve this objective primarily by establishing and maintaining European networks of key stakeholders in the relevant policy sub-fields. Concentrating initially on vocational rehabilitation and training, the material scope of these programmes was later extended (albeit with less intensity) to matters pertaining to mobility and transport, housing, access to public buildings and facilities, service provision and education. Nonetheless, despite the duration and the apparent breadth of these programmes, their immediate policy outcomes were disappointing. Of the few instruments adopted in this context, the most significant was a 1986 Recommendation 'on the employment of the disabled in the Community' – a non-binding instrument, unenforceable by individuals. The member states therefore could – and did – ignore it with impunity.

This lack of progress is most readily explained by the policy context surrounding the EU institutions during these two decades. Later key advances in EU disability policy (from the mid 1990s) emerged from legal bases that existed in the EC Treaty during the life of these programmes. In other words, a lack of policy impetus and political drive precluded progress during this period, not a weakness in legal competence.

While a prohibition against disability discrimination had existed in the United States from as early as the 1970s, no equivalent would emerge among the EU member states until the mid 1990s. Consequently, no member state had an incentive during this period to influence EU policy towards a common level of commitment against disability discrimination, especially one exposing them to any associated costs that might place them at a competitive disadvantage. Similarly, no pressure came from disability NGOs during this period, either at national or EU levels. Only when the British disability rights movement sought in the early 1990s – via EU institutions – to overcome the national political impasse over a prohibition of disability discrimination did an equality agenda began to have any impact at the EU level.

Thus, prior to the 1990s, an equality strategy in the context of disability was simply not on the policy horizon of EU institutions. EU policymakers were instead guided by the member states, whose approach comprised the traditional elements of disability policy. With matters having a direct impact on income security programmes and social services falling outside EU competence, the policy area that presented the greatest opportunity for EU action under these programmes was employment – hence the priority it received.

Nevertheless, instead of pursuing a policy objective that would complement existing disability policies in the member states, the legislative proposals emanating from these EU programmes relied on the same philosophical foundations underlying the traditional elements of disability policy at national levels. Because the member states viewed such matters as core public policy choices (and thus important sources of governmental legitimacy) that were most appropriately dealt with nationally, any EU attempt to standardize such matters was likely to meet considerable resistance. Therefore, the proposal that culminated in the 1981 Recommendation on employment was relegated to a recommendation (rather than a directive), and its content was significantly watered down during the decision-making process. Likewise, legislative proposals on matters (outside these traditional elements) that sought to enhance the rights and interests of people with impairments in the absence of an equality-based logic were likely to lack the necessary policy coherence for the institutional and political support needed for their adoption at the EU level. Unfortunately, such difficulties prevented the adoption of the only proposal under these programmes for a binding regulatory measure, namely the 1991 proposal for a directive 'on mobility and safe transport to work'.

Nonetheless, we should not dismiss the value of the disability action programmes. At a minimum, they generated valuable lessons for EU policymakers in the disability field, not least the need to be sensitive to the legal and political climate surrounding a particular issue at national levels. Nevertheless, more significant is that the activity under these programmes put in place, albeit sometimes unwittingly, the apparatus supporting much of today's more established EU disability policy.

First, due to the practical demands of running these programmes, a dedicated unit within the EU Commission (the disability unit) was established from the early 1980s, to manage their operation. This unit has helped maintain the policy momentum on disability issues within the EU institutions, playing a particularly important role during the mid 1990s in generating the necessary drive and strategic direction for securing the equality-based strategy that dominates EU disability policy today.

Second, throughout these programmes pilot research projects were funded in various areas, most consistently and significantly in the context of employment. The lessons learned from these projects have fed directly into generic EU employment initiatives that operate today and seek to enhance and, where possible, co-ordinate national employment policies, such as the Equal Initiative and the European Employment Strategy. By so doing, these pilot projects have helped to ensure that disability is well represented among these initiatives.

Third, while the 1991 proposal for a directive 'on mobility and safe transport to work' failed to survive the EU decision-making process, its failure nonetheless prompted the development of an action programme dedicated to transport accessibility for people with reduced mobility. This programme subsequently paved the way for many of the recent 'design for all' successes in the context of EU transport policy.

Finally, and most significantly, these programmes provided financial and organizational support for the creation of EU-level disability NGOs. This support eventually culminated in the establishment of the *European Disability Forum* (EDF) – an umbrella organization of disability NGOs throughout the EU. By the close of these action programmes, the EDF had considerably enhanced its ability to effectively lobby EU institutions. By the mid 1990s it was well placed to apply these skills in helping to secure the necessary changes in the EC Treaty that would, in turn, achieve an equality-based strategy at the EU level in the context of disability.

Nevertheless, by 1994 the limitations of the prospects for securing a further action programme on disability had become clear. The intended legal basis for such a programme, as well as the Commission's use of this legal basis, was coming under increasing judicial and political scrutiny at national levels. At the same time, equivalent proposals for the poor and the elderly were meeting considerable resistance from national authorities. Given this legal and political climate, the Commission concluded that investing further energy in the policy trajectory envisioned by these programmes was likely to be ineffective and that an alternative policy agenda was necessary. The result was a radical shift in policy direction, a policy shift that would be dominated by the principle of equal opportunity.

The process of securing the new EU agenda

With the strength of the British disability rights movement advocating an equality-based strategy and the likely rejection of a further disability action programme, the EU Commission was able to pursue a new disability agenda from the mid 1990s, with the prohibition of discrimination as its flagship. In the period leading up to the 1996 Intergovernmental Conference (IGC), organizations of people with impairments – especially the British NGOs, in alliance with their counterparts in the member states holding the EU presidency – lobbied various national authorities to include disability as a prohibited ground of discrimination in the EC treaty. Key to securing this treaty amendment was a report on disability by prominent legal experts, entitled 'Invisible Citizens' (EDF 1995). The report clearly articulated both the discriminatory barriers regularly encountered by people with impairments and the policy rationale for combating these barriers with EU-level regulation. With the ratification of the amending Treaty of Amsterdam in May 1999, Article 13 EC enabled EU institutions to adopt a variety of measures to combat discrimination on a number of new grounds, including disability (Whittle 2000). Even though many actors questioned the added value of this legal basis, it led to the adoption of the Employment Framework

Directive in 2000 (CEU 2000b) – the most significant EU-level development to date in the context of disability rights.

In addition to the inclusion of Article 13, the 1996 IGC attached a non-binding declaration to Article 95 EC (the disability declaration) in the EC Treaty. Article 95 enables the adoption of common design standards for goods and services throughout the member states. On occasion the adoption of such standards – particularly in the fields of telecommunication and transport standards and the design of lifts – has failed to consider the needs of people with impairments and created significant difficulties for them. Therefore, the disability declaration attached to Article 95 requires the EU institutions to take into account the needs of people with impairments whenever they use this provision as a legal basis for decision-making.

Current EU disability policy

Today EU disability policy can accurately be described as a horizontal issue – one that encompasses a range of activities, from the setting of technical standards to fundamental human rights. Because it therefore requires the attention of policymakers operating across an array of policy interests, disability policy at the EU level should no longer be seen as the sole responsibility of the Directorate-General for Employment, Social Affairs and Equal Opportunities and a small number of related services beyond the EU Commission. Similarly, we should no longer view this policy field at the national level as the sole responsibility of policymakers in departments of welfare and labour.

This change in the landscape of disability policy (whether at national or EU levels), stems from the principle of 'mainstreaming'. This principle seeks to ensure that the interests of a particular group are taken into account in a co-ordinated and holistic manner throughout the spectrum of the policy-making arena. This principle therefore promotes an equality of consideration (or attention) from policymakers when competing interests are at stake. Nevertheless, while this approach demands changes to, and creates new opportunity structures within, a given policy field, its increased breadth will also (at least initially) create significant challenges to the capacity of those seeking to influence the field. These challenges are as pertinent to NGOs as they are to policymakers, especially to those (e.g. the EU Commission) with particularly limited resources.

Even though for the purposes of this chapter we have focused on the core components of the EU's disability equality strategy, we stress that the opportunities and challenges associated with these components are not unique to this strategy; they are similarly reflected throughout EU disability policy as a whole. Nonetheless, from these components, the adoption of the Employment Framework Directive in 2000 is the most significant achievement, and it has rightly become the focal point of interest in recent years for EU disability rights activists and commentators. The transposition of this directive (i.e. the insertion of EU legislation in the body of law of the member states) creates new opportunities both collectively and individually. At the collective level it offers opportunities for increasing visibility, participation, voice and influence vis-à-vis public bodies at various levels of governance. At an individual level, it offers new or improved possibilities for pursuing a disability discrimination claim – ensuring the availability of the formal legal mechanisms and structures necessary for enforcing a satisfactory remedy. The key challenge is to ensure that the directive's provisions are correctly interpreted from a disability rights perspective, both at national and EU levels (Whittle 2002), a challenge that would most effectively be met by a test case strategy co-ordinated at the EU level.

The design-for-all component, on the other hand, is comparatively weak from a legal perspective, with the disability declaration (attached to Article 95 EC) forming a procedural obligation at best. Nonetheless, we should not underestimate the potential of this component. Provided that the ethos underpinning this declaration is properly understood and applied at the EU level, this aspect of the equality strategy will generate concrete positive change for people with impairments. Since its inclusion in the treaties, the EU institutions have certainly been more receptive to activities and complying with the declaration. Generally speaking, EU institutions have encouraged the EDF and other disability NGOs to make their representations on particular matters, and recent successes in this context include areas of accessibility standards pertaining to coaches and buses, and telecommunications, and improvements to rail and air passengers' rights. Nevertheless, while the EDF has been very active in ensuring that it receives sufficient attention during relevant committee meetings, etc., within the EU institutions, the challenge will be to maintain this level of vigilance at the EU level across the spectrum of matters that have an impact on disability.

Finally, a common 'conceptual' challenge to the successful operation of these components exists. In essence, this challenge relates to the need for all actors to understand – and to adhere to the implications that emerge from this understanding – that these components are intended to operate within meritocratic systems and are thus subject to the limits that the principle of meritocracy imposes. The connection between the meritocratic principle – that advancement is to be based on individual achievement and ability – and the EU's goal of increasing market participation, forms both the strength and the limitation of these components, as well as the characteristics necessary to justify EU-level regulatory involvement.

The strength of these components lies in the palatability of this principle to both market-based actors and society at large, both of which are likely to favour and give greater priority to allocations given to individuals on the basis of merit or in the absence of 'special' considerations. The limitation is the lack of consideration that will therefore go to other principles of allocation, e.g. need. In other words, the anti-discrimination component is concerned not with compensating for disadvantage associated with living with impairments but with removing the barriers that limit or preclude participation on the basis of the individual's merits. Similarly, the 'design for all' component seeks not to provide special access for any particular group but to simply provide equal access to all groups capable of using a given product or service. Understanding this point and its practical implications will help maintain the credibility of these components and ensure that their policy value is not undermined (Whittle 2005).

The EU equality strategy in national contexts

With every new policy or law comes a danger that its potential will not be fully realized. It may become a victim of implementation deficit or lack of enforcement and, in the worst cases, remain merely a symbolic statement of good intentions. In general, we expect any new policy or law to have a greater impact if it does not appear to challenge pre-existing policy, legislation or institutional arrangements too strongly and if stakeholders can commit themselves to its implementation. Matters may become complicated at the EU level with decisions originating in a multi-level structure of governance and stakeholders.

Even with a unanimous European Council decision, member states may support it on different premises and with different degrees of commitment. Moreover, governments may need to weigh an EU directive against competing national considerations and the interests of affected parties. Not all national governments will be equally keen to push for a rapid and consistent adoption of EU directives. Strong sectional interests (e.g. social partners) are likely to restrain the process if they see the new policy or law as affecting their interests. Other non-governmental actors – in this case, organizations of people with impairments – may be actively engaged in efforts to affect the process.

For the Nordic countries, France and the United Kingdom, we now look at various aspects of the transposition process in relation to the core components of the EU's equality strategy in the context of disability: how have the profiles of national disability policy affected the process of transposition? And how have the established relationships between national governments and organizations of people with impairments influenced the process?

Pre-existing profiles of national disability protection systems

Among the national systems of disability protection compared here, the *redistributive* dimension appears to have been most developed in the Nordic countries, based on rough indicators like the disability benefit recipiency rate and the proportion of gross domestic product (GDP) spent on disability-related provisions (Hvinden and Halvorsen 2003; Eurostat 2005). Conversely, 'Atlantic' (liberal) countries (Ireland and the UK) had lower recipiency rates and spent a lower proportion of GDP on benefits. Continental countries (Austria, Belgium, France, Germany, Luxembourg and the Netherlands) were in an intermediate position.

At the same time *regulatory* disability protection (e.g. employment quotas) had played an important role particularly in continental countries and had existed in the UK (with less significance), but such protection was completely non-existent in the Nordic countries. Meanwhile, variations in the role of regulatory measures, like work environment and job security legislation offering special protection to employees with impairments, cut across the tripartite division between Nordic, continental and Atlantic countries. As we shall see, these variations created strikingly different profiles of national disability protection systems.

For example, Sweden had the broadest repertoire of policy measures for people with impairments, combining regulatory and redistributive measures. In particular, it had one of the strongest frameworks of labour legislation in Western European countries. Finland, France and Norway were in an intermediate position, while Denmark and the UK had the least restrictive employment protection (OECD 1999: Table 2.2). Within the Nordic group, Sweden practised a stricter enforcement of employers' obligations to accommodate people with impairment in the workplace and gave higher priority to wage subsidies for employees with impairments (Vik 1999). Self-operated personal assistance was more clearly considered an individual right in Sweden than in the other Nordic countries, which tended to consider it as a discretionary provision, more in line with other social services that professional helpers defined and controlled (Askheim 2002). Sweden (1999) was the only member state besides the UK (1995) and Ireland (1998) to adopt separate legislation prohibiting discrimination on the grounds of disability before the adoption of the Employment Framework Directive. While Denmark, Finland and France had introduced general prohibitions against discrimination in their criminal codes or constitutions, these actions were more symbolic than practical (Quinn and Degener 2002).

Denmark in particular tended to base its policy on voluntary agreements and commitments from employers, leaving more to employers' prerogatives or discretionary judgements. Collective agreements between the social partners in Denmark served as a functional alternative to statutory labour law. Compared with the other Nordic countries, Denmark relied more on information campaigns and persuasion strategies to influence the behaviour of non-governmental actors.

France put relatively more emphasis than others on special or targeted measures for people with impairments, on the assumption that they were less able and needed special protection. Similar to several other continental countries, France defined clear-cut obligations to employers in terms of quotas for people with impairments. Employers were, however, allowed several opportunities for evading these obligations. In addition, while the state could provide financial support for accommodation, it did not have to do so. In fact, obtaining public support for workplace accommodation in France was associated with much hassle and prolonged waiting periods. Instead, employers tended to rely on money collected from undertakings that did not fulfil their quotas. Consequently, the greater number of employers who fulfilled their obligations relative to these special measures, the less money would be available for accommodation at regular places of work.

The UK's disability protection system most clearly tilted toward the social regulation side. Previous cuts in redistributive provisions had contributed to the prominent role of regulatory measures, combining legislative and educational-oriented means, thereby reinforcing the liberal, market-oriented character of its welfare system. The negligible quota system was dismantled following the passage of the Disability Discrimination Act in 1995, with quotas being viewed as obstacles to business activities and anti-discrimination laws seen as correctors of market imperfections (understood as unnecessary barriers to participation) and promoters of equal opportunities.

The assumption in the UK was that the individual should be treated according to his or her ability, not his or her disability-based limitations. More clearly than in the other countries, its dominant policies in this field embraced libertarian ideals of a limited and contractual relation between state and citizen (Chapter 3). From the 1990s, vocational rehabilitation or 'welfare-to-work' measures were contracted out to non-governmental agencies, with the state limiting its role to regulating, monitoring and purchasing services. The UK was also marked by a strong statutory approach to accessibility (DRC 2002; Statutory Instrument 2003).

By contrast, reports from national governments, ombudsmen agencies and organizations of people with impairments suggested that the Nordic countries lagged behind many other Western European countries in this aspect of disability policy, despite governments' espoused commitment to the principle of 'design for all' for a number of years (Wästberg 1999; NOU 2001). Stated norms of accessibility and usability were either non-binding or not enforced. The Danish government in particular preferred consultations and voluntary agreements to binding standards (Olsen *et al.* 2005). France appeared in the middle. Although the 'design for all' principle had become more common (Senate 2005), there was considerable local variation in the implementation of existing legal provisions (APAJH 2005).

Understanding these differences in the pre-existing national systems of disability protection helps to explain why some governments were more positively inclined towards the legal rights-based and market-oriented direction of the new EU disability equality strategy. Albeit with different points of departure, the UK and Sweden were well positioned to appreciate the ambitions of the European anti-discrimination agenda and to commit themselves to the EU disability equality strategy. Both were proactive in following this strategy, while the other four countries were more reluctant, initially going for minimal changes in national laws.

Relationships between governments and NGOs

National disability NGOs have demonstrated different capacities for and interests in handling the challenges associated with transposing the Employment Framework Directive into national legislation and, eventually, in backing their members in litigation efforts. Among them, they had established different relationships with their governments and developed different perceptions of the problems facing their constituency and the ways of promoting their social inclusion. Moreover, they had varied experience, interests, skills and competencies in handling legal rights on behalf of their constituency, and thus also different degrees of self-confidence and belief in the fruitfulness of a legal anti-discrimination strategy.

The organizations, especially those of people with mobility impairments, often used the lack of access to buildings and transport as a highly visible illustration of their broader message about barriers to participation in different arenas in society (e.g. through media coverage of wheel chair users prevented from using airplanes or accessing public buildings). The Nordic governments sometimes referred to consultations and direct involvement in planning processes on the part of these groups as alternatives to statutory regulations. Such participation presupposed broad and complex expertise, as well as detailed knowledge about the needs of people with very different impairments.

If the organizations could influence the setting of accessibility standards for planning and design processes, their goals would become more manageable. Providing professional and substantial input into setting technical standards would also require a fairly sophisticated and broad competence that not all organizations believed they had. Even so, the implementation and enforcement of EU regulations and standards at national levels would relieve the organizations of some of their time-consuming tasks, e.g. of registering complaints and drawing other people's attention to cases of lack of accessibility and usability. The primary challenge for these groups is being able to influence the EU decision-making process and ensure the full incorporation of the 'design for all' principle within EU standards. Both sets of challenges at national levels are equally pertinent at the EU level. Nonetheless, EU-level disability groups can now co-ordinate activities Europe-wide and benefit from a sharing of resources and expertise. Moreover, given the size of the EU market and the benefits of being able to freely access that market, manufacturers and producers have a greater incentive to ensure the adoption of, and their compliance with, EU standards.

More generally, the representatives of the organizations of people with impairments in the Nordic countries tended to hold a positive and 'benign' view of the state. In particular, those representing people with well-defined diagnoses enjoyed high legitimacy in the political sphere. They had reasons to trust both the political system and their own ability to influence it. The larger organizations had achieved close, informal and co-operative relationships with the civil service. Often moving between positions in these organizations and the civil service, some of these individuals appeared to share many of the same values, judgements and opinions. Their proximity to the government gave the key actors a favourable position in achieving and maintaining their competence to present their case in a manner matching the modus operandi of the public administration.

In the Nordic context, Finland was somewhat an exception, as the organizations there largely maintained the role of service provider, including medical and vocational rehabilitation, counselling, sheltered work, accommodation, work assessment clinics, community and social planning. The economic hardship after WWII delayed the development of the modern welfare state in Finland. Therefore, Finnish organizations of people with impairments had been compelled to develop their own services as substitutes for those missing in the public arena.

Similarly, several of the French organizations played major roles as providers or contractors of health and social services. The parents' associations had a significant role in initiating and administering services for people with impairments – implying that they were responsible for a large number of employees and corresponding budgets – and have developed strong professional expertise in service management. Their role as providers and managers of services largely guided their priorities and occupied much of their energy, with the effect that they developed vested interests in maintaining special and segregated services (Barral *et al.* 2000). As in Finland, these organizations faced more complex expectations from their members, consequently having more composite tasks than those in the other Nordic countries. They therefore could not concentrate solely on the task of representing the interests of their members in political campaigns, lobbying, consulting and negotiating with public authorities. As a result, they appeared less unequivocally as the advocates of people with impairments; they also had obligations as employers and service providers. Ironically, in some instances, the provider role meant that those who benefited from their services perceived them as adversaries.

At the same time, the French organizations had a more ambivalent relationship to the state, due to the French system being less generous and redistributive than those of the Nordic countries – albeit more interventionist than that of the British. The French welfare design was characterized by co-operation among trade unions, professions, business corporations and voluntary associations and was subject to state control.

The organizations of people with impairments often developed solutions in co-operation with the local, regional and central government. The French state authorized them to administer sheltered workshops and provided partial funding. State support secured loyalty to the central government and confidence in consultative forums controlled by the authorities (CES 2003). At the same time, these organizations had historical reasons to doubt whether the state would follow up on its stated intentions and continue to grant the necessary resources. Thus, while the larger French organizations wanted to maintain co-operative relations with the government, they also sought to distance themselves and retain control over the provisions they administered.

The UK was the only country with a genuine disability movement, in the sense of having a sustained and contentious collective of people challenging the power holders 'by means of repeated public displays of their worthiness, unity, numbers and commitment' (Tilly 1999: 257). This was particularly the case among those with clear-cut mobility and sensorial impairments. Consequently, compared to France and the Nordic countries, the NGOs in the UK had a more adversarial relationship to government. In this capacity, they were central in reframing disability as a question of discriminatory practices that are regularly and systematically repeated, sanctioned and maintained by society at large. In contrast to the Nordic countries, representatives of the new British disability movement saw anti-discrimination legislation as the key means of ensuring real opportunities for choice, control, self-management and autonomy (Barnes 1991; Campbell and Oliver 1996).

However, large charities, voluntary associations and self-help groups in the UK complemented a relatively small redistributive welfare state. The disability rights movement opposed these charities and groups, viewing them as promoting a paternalistic and medicalized approach. The experience of this movement with the inadequate measures and under-funding of the British welfare system furthered a more adversarial relation to the state and any organizations associated with it. Thus, in comparison to their peers in the Nordic countries, the UK disability rights movement had less reason to view public authorities as benign.

Generally speaking, the UK disability rights movement viewed the state as giving priority to interests other than those of people with impairments and, as a result, relations between them and the state were largely distant. Complaints often arose about lack of information, limited and unsystematic consultation with state bodies and frustrations about the central government's priority of contact with, and provision of resources to, related charities, voluntary organizations and self-help groups. Perhaps unsurprisingly, participants in this movement preferred an oppositional, uncompromising stance, rather than building coalitions with government. Table 3 summarizes the relations between the national disability organizations and governments in the six countries.

In the different stages pertaining to the adoption of the EU's disability equality strategy, many of these organizations from the four more reluctant countries (Denmark, Finland, France and Norway) were ambivalent or sceptical about the benefits that such a strategy in general, and anti-discrimination in particular, would provide. The opinions of representatives of these organizations and those of the respective national governments partially converged on this point. They shared a concern that individuals would have to go to court and incur legal expenses to ensure fair treatment. Many in the more reluctant countries feared a shift from a collective and

Table 3 Relations between disability non-governmental organizations (NGOs) and national governments before the transposition of the Employment Directive (EC 2000)

	Denmark, Norway Sweden	*Finland, France*	*United Kingdom*
Redistributive welfare state	Large, generous and encompassing	Later or less developed	Relatively less generous (after cuts)
Distinct role of disability NGOs	Pressure group vis-à-vis public authorities to improve public services	Provider and manager of services	Protest and campaigning movement, contestation
Relations to the government	Co-operative, quasi-bargaining system	Substituting for public provisions	Adversarial

solidaristic system of welfare to an individualistic one that would eventually undermine the availability of relatively generous social security benefits and accessible public services.

The leaders of the larger groups in the four countries tended not to subscribe to the general discourse on 'diversity'. They feared that specifying the different prohibited grounds for discrimination in anti-discrimination legislation would lead to unwanted segregation, reinforcing perceptions of people with impairments as being different and requiring special provisions. Similarly, they opposed the proposal for a separate disability ombudsman or monitoring agency (especially in Denmark and Norway). Until the early 2000s many representatives of public authorities, as well as the organizations in these countries, perceived anti-discrimination legislation primarily as a symbolic instrument, not a legal tool likely to generate concrete positive results.

As mentioned earlier, notable differences existed in the views of national groups and among the members of the EDF, with the British movement being the most active in lobbying for an anti-discrimination strategy and the Danish disability NGOs being the most expressively sceptical. As is evident from the outlines of the national policy contexts, the Danes had reasons to perceive the proposed strategy as breaking most clearly with the established national path, while the British could more easily see it as compatible with, or as a continuation of, the policy situation in their own country – not to mention their preferred adversarial approaches.

Conclusion

We have highlighted the way in which EU disability law and policy has evolved since the mid 1990s to reflect the paradigm shift in a large number of countries worldwide towards a rights-based policy agenda – in particular, an agenda that seeks to realize the principle of equal opportunity in the context of disability. We opened this chapter by questioning to what extent people with impairments have achieved new opportunities for active citizenship as a result of the EU's disability equality strategy and how this population group is likely to use them. While this strategy potentially widens the scope for active citizenship, it is a form of citizenship that will only become a reality if individuals with impairments and their representative organizations take advantage of their new opportunities and assert their rights. In this sense the EU disability strategy confronts people with impairments and their organizations with demands for activity based on awareness, knowledge and competence.

Disability NGOs at the EU level have operated successfully to advance and expand EU disability law and policy, in particular the equal opportunity agenda. Yet are they able to use the new opportunities that this agenda has created? Even when limiting ourselves to the six affluent countries in North and West Europe, the emerging picture is quite varied. The constellations of national governments and organizations that have dealt with the challenges of aligning national policies with EU policy most proactively appear to have been the countries where the EU approach was seen as being compatible with the profile of pre-existing disability protection systems (the UK) or where the demands of transposition in other ways had been anticipated (Sweden). Conversely, the more passive or reactive constellations in other countries resulted from domestic concerns about the EU's approach either undermining or interfering with established national arrangements for public disability protection or with existing relationships between governments and non-governmental actors.

The fact that the UK and Sweden emerged as the most proactive of the six countries, especially as they in many respects represented quite different welfare policy traditions, may appear surprising. While it is beyond the scope of this chapter to account for the historical – institutional configurations in which the national systems of disability protection have developed – the different profiles emerging from combined regulation and redistribution measures have amounted to different degrees of compatibility with the EU's new disability policy. Both Sweden and the UK had already developed similar anti-discrimination legislation, despite other differences in their overall national configurations of disability policy. Both the Swedish and British disability NGOs and the public authorities were accustomed to such measures, already considered them desirable, and could thus comfortably follow established patterns. Moreover, Sweden and the UK, more than the other countries, had adopted the statutory approach implied in the 'design for all' component of the EU's disability equality strategy, albeit with the effectiveness of their enforcement remaining open to question.

In countries with more passive or reactive constellations (Denmark, Finland, France and Norway), the process has been characterized by uncertainty and even reluctance on the part of both national governments and organizations of people with impairments. Both parties first attempted to comply with the Employment Framework Directive by way of minimum changes to existing national arrangements. Given the relatively broad scope of the directive, we can assume that the manner in which the transposition process has so far taken place in these countries will result in a partial implementation deficit that would be open to challenge.

Similarly, an appropriate level of awareness has been lacking in these four countries as to the potential significance and benefits associated with the design-for-all principle and the development of common standards in products and services. With transparent statutory regulations for goods and services, disability NGOs, national authorities and market actors could all be relieved of many of the uncertainties and unpredictable outcomes associated with the use of discretion, the one-sided emphasis on information, and the user involvement that tends to typify current construction, design and manufacturing processes. The NGOs would certainly need less professional and technical expertise to monitor many of these processes if the development of common EU accessibility standards was given higher priority.

At the same time, however, developing new and innovative ideas (so as to co-ordinate expertise and the development of common standards) would require earlier interventions and a dialogue with designers and producers of goods and services. Clearly national organizations of people with impairments have in this respect – at least so far – missed some opportunities in the transposition and implementation of the 'design for all' component of the EU equality strategy. At the same time, disability NGOs in the more reluctant countries, have to various degrees, started to reconsider their positions.

Even though it may not necessarily be too late to correct the implementation deficits, some windows of opportunity may be closed while the new legislation comes into effect and the supervisory bodies set out to do their job. Consequently, the potential impact of the EU disability equality strategy, in terms of increasing and enhancing the possibilities for active citizenship, has not been fully realized in these four countries – at least not to date.

14 Enlarging freedom of choice

Pension reforms in the Nordic countries and Germany

Karl Hinrichs

Introduction

In the first decade of the twenty-first century, a number of factors are pushing for more freedom of choice in pension provision. First, faced with the challenge of adjusting national pension systems to a changing economic and demographic environment, the elites in politics, media and epistemic communities are calling for reducing state and collective solutions and, consequently aim at transforming passive citizens into active consumers (Gillion *et al.* 2000; Queisser 2001). These elites are ideologically committed to freedom of choice as a value in itself.

Second, more individual choice may come about as a concomitant of the state having shifted more responsibility for social protection to the individual on the premise that existing public schemes are unsustainable. In this context, the positive connotation of 'choice' may help governments to persuade the public to accept a reduced level of public protection.

Third, the ongoing process of individualization – in the sense of more diverse life-styles and varying preferences – makes fixed retirement ages or standardized old-age benefit packages less appropriate. To the extent that pension reforms respond to demands from 'below' and enlarge individuals' scope for exercising choice and responsibility in relation to welfare, they are highly relevant for active citizenship in the libertarian sense.

This chapter examines the ways in which and the extent to which self-responsibility and freedom of choice are enlarged, how this process came about, and what outcomes (after reforms have been put into practice) are possible, by comparing recent reforms in Finland, Germany, Norway, and Sweden. Public provision has dominated the pension systems in these countries. While Sweden's recent pension reform was carried out in one stroke, substantial changes in Finland and Germany resulted from a series of reforms. Norway has just joined the pension reformers, with a parliamentary majority agreeing on the principles of an extensive pension reform in the summer of 2005. Rather than detailing all aspects of the reforms in these four countries, this chapter analyzes these reforms for how they promote and affect issues of individual choice and responsibility.

Individual choice in contemporary pension reform

In Germany, Sweden, Finland and Norway, public pension systems, applying the defined benefit principle, have constituted the backbone of national social policy. In the late 1950s or early 1960s, all four countries embarked on a path that gave states the predominant role in replacing earnings after retirement. Until the 1990s, incremental policy change never touched this paradigm, and development remained clearly path dependent. During the 1990s, however, substantial pension reforms occurred in Finland, Sweden and Germany. These reforms, at least in Sweden and Germany, entailed a paradigm shift and a more pronounced turning towards the 'multi-pillar approach' in retirement income provision, combined with a greater scope for individual choice.

A paradigmatic change in the German pension system

Before 1957, the German public pension scheme offered only low benefits that, very often, were insufficient for raising blue-collar workers in particular above the poverty line. The immediate effect of the 1957 structural reform was that, at the end of a full occupational career (and throughout retirement), the public scheme provided true replacement of lifetime earnings of about 70 per cent. Despite much rhetoric about a 'three-pillar model', the reform actually meant the birth of a state-dominated one-pillar approach: the high level of public benefits discouraged the development of occupational pensions, and voluntary private provision for old age was largely confined to the better-off parts of the work force. In general, no paid work was necessary after age 65, and status maintenance was not contingent upon private pensions (Hinrichs 1998, 2005).

Since the late 1980s the German pension system has been the target of three larger reform packages (legislated in 1989, 1996 and 1997) aimed at containing public pension expenditures and further rises of the contribution rate. Later reforms in 2001 and 2004 also called into question the principle of status maintenance. The reform of 1989 was a comparatively early attempt to cope with imminent population ageing. Among other things, it stipulated that all pathways into early retirement would phase out, while *flexible retirement* beginning at age 63 (after 2012, age 62) would remain possible for workers with an insurance record of 35 years. However, taking out a first pension before reaching age 65 now implies a permanent benefit reduction of 0.3 per cent per month whereas, previously, fewer years of contributions had merely meant reduced entitlements. While such a rate is budgetary neutral for the pension scheme, it still offered an incentive for early retirement.

Immediately after coming into office in 1998, the Red-Green government suspended the 'demographic factor', which was the central element of the 1997 pension reform. This factor was designed for containing the contribution rate as further life expectancy at age 65 was integrated into the formula determining both the initial benefit level and annual adjustments. Ultimately, the target replacement ratio would have dropped to 64 per cent.

As early as June 1999, however, the government proposed a reform that would have led to an even lower replacement ratio. Inspired by the Swedish example, the plan included a mandatory contribution of 2.5 per cent of earnings to private pension plans to offset the decline. Due to vehement all-round protests, this element was dropped after 1 week; instead, as a tax-subsidized vehicle to voluntarily compensate for lower public benefits, *voluntary private pensions (the Riester-Rente)* became the cornerstone of the reform package of May 2001. Since 2002 the government has been providing direct subsidies or tax privileges to persons who pay contributions to certified saving plans, limited to 4 per cent of gross earnings from 2008. The design of these subsidies and tax privileges favour families raising children and high-income earners. These incentives also apply if, alternatively, a proportion of earnings is converted into contributions to an employer-sponsored occupational pension plan.

The *Riester-Rente* largely opened up freedom of choice, i.e. whether to participate at all and, if so, with a variety of private pension products as choices. Moreover, it clearly represented a paradigm shift for two reasons (see Hinrichs 2005). First, it stipulated that the contribution rate to the public scheme *must not* exceed 20 per cent until 2020, and 22 per cent until 2030. These upper limits became law in 2004. Calculations from before the 2001 reform had turned out to be overly optimistic; thus, to not miss the contribution targets, the benefit (adjustment) formula was changed again. It now includes a 'sustainability factor' that accounts for the changing numerical ratio of pensioners to contributors. As a result, the *net* standard replacement rate is going to drop from about 69 per cent in 2000 to about 52 per cent in 2030 if the change in pension taxation is allowed for in the projection (Hain *et al.* 2004: 344). Therefore, in 2001 the government sent out the message that public pensions alone will no longer provide adequate wage replacement, and it has repeated this message ever since.

Second, when institutionalizing voluntary private pensions (*Riester-Rente*) as part of retirement income, the Red-Green government did more than make up for the 'forgotten' compensation in the 1997 reform of its predecessor. By extending retirement income policy, the government also irrevocably shifted the German pension system towards a multi-pillar approach again after this system had largely consisted of a *public* pension policy and a one-pillar approach since 1957.

But why exactly did a government led by Social Democrats carry out the paradigm shift and insert private pensions into an emerging multi-pillar system? Two plausible and connected reasons exist, as the next few paragraphs will show.

The first part of the answer relates to demographic ageing, which makes all retirement schemes more expensive. Within the political discourse of the

1990s, an interpretative pattern developed and solidified, to the effect that demographic ageing must not lead to (substantially) higher contributions to the public scheme because of the detrimental effects on employment and inequitable outcomes in inter-generational terms. Within the frame of the ageing issue, enlarged individual responsibility appeared sheer necessity (see Marschallek 2004; Bönker 2005).

After recurrent policy adjustments and still uncertain prospects regarding security in old age, by the end of the 1990s public pension policy had lost its credibility and the institution as such had used up plausibility. Simply re-turning well-known 'adjustment screws' and afterwards declaring 'less' as more 'secure' would have been absolutely pointless for restoring confidence. Likewise, asking for higher contributions to a collective arrangement was hardly suitable for promoting expectations of reliability after this branch of public provision for the economic security of citizens was perceived as insecure in itself. When providing the opportunity to put subsidized savings into pension plans that offer both freedom of choice and true property rights (and a sense of ownership instead of insecure 'entitlements'), the government could even hope to improve its reputation. The government thus enabled employees to pursue an 'investment strategy'. Such a strategy demands sacrificing consumption now so as not to be worse off (than the present generation of pensioners) later, when a declining replacement ratio of public pensions is offset by a parallel increase of the *Riester-Rente* or the alternative, the new *defined contribution* (DC) type of occupational pensions.

The second part of the answer relates to the modernization of German social democracy, a trend placing self-responsibility and efficiency on equal footing with its traditional troika of principles: freedom (emancipation), solidarity and social justice. Individualistic solutions to securing a sufficient level of pensions in view of *individualization* as a societal 'mega-trend' clearly matched the new credo (Chapter 1). Purely collectivist solutions were discarded and numerous statements by leading Social Democrats in Germany verified this reorientation when the government asked citizens to say farewell to a welfare state that paternalistically relieved them of individual responsibility for their lives.

Nevertheless, within the party a shift of the respective roles of the market and the state in pension provision was not universally accepted (Hering 2004). In 2001, as well as before the final vote on the 2004 reform package, the government had to make some symbolic concessions to the 'traditionalists' for a majority vote. Moreover, since there was also no principled dissent between political parties about private pensions as such, freedom of choice as a value in itself played no prominent role in the parliamentary debates.

Shifting risks in the Swedish pension system

The political conflict over universalizing access to earnings-related pensions during the late 1950s developed into one of the fiercest in Swedish history.

The central controversy between two political blocs (the non-socialist parties and the Social Democrats along with their ally, the blue-collar union) was about the accumulating funds in a state-run pension plan, because during a long maturation, incoming contributions would exceed pension outlays. Placing these surpluses in public buffer funds provided the government with an enormous power to control the economy ('pension fund socialism'). In the end, the Social Democrats prevailed, in 1959 enacting a public earnings-related pension scheme (ATP).

In the early 1990s, when a parliamentary commission on pensions presented its first report, Sweden entered into a deep economic crisis. The report emphasized the costs of the ATP scheme as strongly dependent on economic growth and vulnerable to increasing longevity. Moreover, the report confirmed the unfairness of the 15/30 rule (i.e. a 'full' pension earned after 30 years of employment, calculated on the basis of the 15 'best' years) to workers with a flat earnings profile and to blue-collar workers of both sexes in particular. Finally, the future depletion of the ATP funds would endanger an adequate national savings rate.

These undeniable problems were the starting point of a pension reform group, appointed by the new non-socialist government in 1991, with experts from all seven parties in parliament. Even though the institutional changes resulting from the group's work were at least as radical as the state pension system created 30 years earlier, they was incomparably less controversial. From the beginning, all parties agreed that even in the long run, a reformed pension system should not become more costly than it had been in the early 1990s, when the total contribution rate had been about 18.5 per cent. Additionally, for political stability, all parties concurring in the reform framework agreed to support any refinements and further amendments (Lindbom 2001).

A central feature of the compromise between the four non-socialist parties and the Social Democrats was the transition of the ATP scheme into the *notionally defined contribution* (NDC) system. This version of a pay-as-you-go scheme almost perfectly mimics a *fully funded pension plan* (FDC). While it provides nearly as much choice for the participants – with regard to retirement age, withdrawal options, and sharing pension rights with spouses – it also contains risks inherent in any funded plan. The new scheme is based on *lifetime* accounts, with benefits explicitly linked to contributions paid and individually calculated according to further cohort life expectancy at age 65, when the NDC wealth is actually converted into an annuity.

In the NDC scheme, the accumulation of entitlements becomes transparent, thus creating stronger property rights and a sense of actuarial fairness. While it minimizes distortions, pensions become less predictable: contributions yield an 'interest rate' corresponding to the growth of per capita income subject to contributions. When the accumulated (but in fact notional) pension wealth is converted into an 'annuity' at the end of a working life, the actual replacement ratio depends on further life expectancy of the person's cohort. Finally, the new NDC scheme will always operate on a contribution rate of 16 per cent. If this target rate becomes endangered, an 'automatic balance mechanism', by which NDC pension wealth and actual pensions are temporarily indexed at a lower rate, will be triggered (Settergren 2001). This automatic balancing may possibly become the Achilles heel of the NDC scheme because 'property rights' of working-age people and pensioners are violated when this mechanism is actually triggered.

In addition, 2.5 percentage points of the total contribution rate (18.5 per cent) are channelled into individual pre-funded accounts for a premium pension. This partial privatization of the mandatory pension system was a most controversial issue. Calculations showed that a contribution rate of 16.0 per cent to the NDC scheme would suffice to honour all earned entitlements, but future benefits were lower than hitherto provided by the ATP scheme. The non-socialist parties proposed to levy a compulsory rate not higher than 16.0 per cent and to leave the decision about saving for higher pensions to individual citizens. The Social Democrats insisted on sticking with the present 18.5 per cent rate, which would have entailed an additional build-up of collective funds. The political compromise, a mandatory layer of funded pensions assuring adequate wage replacement, satisfied the Social Democrats while serving the non-socialist parties' interests in private ownership and individual choice. The compromise resulted in a highly regulated but not very cost-efficient arrangement. This arrangement allows individuals to place their contributions with a maximum of five fund managers from a list of more than 700 fund managers (and to move accounts between them without extra charges); alternatively they may not choose a placement, in which case their contributions are automatically transferred to the publicly managed 'default fund'. This part of the mandatory system offers a wide spectrum of options for the timing and form of withdrawal, but ultimately pension wealth has to be converted into an annuity, either as a pension that is fixed for lifetime or one that is annually adjusted.

The parliament approved the framework legislation in 1994. The age-related conversion factor of the NDC scheme (continually adjusted to cohort life expectancy) also helped to avoid another potential controversy, namely raising the 'official' retirement age that has been an issue in France, Italy and Germany. Nevertheless, so as not to impede economic growth through early retirement, workers cannot draw either the NDC or the premium pension before age 61 – with no upper age limit for acquiring further entitlements from employment.

Moreover, the legislation raised the right of job retention to 67 years of age. Still, age 65 remains the central chronological marker, because contractual pensions are still related to it, and disability pensions are converted into old-age pensions at this age. Furthermore, the guaranteed pension tested against the NDC and premium pension is not available before age 65, thereby preventing self-inflicted eligibility for people retiring earlier with 'too low' entitlements from the NDC and FDC schemes.

In this way, the potential retiree enjoys extended freedom of choice and always pays an actuarial 'price' for his or her decision of when to claim the pension and whether to take it in full or to combine employment with a partial benefit or to take out the NDC and the premium pension at different times (Ministry 2002a: 32–3, 50–1; OECD 2003a: 49–53). Even though internalizing the costs of retirement decisions discourages early exit, it remains to be seen if the reformed system actually encourages deferred retirement, given the strong preference for early retirement (Pensionsforum 2003).

With the new public system phasing in after 2000, contractual and individual pensions became all the more relevant, since public earnings-related benefits were to be lower (unless one defers retirement beyond age 65) and less predictable, and the pension income ceiling for the NDC scheme would amount to only 144 per cent of the median wage of the working population. Contributions to private (unit-link) insurance and individual retirement saving accounts are tax-deductible up to a ceiling. Withdrawals have to be phased over at least 5 years and must not start before age 55. Particularly among women and older workers, those saving contracts have spread enormously since 1990: in that year about 17 per cent of the working age population invested in private pensions, while in 2002 about 40 per cent did so, and many more have entered other saving arrangements (Palme 2003: 67; Pensionsforum 2003). The NDC scheme paying no widow's benefits for persons born after 1944 partly explains the steep rise in voluntary provision; another reason is the spontaneous reaction of the public to anxieties about a future lower level of public pensions.

All in all, the reformed Swedish pension system offers the participants great transparency. Annual statements explicitly show the accumulated pension wealth and the return of contributions to the individual NDC and the premium pension accounts. The reform implies an almost complete transition towards DC pensions (including most contractual plans that altogether cover about 90 per cent of employees). Concomitant features are a clear trend towards a higher degree of pre-funding and expanded private components within a now advanced multi-pillar approach. Consequently, within the new system all risks incorporated in the single plans (wage growth, performance of capital markets, increased life expectancy etc.) are inevitably shifted to the future retiree, a big change from the former *defined benefit* (DB) approach that left all risks with the plan's sponsor.

Finnish reform: flexible retirement age as freedom of choice

The Swedish reform of 1959 paved the way for broadly similar policy changes in Finland 2 years later, when earnings-related pensions came about by collective agreement among social partners, initially confined to the permanent workers in the private sector and later confirmed by a corresponding pension act (TEL). Ultimately, the whole economically active population became compulsorily covered with the creation of a decentralized, occupationally segregated system of nine statutory schemes. Different from Sweden's ATP, these partially pre-funded schemes are privately administered through financial institutions (insurance companies and pension funds), but are strictly state regulated. This system offered considerable choice (and control over investment capital) for individual employers.

Routes into early retirement had been extended in the mid 1980s. When Finland faced extremely high unemployment in the early 1990s, most elderly workers left the labour market well before age 65. Even though retiring early was an attractive option for older workers, it was costly for the pension system. Since demographic ageing proceeds more rapidly in Finland than in other Scandinavian countries, the major objective of pension reforms was to create disincentives for retirement, to prevent future labour shortages and to achieve higher economic growth. The issue of *individual choice* thus mainly relates to pathways into, and the timing of, retirement. The reforms did not change the central role of the semi-public mandatory scheme for providing retirement income and only indirectly affected voluntary occupational and private pensions.

The most significant step of a series of reforms that started in 1993 came about in the fall of 2002, when the labour market organizations in the private sector finally agreed upon a detailed package of changes. As in 1961, the reform originated from an expert committee's recommendations. The reform of July 2004 saw similar changes in the schemes covering employees in the public sector. The reform reinforces actuarial fairness, because average lifetime earnings will determine benefits when the new formula takes effect from 2005–11, even though the link is not completely straightforward. The 'reference' age for claiming an old-age pension will be 63. It is calculated according to the credits that have accrued by then. Continuing employment after that age accelerates entitlements, because the period of pension receipt is reduced and additional credits are earned.

Therefore, the ceiling on the replacement ratio (hitherto 60 per cent at maximum) is lifted; theoretically, an individual who was continuously employed from age 18 until age 68 (after which age no more credits accrue) may end up with a pension that replaces 94 per cent of his or her average career earnings. While accounting for a complete employment history (as in Sweden and Germany) makes the scheme more equitable to those with a flat lifetime earnings profile, the age-dependent progressive accrual rate nevertheless maintains the privileges of white-collar employees, because they have a better chance of working longer than manual labourers.

The progressive accrual rate encourages older workers to retire later. They can claim an old-age pension already at age 62, but then it will permanently be reduced by 7.2 per cent. Other benefit types that had facilitated early exit either were further restricted or will phase out completely (OECD 2004a: 76–8). Whether to take out a part-time pension after age 58, retire at 62 or continue working until age 68 is the only choice that the Finnish core pension system provides.

Finnish pension reform – a piecemeal process with a considerable cumulative impact (Hinrichs and Kangas 2003) – proceeded very peacefully. A major reason may be that the earnings-related pension system, although covered by comprehensive legislation, is the least 'statist' among these four countries. The willingness of the social partners to compromise on reforming 'their' scheme largely rendered government intervention unnecessary, although the government was involved in tripartite negotiations and maintained a stake in the reform process when it came to tax money (e.g. child care credits) or protecting certain beneficiaries (indexing of disability pensions). Party politics played almost no role. Rather, tensions were strongest among trade unions when organizations of white-collar employees and academic professionals tried to defend their traditional privileges, but they eventually gave in. Partial pre-funding of the system (which will be increased over the next decades) excluded further privatization as a strategic (or, in Sweden, ideological) reform element meant to sustain the pension system.

Since the pension reform in Finland implied no risk-shifting (beyond a life expectancy coefficient, 'borrowed' from the Swedish reform package) and no lower benefits if workers retire later, individual choice is related to supplementary private pensions that mainly bolster the consequences of individual retirement decisions in the mandatory system. These pensions are not an integrated component of the Finnish pension system, nor are employer-based pensions, which have declined to near insignificance.

On a steep increase, however, are personal pensions. Younger birth cohorts take out those tax-deductible policies most frequently. At the end of 2002, about 12 per cent of the working age population paid into personal pension plans (Hietaniemi and Vidlund 2003: 115–16, 123). As in Sweden, two motivations stand out: mistrust and the desire for an early retirement. Even though confidence in the core system has improved (Ministry 2002b), some mistrust persists as to whether the actual pension level will turn out to be as high as expected. A supplementary personal pension would then fill a potential gap ('just in case . . .'). As an alternative to such precautionary saving, the accrual of a personal pension scheme can compensate for a lower benefit when someone retires at the preferred age or on a part-time pension, i.e. it serves to 'buy an extra year of retirement'. Increased freedom of choice as to retirement age widens the scope for private pensions to some extent, and individual decisions about the respective financial market products go along with the usual risks.

Norway: emulating the Swedes again?

As in Finland, the Norwegian pension reform of 1966 was influenced by the Swedish model. Nonetheless, the constellation of collective actors approving or opposing public supplementary pensions differed somewhat from that in Sweden. During the reform struggle, the stands of the labour market organizations and political parties largely converged, and all political parties supported the introduction of *Folketrygden* (FT), a lean version of the Swedish ATP model.

Compared to its neighbours, Norway faces less pressure to reform its pension system, because demographic ageing there is expected to be more moderate. The employment rate in the upper age brackets is well above the average of the members of the Organization for Economic Co-operation and Development (OECD), and the public scheme is less generous. Even though the government could earmark considerable assets of the FT Fund and the Petroleum Fund for future pension financing, they would be insufficient to cope with the steep increase in the GDP ratio of pension expenditure over the coming decades (Pensjonskommisjonen 2002; NOU 2004). Nevertheless, concerns about long-term sustainability and future labour shortages, aggravated by a decreased retirement age, led the then Social Democratic minority government to set up a pension commission in the spring of 2001.

To achieve a consensual reform package, the government appointed commissioners comprising representatives of all parties in the parliament (and a few experts), limiting other actors in the pension policy arena (social partners, financial service industry) to membership on an advisory board or to speaking later. An informal understanding was that, to give political weight to the proposals in the subsequent legislative process, the compromise should receive support from at least the Social Democratic, Conservative, Christian, Centre and Liberal parties. Nevertheless the political parties had developed quite different positions before the commission convened (Ervik 2001), so that the commission's interim report (Pensjonskommisjonen 2002) included two extreme alternatives.

The first was to maintain a tax-financed universal flat-rate pension of about the same level, to be topped up with voluntary contractual and individual pensions. The second was a modernized version of the FT scheme (including public earnings-related pensions), borrowing from the recent Swedish reform and aimed at not only increasing pre-funding but also possibly creating pensions providing individual ownership and freedom of choice (Pensjonskommisjonen 2002: 68–9). The majority proposals in the commission's final report (NOU 2004) favoured the second alternative, a watered-down version of the Swedish reform.

At the beginning of the 2000s, about 60 per cent of all employees were entitled to retire within a window of 5 years (ages 62–67). Flexible early retirement, the only individual choice offered so far, came about in 1988 with the introduction of the AFP (*Avtalefestet pensjonsordning*) arrangement. This publicly subsidized scheme, based on agreements between the social partners, originally intended to offer tired long-term workers a decent way of exiting employment without suffering cutbacks in their old-age pensions, which start at age 67. These incentives, however, also made the scheme attractive to healthy workers in less strenuous jobs. AFP has thus not affected the high recipiency rate of disability pensions. Voluntary (and sometimes involuntary) retirement on AFP benefits contributed to the considerable drop in effective retirement ages (NOU 2004: 177–81; OECD 2004b: 45, 57–9, 67–72). To effectively reverse this trend, the commission proposed to end government subsidies to the AFP scheme.

A minority voted for mandatory contributions to individual accounts offering investment choices. Inspired by their Swedish counterparts, commission members from the Conservative, Christian, Liberal and Centre parties pleaded for this component (NOU 2004: 233–45), although they did not particularly emphasize arguments of ownership or freedom of choice. In contrast, left-wing members took a minority position favouring mandatory occupational pensions as a means of covering workers (particularly in low-wage, female-dominated sectors) who tend to be excluded today (NOU 2004: 273–4).

After a fairly heated public debate in early 2005, a parliamentary majority voted for the principles for a modernized FT scheme in May 2005 (Innst. S. nr. 195 2004–5, Forh. S. Nr. 160–2, 2004–5). The majority consisted of the parties supporting the then incumbent minority government (the Christian, the Conservative and the Liberal Parties) and the largest opposition party (the Social Democrats) and the Centre Party. The majority supported most of the commission's proposed reform elements, which the government later adopted in its report to the parliament (Stortingsmelding nr. 12 (2004–5)).

The compromise included a closer link between lifetime earnings and benefits: pension calculations were now to consider the complete employment career (instead of the 20 'best' of 40 years) so as to abolish inequities resulting from different distributions of the same lifetime income and to reward employment of more than 40 years (cf. NOU 2004: 72–5). Employment income of up to about 133 per cent of the average wage earns entitlements, and the reformed FT scheme retains its defined-benefit feature: the benefit formula becomes biased in favour of low-income workers. Three further elements are Swedish 'imports': pension credits for periods spent in care work and military service become entitlements earned through employment; a guaranteed pension for retirees with insufficient earnings-related pensions replaces the universal minimum state pension; and a life expectancy coefficient prevents an implicit expansion of the scheme. Older workers may postpone retirement to offset a lower pension when their cohort is expected to live longer. Finally, the assets of the Petroleum and the FT funds will merge into a Government Pension Fund. This fund will operate as a buffer when contribution revenues (out of a stable rate of 17.5 per cent, equally shared between employers and employees) cannot completely cover expenditures.

To make the reform more palatable to the trade union movement, feminist groups and the rank-and-file of the Social Democratic Party, the government had to give in on two issues. First, flexible retirement after age 62 will remain possible. The current AFP scheme will continue in a modified form (details to be determined when collective agreements are up for renegotiation in 2006 and possibly extended to all workers in the private sector). The idea is that individuals opting for early retirement should shoulder the main burden of the costs related to their choice but receive a higher annual pension if they delay retirement. Even though standard retirement age will remain at 67, workers can earn pension entitlements even beyond age 70.

Second, after a joint proposal by the social partners and a corresponding bill drafted by an expert committee (NOU 2005: 15), the parliament decided that, starting in 2006, all employees in the private sector have to be covered by occupational pension schemes with an employers' contribution rate to DC-type plans of at least 2 per cent (or an equivalent level for DB-type plans). After the Swedish experience caused the general enthusiasm for individual FDC accounts to wane, the non-socialist parties found it much easier to agree to mandatory occupational pensions.

The broad consensus on the main reform principles ensures the continuation of the process, although a number of important details need settling before the reform goes into effect in 2010 and fully affects cohorts born in 1965 and later. Yet it seems clear that Norway will implement a lean version of the commission's proposal, providing more individual choice, primarily over the timing of retirement age.

Patterns of enlarged freedom of choice

A central idea of active citizenship is to leave decision-making to the discretion of individuals and to enable them to exercise self-responsibility (Chapter 3). Self-responsibility and freedom of choice as welfare-enhancing devices have always been central values for liberals. Therefore the fact that Social Democratic governments in Sweden, Germany and Finland have carried out reforms increasing freedom of choice is remarkable.

In Sweden and Germany in particular, the reforms departed from features hitherto seen as characterizing Social Democratic or Conservative pension schemes, namely a high level of public benefits securing adequate retirement income. In both these countries the Social Democratic elite appears either to have upgraded values like individual responsibility and freedom of choice at the expense of traditional values like solidarity and distributive justice (Germany) or to be prepared to surrender those tenets for the sake of compromise (Sweden). Such shifts fit into the overall move from simply *protecting* citizens against market forces while in or outside employment to *enabling* them to individually satisfy their welfare needs within markets of all kinds (Esping-Andersen 2002). In contrast, Finnish pension reform was not accompanied by such frame shifts, whereas in Norway the Social Democratic elite was more intransigent about demands for increasing individual choice – at least in the more radical form of individual accounts.

When variants of such accounts played a prominent role in the reform debate in Germany and Sweden, Social Democrats there had embraced the paradigm shift towards a multi-pillar approach. Individual accounts developed as an inevitable consequence of the respective route of reform that followed from the specific legacies of established pension systems. They are by-products of public pension reforms aimed at financial sustainability and intergenerational equity and are therefore meant to fill a growing benefit gap. These DC-type pension plans provide future pensioners with true property rights while also shifting all inherent risks to them. They not only *facilitate* more individual choice but also *require* the ability and willingness to choose according to one's preferences and degree of risk aversion. This aspect of the reforms did not result from a clear ideological shift, nor did it speak to a strong demand for variety 'from below'. Instead, it represents a fairly strong popular demand for more flexibility in the timing of retirement and, so far, for extended options to early retirement.

New demands on citizens

Mandatory membership in public pension schemes or in occupational pension plans has largely relieved employees from retirement planning and the need to assess the risks of welfare markets. The shift from schemes providing DB-type benefits towards an enlarged role of DC-type components increases the demand for individual risk management or 'do-it-yourself social policy' (Klein and Millar 1995). Changes in pension policy involving a transfer of responsibility and demanding individual initiative are not part of efforts to strengthen 'active citizenship'. Instead, these reforms presuppose citizens who are able to behave as active and knowledgeable consumers responsible for their own well-being. Shifting risks back to citizens, thereby offering them more choice, does not guarantee the emergence of active consumers, able to cope with inherent risks and simultaneously trust-regulated welfare markets (Taylor-Gooby 1999; International Monetary Fund 2005: 71–89). Such a rational approach to consumer choice suffers from serious human limitations, of which three closely interrelated kinds are most central: financial illiteracy, procrastination and short time horizons.

Pensions are complex products, and individual retirement planning becomes more complicated the more the income package in old age will consist of different components over which considerable scope of agency exists. Knowledge thus becomes all the more important (OECD 2005a). Nevertheless, even public schemes are incomprehensible to the ordinary citizen, and people often overestimate their future entitlements to public pensions and neglect the cumulative impact of previous retrenchments (*Institut für Demoskopie* 2003; Leinert 2003). For example, fewer than 40 per cent of respondents in a Swedish survey reported that they had 'good knowledge' about the reformed (NDC) system, and about one-third did not even care at all (Sundén 2005). Private pensions are even more complicated, requiring broad financial literacy for making informed choices. Numerous empirical studies have revealed that those skills are largely lacking. Few people know about their provisions or the actions they need to take to improve them.

Knowledge of this kind generally depends upon income and education (Mayhew 2003; Leinert 2004).

Retirement planning is time-consuming. For most people it is an unpleasant exercise that they tend to postpone in favour of more 'important' or more satisfying activities, especially if the decisions at stake only become important years or even decades later (Loewenstein 2000). Such problems of procrastination show up in an inertia based upon the false belief that acting later will produce no other result than acting right away. Another example is status quo bias: once an individual has made an active choice, that person tends to stick with it, almost never searching for more advantageous alternatives (Cronqvist and Thaler 2004: 427; Thaler and Benartzi 2004: 167–68). A recent Swedish study shows that higher education and/or income, existing personal pension savings, and being born in the Nordic countries are among the most relevant determinants of whether people actually choose from the available funds or reallocate their portfolios (Engström and Westerberg 2003).

Research on the Swedish premium pension scheme provides further insights. In 2000, when the gainfully employed could decide upon their portfolios for the first time, 68 per cent made an active choice. At that time equity markets were 'bullish', and the new premium pension plan received much attention. In 2004, among the new (mostly young) entrants, only 10 per cent made an active decision (Sundén 2004; *Statens offentliga utredningar* 2005: 78–80). People's avoidance of making choices naturally relates to their limited financial experience. They become confused and demotivated when facing a bewildering range of over 700 fund alternatives. Therefore, a committee that evaluated the premium pension scheme, among others, recommended drastically reducing the number of fund management alternatives and improving guidance for largely ignorant participants, to encourage them to make active and better choices (*Statens offentliga utredningar* 2005). In Germany, the consequences of ignorance and non-choice are even more acute, since taking out a *Riester-Rente* or enrolling in the new occupational pension plans is voluntary (not mandatory, as in Sweden). Even though most German workers are aware of the need to save for retirement, only about 25 per cent of eligible workers make use of the new opportunities. Financial illiteracy and perceived difficulties about making oneself knowledgeable are the most important reasons for constantly postponing a decision (Leinert 2003, 2004).

Even though deliberate procrastinators act on a short time horizon, the capacity to plan for long periods ahead is only one dimension of social inequality. A 2004 German survey shows that retirement planning is largely restricted to people with high and secure incomes and who have real control over their future (Allianz 2004): the rest of the population acts on a short time horizon when it comes to financial planning, even if intensified individual efforts to save for retirement are considered necessary. If citizens are to take greater responsibility for their financial security in old age and, consequently, are to be granted more choice, governments have to factor in persistent financial illiteracy, people not taking action at all (or too late) and people making bad choices that are costly to revise. That financial education, transparent information and more comprehensible pension products can fully remove those unequally distributed limitations to intelligent decision-making is quite unlikely.

New risks and new options

The fact that new risks have become significant, especially in the German and Swedish pension systems, does not mean that future pensioners will fall into an abyss. Obviously, private pre-funded schemes face financial market risks, which may hit without prior warning and ruin even careful retirement planning. Most important are *investment risks*, because the value of assets at the time of retirement is contingent upon the management of the pension fund, the portfolio chosen and the performance of financial markets during the whole accumulation period. Nevertheless there are also *annuity risks* (as current interest rates and mortality rates determine the level of the periodic payment until the death of the annuitant) and post-retirement *inflation risks*. Given the still dominant role of public schemes for preventing poverty, however, any potential loss should not be drastic, although rising expectations of financial security in old age may not be met and consumption plans could fail. Because governments (or social partners) compel or strongly encourage employees to contribute to private pensions that, with no individual blame, turn out to be bad investments, disappointment can then become an increasing problem.

Among the individual options that have been enlarged, those concerning a flexible retirement age appear the least risky, although by involving a complex decision they are immediately welfare-improving, because the range of choice about the time path of consumption is increased. This welfare argument holds true as long as individual agency is truly unconstrained. In Finland, Sweden and Germany, the departure from a schematic transition from employment into retirement was continued despite the closing or systematizing of several pathways into early retirement. Pre-existing opportunities for early exit hid open unemployment among older workers and facilitated a decent exit from working life for tired but not completely incapacitated employees.

In contrast, the incentives accompanying extended options for individually determining one's full or partial exit from employment are meant to achieve just the opposite, namely to break up an established early retirement culture and to make employment until statutory retirement age or even beyond more attractive. Thus, they provide a kind of guided choice, because the implicit tax on prolonged employment is lowered and the financial consequences of individual choice are intensified. That way, at least in Sweden and Finland, the unpopular issue of raising the statutory retirement age has become depoliticized.

Conclusions

This chapter has shown that individual options, as well as individual responsibilities for choosing one's retirement age and/or retirement income have been – and in the case of Norway, will be – expanded. It remains questionable, however, whether those elements of pension reform actually provide more real free choice. For example, the premium pension in Sweden, on top of the NDC pension, is intended to close the gap that has arisen from the abolition of the previous ATP scheme. It is paternalistic because it not only makes future pensioners better off than without such a supplement but also involves coercion: all employees who contribute to the NDC scheme also pay into the pre-funded component (and the same is true for the quasi-mandatory occupational pensions based on collective agreements). Individual choice comes only second. Regardless of whether employees exercise their right to choose from the menu of investment funds or not, financial market risks remain so that in the worst case, paternalistic intentions – i.e. the government defining a target for 'appropriate' earnings replacement – will be nullified. Nevertheless, the present German approach that banks on individuals' voluntary decision to additionally save for retirement (and provides financial support as an incentive) will hardly attain a take-up rate of 100 per cent and cannot ensure that contributions are paid without interruptions and always at the recommended rate. A considerable proportion of retirees remaining without supplementary private pensions will create further income inequality in old age.

All four countries have extended individual options for the timing of first pension payments and strengthened the trade-off between later (or earlier) retirement and higher (or lower) benefits according to actuarial criteria. In Sweden, the extension of flexibility even meant an almost complete abolition of a statutory retirement age. Sensible older individuals will choose an exit age that balances their fatigue from paid work against their income needs during retirement. Older workers often underestimate those income needs or inflate the attractiveness of post-employment life, so that they retire too early. Having left their job, they find re-entry into the labour market at a similar wage rate just about impossible.

In other cases, impaired health, reduction in work capacity, job loss, or inability to find a job constrains older workers' free choice about the timing of retirement. If investments in private pensions have performed worse than expected, the choice of the preferred age of labour market exit is further constrained. Finally, if public pension reforms imply that working longer is necessary for obtaining benefits of the present level, the 'choice' of one's retirement age becomes almost fictitious. Taken together, the promise of a flexible retirement age may either entail inferior choices or ultimately reveal the absence of any real choices at all.

15 Conclusions

Remaking social citizenship in the Nordic welfare states

Bjørn Hvinden and Håkan Johansson

Introduction

In the introductory chapter we pointed to a number of ongoing changes in contemporary societies and welfare states, changes calling for a more dynamic, multifaceted understanding of citizenship. These changes include attempts to establish stronger links between public income maintenance and employment policy, a new division of responsibility between public and private in social risk protection, a redefined relationship between the state's roles as providers of resources and regulators of market behaviour, and the blurring of the boundaries between national and supranational influences in welfare policy. We illustrated some of the ways in which these changes interact with each other and are connected to two broad transformations of contemporary societies: the first is greater economic openness and more prominent roles for market competition and competitiveness as issues for public policy consideration, including welfare policy ('globalization', 'Europeanization'); the second is greater autonomy of the individual, based on competence and economic independence, as enabled and supported by rights granted by the welfare state ('individualization').

Finally, we outlined and discussed some of the main ways in which citizenship has been conceptualized in social theory. In particular, we contrasted socio-liberal, libertarian (or neo-liberal) and republican models of citizenship. We identified an underlying active-passive dimension in all three models of citizenship, with the exact meaning of this dimension dependent on the model in question.

To investigate these issues and questions, the authors selected a range of policy areas and welfare reforms for more detailed case studies. These case studies have covered the following areas of welfare policy, legislation and practice:

- Activation – and reforms linking income maintenance and employment promotion.
- The scope for participation of marginal groups in deliberation and decision-making.

- The impact of human rights legislation for welfare, legal protection against discrimination and social barriers to equal market participation.
- The co-ordination of social security systems to facilitate cross-border mobility.
- Pension reform – and efforts to make pension systems sustainable.

To see to what extent the case studies have clarified our three broad questions, in Table 4 we summarize the main implications of the case studies for the remaking of social citizenship – most directly within the Nordic welfare states but potentially beyond them.

Implications of activation reform

Activation reform has indeed given the fulfilment of duties or activation requirements greater emphasis within the income maintenance system for people of working age. Compliance with such requirements has more or less become a condition for receiving cash benefits, e.g. social assistance, unemployment benefits or disability-related payments. This implicit condition clearly shows that underlying notions of a balance between rights and duties, associated with the original socio-liberal understanding of citizenship – as codified by T. H. Marshall – have gained new or renewed significance.

Even more striking is the way in which activation reforms have adopted notions of user participation, co-determination, and choice, especially in the joint formulation of individual action plans for helping the unemployed citizen become economically self-sufficient.

The use of these notions of choice seems paradoxical, given that the initial or continued granting of benefits is increasingly conditional on the fulfilment of activation requirements, while non-compliance is met with sanctions (reduction or termination of payments). In other words, to the extent that an individual depends on cash benefits an element of compulsion appears to contradict the notion of freedom of choice. Yet, according to the case study of activation reform in Finland reconciling these elements is possible.

On the other hand, the more diverse cases of Norway and Sweden suggest that the combination of forced and voluntary participation in activation reform has been less consistent and convincing there. The experiences reported by unemployed citizens claiming social assistance in those two countries indicate that the element of compulsion predominated over those of involvement and co-determination in individual action plans (if such plans existed at all). A more general implication of these findings is that when governments attempt to combine elements associated with different models of active citizenship, some may be suppressed, ignored, or negligible in practice. More detailed research must clarify under what circumstances such suppression can be avoided.

Table 4 The remaking of social citizenship as highlighted by case studies

Areas of national and European welfare policy, legislation, practice, and citizenship	1) Renewed emphasis of the active side in each model of citizenship ('opening within')	2) Interplay of aspects from several models of citizenship ('opening between')	3) Interaction between European and national citizenship within social policy ('denationalization')
Activation reform – the linking of income security and employment promotion	Increased weight to the fulfilment of duties and activity requirements as conditions for being granted (continued) cash benefits (Chapters 4–6)	Stronger emphasis of rights/duties balance, as well as participation, even choice, in individual action plans (Chapter 5, less consistently in Chapter 6)	The EU's promotion of active measures and active social policy; corresponds more or less to national emphasis (Chapter 4)
Scope for participation of marginalized groups in deliberation and decision-making	In spite of official calls for 'user involvement', ambivalence on the part of national and local government towards collective and individual voice (Chapters 7–9)	Unintended consequence of stricter enforcement of activation requirements: facilitates self-organization and voice on the part of recipients (Chapter 7)	The European Commission's legitimizing of and support for marginalized groups at European level; providing a source of influence at national level (Chapters 9 & 13)
Human rights and anti-discrimination legislation and removal of barriers to equal market participation	Human rights and anti-discrimination provisions require active citizens to have practical significance; competent agency is necessary for realizing their potential (Chapters 10, 12 & 13)	Human rights provisions might constrain the nature of activity requirements imposed on claimants; some redistributive provisions might help to combat discrimination (Chapters 7, 10 & 13)	The EU has introduced binding legislation, now incorporated in national legislation; transnational and national networks have campaigned for this (Chapters 10, 12 & 13)
Co-ordination of social benefit systems to facilitate cross-border mobility	Individuals are expected to make more use of the opportunities and scope for choice in the European labour market (Chapters 10 & 11)	Efforts to prevent national social benefit rules from creating disincentives for the full realization of market citizenship (Chapters 10 & 11)	The EU regime of co-ordination constrains national control of social benefit systems (Chapters 10 & 11)
Pension reform – efforts to make pension systems sustainable	Increased weight given to encouraging citizens to exercise self-responsibility and choice regarding personal pension planning and timing of retirement (Chapter 14)	Economic security in old age to be based on a combination of public and private provisions, public entitlements and private contracts, and property rights (Chapter 14)	The EU seeks to stimulate national reforms of pension systems to make them sustainable and compatible with increased and prolonged labour market participation (Chapters 1 & 9)

Finally, the introduction or stronger activation requirements in income maintenance systems throughout the 1990s became part of European Union (EU) policy. Expressed within the European employment strategy, policy changes at European level suggest that such activity requirements have – or are about to – become an aspect of social citizenship in a great number of European countries. At the same time existing knowledge from comparative welfare state research gives reason to expect that the extent to which, and the ways in which, activation requirements are put into practice will vary considerably between countries. Perhaps with the exception of Finland, the adoption of activation goals Europe-wide has in no obviously significant way influenced the introduction or reinforcement of activation requirements in the Nordic countries. To the contrary, Sweden and Norway in particular had for a long period based their income maintenance systems on the 'work line', involving activation requirements for working age people claiming cash benefits. Moreover, the policy shift to activation happened in Denmark, Norway and Sweden in the late 1980s and early 1990s, long before activation was firmly established as an operational part of EU policy.

Whether the trend towards an activation rationale represents a novelty varies considerably from country to country. Traditionally, welfare states belonging to the southern and western parts of Europe have much less than the Nordic countries subscribed to an activation rationale, with continental welfare states in the middle. In other words, many welfare states have relied on other mechanisms for promoting labour market participation and self-sufficiency than activation requirements. The simplest of these mechanisms has obviously been the assumed or actual work-promoting incentive of low or non-existent income security benefits.

The Nordic welfare states have, from the start, viewed activation requirements not only as a way of preventing excessive demand for cash benefits from citizens of working age but also as expressions of a reciprocal 'moral' relationship between rights and duties, on the parts of both the individual and the state. In spite of Nordic welfare states' general claim of universality, the rights to cash benefits associated with social citizenship have greatly depended on the efforts of individual citizens, in the form of either past employment and earnings or of current fulfilment of activation requirements towards becoming re-employed.

This aspect of Nordic welfare policy has undergone a renaissance since the beginning of the 1990s. Against the backdrop of new patterns of unemployment, as the perception of an excessive demand for cash benefits, and restated political goals for inclusion and participation, important new elements have been joined with the traditional Nordic commitment to an active policy of social protection. This change does not mean that public systems mainly providing income maintenance for people of working age (i.e. 'passive' provisions) have ceased to exist. Rather, we have seen the emergence of a more complex, dynamic relationship between the passive and active dimensions of the Nordic version of socio-liberal citizenship.

Implications of marginal groups' scope for participation

Recent changes in society and public policy have improved the possibilities for visibility and voice for marginal groups in the public sphere. These expanded opportunities have partly resulted from public policy, e.g. policy aimed at encouraging voluntary engagement and activity, self-help, dialogue and consultation with groups whose lives are affected by welfare provisions. National and local authorities have also provided some financial and practical support to grass-root associations. Moreover, a more open, tolerant, social and cultural climate has contributed to the more favourable situation for collective action on the part of marginal groups such as unemployed people claiming income maintenance benefits, people with impairments, and people belonging to ethnic minorities.

From these changes some might argue that the ideals of active participation in deliberation and decision-making in society, associated with republican citizenship, now also apply to groups previously excluded or absent. Nevertheless, the case studies that have examined the scope for active participation of marginal citizens give a more mixed picture. These studies indicate that attempts by marginal groups to assert themselves in the public sphere and vis-à-vis political authorities and other more well-established actors can encounter considerable ambivalence. This reaction suggests that the legitimacy of active participation and independent voice on the part of marginal groups is still contested.

On the other hand, both the experiences of the grass-root groups in Denmark and Norway and the network of social NGOs in Sweden look promising because, despite resistance from more powerful actors, they succeeded in gaining greater visibility and influence for their constituencies. By contrast, the Russian women in Norway met greater obstacles in their struggle to gain legitimacy for their voice and obtain access to arenas that would allow them to develop further their capabilities. These obstacles were greatly related to a combination of discrimination because of gender and nationality.

Furthermore, the case studies also showed another striking interaction between elements associated with different models of citizenship. In Denmark and Norway the stronger enforcement of activity requirement in income maintenance systems partly served as an impetus to the formation of grass-root associations of unemployed citizens and partly helped to establish contact among those who eventually took the organizational initiative.

Finally, the case studies have also illustrated how the EU, represented by the Commission, has contributed significantly to the formation and operation of transnational networks of national associations of marginal citizens. By so doing, the Commission has also indirectly strengthened the position of networks and associations at the national level, by providing legitimacy, valuable knowledge and support, and assistance in the building of political capacity and self-confidence among group leaders and key activists. This strengthening has obviously improved the potential of the national networks and organizations for influencing public policy and creating greater scope for participation for marginal citizens in deliberation and decision-making in general.

Implications of human rights and anti-discrimination legislation

The incorporation of human rights and anti-discrimination provisions in national legislation represents a major challenge to established ways of thinking about social citizenship. This challenge holds particularly true in the Nordic countries, where the welfare state has mainly been seen as provider of benefits and services to the whole population. Less systematic attention has been given to the role of the state as regulator of the behaviour of other, largely non-governmental actors. This regulation takes place through a range of monitoring, supervising and arbitrating bodies and, eventually, through the court system. To a great extent, the rights that the regulatory system provides can be realized and implemented only to the extent that individuals – or agencies acting on their behalf – make competent use of them through filing complaints or litigation. In this sense, human rights and anti-discrimination provisions require active citizenship for practical significance.

Even though how social regulation provisions actually affect the ways in which individuals exercise social citizenship needs further analysis, the case studies nonetheless are illustrative. For instance, one chapter analyzes how immigrant women in Denmark and Norway have promoted their welfare by taking cases of discrimination on the combined grounds of gender and ethnicity to court, on the basis of human rights provisions. Another chapter has demonstrated how the ongoing implementation of the Frame Directive on equal opportunities in employment gives people with impairments in Europe additional instruments for finding and keeping suitable work. Other chapters have discussed how human rights provisions (e.g. protecting the individual's dignity) have been used to question the nature of requirements imposed on participants in activation measures in Denmark. Moreover, in some European countries, the employers' duty to provide reasonable accommodation for job seekers or employees with impairments may be undermined unless public financial support can cover a part of the costs of accommodation. Such cases will demand the combined active use of both regulatory and redistributive legal provisions.

Finally, as already indicated, both human rights and anti-discrimination legislation clearly show a denationalization of citizenship, in that they involve rights that are shared by the inhabitants in several countries and are thus less dependent on nationality or residence in a particular national territory. Transnational networks acting on behalf of citizens in Europe have also campaigned and lobbied for the adoption of European legislation in this area.

The significance of the European regime for co-ordination of social benefit systems

The EU seeks to promote cross-border mobility of labour. As one means of achieving this goal, it has established a legal framework for co-ordinating national social benefit systems. We can see this action as part of wider efforts to encourage the citizens of Europe to make active use of the opportunities provided by a single European market, both as workers and as consumers. As a result, national welfare states lose some control over the demand for their social provisions – and potentially lose the funding of these provisions. Member states can somewhat restrict welfare provisions to their own citizens, and they lose the control over the spatial location of their consumption; e.g. benefits provided by one state may become portable to others. European citizens have also gained wider scope for consuming welfare services in other countries, with the costs reimbursed by benefit systems operating in their own country. This extension of the rights provided under national social citizenship challenges the financial and administrative control of national welfare authorities.

To the extent that European citizens seek to make active use of the opportunities provided by the wider European market, the market will become a more important means of promoting the individual's welfare, while belonging to a particular national welfare state will become relatively less significant. In this way more extensive cross-border mobility in Europe may contribute to a more long-term shift towards an increasing role for 'market citizenship' in general, as well as to the complex process referred to as 'individualization'. More specifically, the shift to co-ordinating social security is making the provisions of national systems accessible to non-nationals, workers from other countries and other families. As this book discusses, this process raises complex normative issues that are yet to be settled, not least because they relate to the question of what a future European social citizenship could entail.

Pension reform – efforts to make pension systems sustainable

Contemporary pension reform in many countries explicitly aims at strengthening the role of self-responsibility and choice, in line with core normative ideas of libertarian or neo-liberal citizenship. Pension reforms are often meant to contribute to a greater role for market citizenship. The comparative analysis of national pension reforms in Finland, Germany, Norway and Sweden, however, indicates that various factors have constrained these efforts. More extensive scope for exercising individual choice has been provided only in Germany and Sweden. Yet even here it is more than doubtful that a large proportion of the population are fully aware of the choices open to them or feel competent to use the opportunities for exercising self-responsibility and choice regarding their economic security in old age. For many people in the four countries, the main choice they exercise concerns the timing of their retirement – and even this decision is fraught with difficult judgements for the individual.

Currently, many governments not only make strong efforts to persuade people in their late middle age to postpone their retirement but also provide financial incentives for such postponement. We can easily imagine a situation in which governments will increasingly present the idea of staying employed longer than many people would prefer as something like a 'moral duty' to society. Thus 'active ageing' can be constructed as an additional aspect of active citizenship. If so, the main reason will be that for most people the elements of private or market-based provisions for old age will only be smaller supplements to people's entitlements through public pension systems.

Do we see a shift towards libertarian and republican citizenship in the Nordic countries?

The case studies in this book show that a more complex mix of elements associated with different models of citizenship is emerging in the Nordic countries. At least in terms of stated aims and the adopted rhetoric, we see that more established forms of cash benefits, employment, and social services are infused with notions of participation in decision-making, co-determination, (user) involvement, (user) choice and self-responsibility.

Yet that these transformations are very deep or consequential is not obvious. One exception is that groups of marginal citizens – through a combination of self-organization and recognition from their political environment – have gained greater scope for visibility and choice in the public sphere, consequently improving their chances for participation in deliberation and decision-making. Moreover, some substantial cuts have been made in some public income maintenance systems and services.

At the same time private and market-based provisions based on consumer choice, contract and property rights clearly play a greater role than before, although their overall role is still one of marginal supplements rather than that of substitutes for public provisions. It is also clear that new forms of regulatory legal provisions have strengthened citizens' rights as workers and consumers, thus adding new elements to what we have referred to as 'market citizenship'. Yet, all in all, we cannot conclude that libertarian and republican citizenship have replaced socio-liberal citizenship in the Nordic countries. Socio-liberal citizenship still predominates. Nonetheless, it is now to a greater extent than ever complemented – and challenged – by elements of libertarian and republican citizenship.

Conclusion: towards a more open conceptualization of social citizenship

Our answers to the three broad research questions with which we began are as follows:

- Policymakers and welfare reforms have indeed given stronger emphasis to the 'active' side of citizenship (as framed within each of the three ideal-type models), and this shift has been related to the transformations of societies and welfare policies.
- Normative ideas conventionally associated with different models of citizenship – for instance 'fulfilling duties' (socio-liberal citizenship), 'exercising choice and self-responsibility' (libertarian citizenship), 'participating in deliberation and decision-making' (republican citizenship) – are usually combined or intertwined in practice. At least in the context of activation reform, these elements appear to sit together uncomfortably, leading in some cases to the suppression of some elements in practice.
- We can also clearly observe a weakening of the strong bonds traditionally found between national welfare states and social citizenship, in the sense that the actual content of social citizenship is more greatly determined by international influences or interactions between national and supranational levels of government. Thus we see a trend toward the denationalization of social citizenship; not only in the Nordic countries, but throughout Europe. The trend towards denationalization appears to facilitate or reinforce two other trends: individualization and the marketization of citizenship.

Based on these answers we have tried to substantiate the claim that there is need to open our conceptualization of social citizenship:

First, we have indicated that this is partly a question of avoiding an arbitrary focus either on passive *or* active dimensions of social citizenship (regardless of how 'passive' or 'active' is constructed), and rather see these aspects in relation to each other and how they even may be mutually conditioning each other ('opening within').

Second, we have suggested that there is a tendency to limit the researcher's attention to one of several possible perspectives or approaches to social citizenship, rather than asking how the elements of reality each of them focus on, may co-exist and interact with each other ('opening between').

Third, we have argued that existing conceptualizations of social citizenship tend to be too strongly restricted to the nation-state as a space for citizenship. We need a more open conceptualization of social citizenship that can capture the ways in which the substance of social citizenship is also determined by international influences, market processes and interactions between national and supranational levels of government ('denationalization'). This also means widening the horizon from only considering the direct public and redistributive basis for social citizenship (systems of taxes/contributions and transfers/services granted, provided or guaranteed by public authorities), to also including social regulation (how governments can seek to promote social objectives by influencing the behaviour of non-governmental actors, which may or may not serve as functional substitutes for direct redistributive public provisions).

Currently the active dimensions of citizenship and their combination are of particular interest, given the focus of debates about welfare reform in Europe and most member states. This means that we see attempts to combine notions like: fulfilling duties (obligations), exercising choice and self-responsibility, and participating in deliberation and decision-making.

Consequently, one important task for future research is to describe and analyze how the new and 'hybrid' forms of social citizenship give rise to tensions, conflicts and ambiguities. Another task for research is to gain more systematic knowledge about how denationalization of social citizenship may promote a relative shift in the overall configuration of social citizenship; e.g. a strengthening of libertarian or republican components at the expense of socio-liberal components. In other words, this approach will give us a vocabulary for describing and analyzing the possible strengthening of libertarian notions of citizenship (cf. 'market citizenship' or 'consumer citizenship') at the expense of solidaristic and redistributive notions of social citizenship.

References

Official publications

Act (1998) on Active Social Policy (Consolidated Act 709 2003 Denmark), available at: www.retsinfo.dk (accessed 29 June 2006).

Act (2003: 308) amending the Act (1999: 130) on the elimination of discrimination because of ethnicity on the labour market (Sweden).

Act No. 30 of 21 May 1999 relating the strengthening of the status of human rights in Norwegian law (The Human Rights Act) (Norway), available at: http://lovdata.no (accessed 28 June 2006).

Act No. 375 of 28 May 2003 on Danish Courses for Adult Aliens, etc. (Denmark), available at: www.retsinfo.dk (accessed 29 June 2006).

Act No. 388 of 30 May 2000 on Equality between Women and Men (Denmark), available at: www.retsinfo.dk (accessed 29 June 2006).

Act No. 398 of 6 June 2002 amending the Act on Social Services (Denmark), available at: www.retsinfo.dk (accessed 29 June 2006).

Act No. 417 of 10 June 2003 amending the Active Social Policy (Denmark), available at: www.retsinfo.dk (accessed 29 June 2006).

Act No. 459 of 12 June 1996 on the Prohibition of Different Treatment in the Labour Market (Denmark), available at: www.retsinfo.dk (accessed 29 June 2006).

Aetat (2004) Årsstatistikk om arbeidsmarkedet 2003, Oslo: Arbeidsdirektoratet.

Case 41/84, Pinna v. Caisse d'Allocations Familiales de la Savoie [1986] ECR 1 (Pinna1), available at: http://eur-lex.europa.eu/RECH_jurisprudence.do (accessed 29 June 2006).

Case 302/84 Ten Holder [1986] ECR 1821, available at: http://eur-lex.europa.eu/RECH_jurisprudence.do (accessed 29 June 2006).

Case C-20/96 Kelvin Snares v. Adjudication Officer [1997] EI-6057, available at: http://eur-lex.europa.eu/RECH_jurisprudence.do (accessed 29 June 2006).

CEDAW (1979a) Convention on Elimination of all Discrimination Against Women (of 18 December 1979).

CEDAW (1979b) Convention on the Elimination of All Forms of Discrimination against Women, General Assembly resolution 34/180 of 18 December 1979, available at: www.un.org/womenwatch/daw/cedaw (accessed 29 June 2006).

CEDAW (2002) Concluding Observations of the Committee on the Elimination of Discrimination Against Women: Iceland 07/05/2002 A/57/38, (part 1), paras. 235–36, & Denmark: CEDAW/C/2002/IICRP.3/Add.3 para. 18.

CEDAW (2003) and Norway CEDAW/C/2003/I/CRP.3/Add.2/Rev.1 paras. 20–21.

CES (2003) *L'insertion professionnelle en milieu ordinaire des personnes en situation de handicap*, Conseil Economique et Social. Paris: Journaux officiels.

CEU (2000a) Council Directive 2000/43/EC implementing the principle of equal treatment between persons irrespective of racial or ethnic origin, *Official Journal* L 180, 19/97/2000, p. 0022–26.

CEU (2000b) Council Directive 2000/78/EC of 27 November 2000 establishing ageneral framework for equal treatment in employment and occupation, *Official Journal* L 303, 02/12/2000 p. 0016.

Charter of Fundamental Rights of the European Union, *Official Journal of the European Communities*, 18.12.2000 C 364/1.

Consolidated Act No. 709 of 13 August 2003 on Social Policy (Denmark), available at: www.retsinfo.dk (accessed 29 June 2006).

Consolidated Act No. 764 of 26 August 2003 on Active Social Policy (Denmark), available at: www.retsinfo.dk (accessed 29 June 2006).

Consolidated Act No. 1035 of 21 November 2003 on the Integration of Aliens (Denmark), available at: www.retsinfo.dk (accessed 29 June 2006).

Consolidated Integration Act No. 839, Consolidation of the Act on Integration of Aliens in Denmark, Danish Ministry of Refugee, Immigration and Integration Affairs, 5 September 2005, available at: www.retsinfo.dk (accessed 29 June 2006).

Council Directive 90/365/EEC of 28 June 1990 on the right of residence for employees and self-employed persons who have ceased their occupational activity, *Official Journal*, L 180, 13.7.1990, p. 28–29.

Council of the European Union, press release 163, no. 9507/04, 2/6/2004.

Council Regulation (EC) No. 1408/71 on the application of social security schemes to employed persons, to self-employed persons and to members of their families moving within the Community, *Official Journal* L 149, 5.7.1971, Consolidated version OJ No L 28 of 30.1.1997.

Council Regulation (EEC) No. 574/72 laying down the procedure for implementing Regulation (EEC) No. 11409/71 on the application of social security schemes to employed persons, to self-employed persons, to self-employed persons and to their families moving within the Community (*Official Journal* No. L 74, 27.3.1972, Consolidated version, *Official Journal* No. L 28 of 30, 1.1997).

CRC (1989) Convention on the Rights of the Child Adopted and opened for signature, ratification and accession by General Assembly resolution 44/25 of 20 November 1989, available at: www.unhchr.ch/html/menu3/b/k2crc.htm (accessed 29 June 2006).

Danish Constitution 1849 with latest amendments 5 June 1953.

Danish Government (2001) Report 1407 On Incorporation of Human Rights Conventions into Danish Legislation, Copenhagen.

Danish Ministry of Refugee, Immigration and Integration affairs (2005) *A new chance for everyone – the Danish Government's integration plan*, Summary May 2005, Copenhagen.

Danish Ministry of Social Affairs (2000) *Socialpolitik som investering, Socialpolitisk Redegørelse 2000 – Sammenfatning*, Copenhagen.

Danish Supreme Court (2003) *Højesterets dombog*, Dom avsagt 22. desember 2003 i sag 493/2002 mot Den Social Ankestyrelsen, available at: www.retsinfo.dk (accessed 29 June 2006).

D'Hoop (C-224/98) Union Citizenship (ECJ case), available at: http://eur-lex.europa.eu/RECH_jurisprudence.do (accessed 29 June 2006).

Discrimination Act (LOV-2005-06-03-33), available at: http://lovdata.no (accessed 28 June 2006).

Draft treaty establishing a constitution for Europe, *Official Journal* C 169, 18 July 2003, with final changes of June 18, 2004 CIG 81/04 amended by document CIG 85/04 and 50/03.

DRC (2002) *Code of Practice. Rights of Access. Goods, Facilities, Services and Premises*, The Disability Discrimination Act 1995. Disability Rights Commission.

DS 2002:54, Swedish and Foreign marriages, Ministry of Justice, Stockholm.

EC (2000) Council Directive 2000/78/EC of 27 November 2000 establishing a general framework for equal treatment in employment and occupation, *Official Journal*, L180/22.

EC (2003) *Employment in Europe 2003. Recent trends and prospects*, Luxembourg: Office for Official Publications of the European Communities.

ETS No. 157 (1995) *Framework Convention for the Protection of National Minorities*, Strasbourg: Council of Europe.

EU (1997) *Consolidated Version of the Treaty Establishing the European Community, in Consolidated Treaties*, Luxembourg: Office for Official Publications of the European Communities.

EU (2000) Charter of Fundamental Rights of the European Union, 2000/C 364/01, *Official Journal*, 18/12/2000.

European Commission (2001) *Draft Joint Report on Social Inclusion*, Communication from the Commission, COM (2001) 565 Final.

European Commission (2003) *Modernising Social Protection for More and Better Jobs: a Comprehensive Approach Contributing to Making Work Pay* COM (2003) 842(01).

European Commission (2005) *Working Together for Growth & Jobs, A New Start for the Lisbon Strategy*, Commission Communication to Spring European Council.

European Convention of Human Rights (1950) European Convention for the Protection of Human Rights and Fundamental Freedoms (with amendments), available at: www.echr.coe.int/echr (accessed 29 June 2006).

European Council (2000a) *Lisbon European Council. Presidency Conclusions*, March 2000, available at: http://europa.eu/european_council/conclusions/index_en.htm (accessed 26 June 2006).

European Council (2000b) *Nice European Council. Presidency conclusions*. December 2000, available at: http://europa.eu/european_council/conclusions/index_en.htm (accessed 26 June 2006).

European Court of Human Rights, Leyla Sahin v. Turkey, judgement of 10 November 2005, available at: www.echr.coe.int/ECHR/EN/Header/Case-Law (accessed 20 June 2006).

European Social Charter (1961) European Social Charter (revised 1996) CETS No. 163, available at: www.coe.int/T/E/Human_Rights/Esc (accessed 29 June 2006).

Eurostat (2005) *European Social Statistics. Social Protection 1994–2002*, Luxembourg: Office of Official Publications of the European Communities.

Eurostat (2006) *European Social statistics, Social Protection, Expenditure and Receipts*, Luxembourg: Office for Official Publications of the European Communities, available at: http://europa.eu.int (accessed 1 May 2006).

Finnish Constitution 11 June 1999.

Forh. S. Nr. 160–62 (2004–5) Forhandlinger i Stortinget, pp. 2349–88, 2403–7.

Høringsnotat om innarbeidning av kvinnekonvensjonen i norsk lov, June 2003, (Norway), available at: http://odin.dep.no/filarkiv/182660/Horingsnotat_FNs_kvinnekonvensjon.pdf (accessed 30 June 2006).

ILO (1989) *Convention no. 169 Indigenous and Tribal Peoples Convention*.

Innst. S. Nr. 195 (2004–5) Innstilling fra finanskomiteen om pensjonsreform – trygghet for pensjonene.

International Monetary Fund (2005) *Global Financial Stability Report: Market Developments and Issues*, April 2005, Washington, DC: IMF.

Klagenemda for likestilling. Vedtak av 29.08.2001(Norway), available at: www.likestillingsombudet.no/vedtak (accessed 30 June 2006).

Martínez Sala case (C-85/96) Union citizenship (ECJ case), available at: http://eur-lex.europa.eu/RECH_jurisprudence.do (accessed 29 June 2006).

Ministry for Social Affairs (2003) *Denmark's National Action Plan to Combat Poverty and Social Exclusion*, available at: www.sm.dk/netpublikationer/2003/peactionplan0909 (accessed 29 June 2006).

Ministry of Health and Social Affairs (2002a) *National Strategy Report on the Future of Pension Systems – Sweden*, Stockholm.

Ministry of Health and Social Affairs (2002b) *Finland's National Pension Strategy Report*, Helsinki.

Ministry of Labour (2003) Employment Report 2003, Helsinki: Ministry of Labour, available at: www.mil.fi/english/reports/index.html (accessed 29 June 2006).

National Action Plan against poverty and social exclusion (NAP) (2001) Swedish Ministry of Health and Social Affairs, Stockholm.

National Action Plan against poverty and social exclusion (NAP) (2003) Swedish Ministry of Health and Social Affairs, Stockholm.

Norwegian Constitution of 17 May 1814 with later amendments.

Norwegian Ministry of Children and Family Affairs (2004) Press release No. 04012, 3 March 2004.

NOSOSCO (2005) *Social Protection in the Nordic Countries 2003*, Copenhagen: Nordic Social Statistics Committee.

NOU, 2001: 22 *Fra bruker til borger.* Oslo: Norges offentlige utredninger 2001: 22.

NOU, 2004: 1. *Modernisert folketrygd. Bærekraftig pensjon for framtida*, Oslo: Norges offentlige utredninger 2004: 1.

NOU, 2005: 15. *Obligatorisk tjenestepensjon*, Utredning nr. 13 fra Banklovkommisjonen, Oslo: Norges offentlige utredninger 2005: 15.

OECD (1995) *The OECD Jobs Study: Implementing the Strategy*, Paris: Organization for Economic Co-operation and Development.

OECD (1999) 'Employment protection and labour market performance', in *Employment Outlook*, Paris: OECD.

OECD (2003a) *Ageing and Employment Policies: Sweden*, Paris: OECD.

OECD (2003b) *Transforming Disability into Ability: Policies to Promote Work and Income Security for Disabled People*, Paris: Organization for Economic Co-operation and Development.

OECD (2004a) *Ageing and Employment Policies: Finland*, Paris: OECD.

OECD (2004b) *Ageing and Employment Policies: Norway*, Paris: OECD.

OECD (2005a) *Improving Financial Literacy: Analysis of Issues and Policies*, Paris: OECD.

OECD (2005b) *OECD Employment Outlook*, Paris: Organization for Economic Co-operation and Development.

Ot.prop. nr. 28 (2002–3) *Om Introduksjonsloven.*

Ot.prop. nr. 50 (2003–4) *Om lov om endring av introduksjonsloven.*

Østre Landsret (2002) Dom avsagt 14.01.2002 af Østre Landsrets 21. avdeling nr B-018901 og nr. B-0190-01 mot Kommunernes Landsforening som mandatar for Køge kommune.

Pensjonskommisjonen (2002) *Mål, prinsipper og veivalg for pensjonssystemet*, Foreløpig rapport fra Pensjonskommisjonen, Oslo.

Proposition (Government Bill) 2002/03:65, *Ett utvidgat skydd mot diskriminering*. Stockholm.

Regulation (EC) No 883/2004 of the European Parliament and of the Council of 29 April 2004 on the coordination of social security systems (*Official Journal of the European Union* L 166 of 30 April 2004, Corrigendum, *Official Journal* 200 of 7.6.2004, 1–49).

Regulation (EEC) No. 1408/71 of 14 June 1971 on the application of social security schemes to employed persons, to self-employed persons and to the members of their families moving within the Community.

Regulation (EEC) No. 1612/68 of the Council of 15 October 1968 on freedom of movement for workers within the Community.

Senate (2005) Minutes. Compte rendu analytique officiel de la discussion du projet de loi pour l'égalité des droits et des chances, la participation et la citoyenneté des personnes handicapées, JO du 12 février 2005 – p.2353–88 Paris.

Sør-Varanger Avis, 31 August 2000, *Ansvar og frihet.*

Socialstyrelsen (2000) *Nationellt stöd för kunskapsutveckling inom socialtjänsten,* SoS-rapport 2000:12, Stockholm: Socialstyrelsen.

St.meld. nr. 14 (2002–3) *Samordning av Aetat, trygdeetat og sosialtjeneste,* Oslo.

St.meld. nr. 49 (2003–4) *Mangfold gjennom inkludering og deltakelse,* Oslo.

Statens offentliga utredningar (2005) *Svårnavigerat? Premiepensionssparande på rätt kurs,* SOU 2005:87, Stockholm: Fritzes/Nordsteds juridik.

Statistics Denmark (2004) *Statistisk Årbog,* Copenhagen.

Statistics Norway (2003) *Statistisk årbok,* Oslo.

Statistics Norway (2006) *Immigration and immigrants,* available at: www.ssb.no (accessed 30 May 2006).

Statutory Instrument (2003) No. 1673. The Disability Discrimination Act 1995 (Amendment), UK.

Stortingsmelding nr. 12 (2004–5) Pensjonsreform – trygghet for pensjonene, Oslo: Finansdepartement.

Swedish Constitution 1 January 1975 with later amendments.

TEC (2002) Consolidated version of the Treaty establishing the European Community, *Official Journal of the European Communities,* C 325 of 24.12.2002, 33–185.

TEC (2004) Treaty establishing a Constitution for Europe, *Official Journal of the European Union,* C 310 of 16 December 2004, 1–474.

U 2001.1258H (SC): The right for a disabled student to export rehabilitation benefit (Danish supreme court case).

U.2006.770H (SC) Repeated refusal of activation offers (Danish supreme court case), available at: www.retsinfo.dk (accessed 29 June 2006).

UN Doc A/44&49 (1989) *Convention on the Rights of the Child,* G.A. res. 44/25, annex, 44 U.N. GAOR Supp. (No. 49) at 167.

Van der Mussele v. Belgium appl. 00008919/80 Article 4 compulsory labour (Strasbourg court case), available at: www.echr.coe.int/ECHR/EN/Header/Case-Law (accessed 29 June 2006).

UN (2006) *Convention on the Rights of Persons with Disabilities: Draft text adopted on 25 August 2006,* New York: United Nations, Ad Hoc Committee, available at: www.un.org/esa/socdev/enable/ (accessed 20 November 2006).

Vestre Landsret (2004) Dom afsagt 25.03.2004 af Vestre Landsrets 6. afdeling i 1. instanssag B-2153-02 mot Kolding Kommune, available at: www.retsinfo.dk (accessed 29 June 2006).

Work environment Act (LOV-2005-06-17-62), available at: http://lovdata.no (accessed 28 June 2006).

Bibliography

Ala-Kauhaluoma, M., Keskitalo, E., Lindqvist, T. and Parpo, A. (2004) *Työttömien aktivointi. Kuntouttava työtoiminta-lain sisältö ja vaikuttavuus* (Activating the unemployed. Rehabilitative work experience – the content and effectiveness of the Act), Research 141, Helsinki: STAKES.

Allianz (2004) *Lebensziele – Menschen in Deutschland, Eine Studie der Allianz Group,* München.

Andersen, N.Å. (2004) *Borgerens kontraktliggørelse*, Copenhagen: DJØF forlag.

Anker, J. (2004) 'Contesting the meaning of active citizenship: The dynamics and strategies of unemployed persons in Denmark', *International Journal of Contemporary Sociology*, 41, 1: 11–39.

APAJH (2005) *Personnes Handicapées. Le Guide Pratique,* Paris: Prat éditions.

Arendt, H. (1958) *The Human Condition*, Chicago: Chicago University Press.

Askheim, O.P. (2002) 'Personlig assistanse for funksjonshemmede', *Tidsskrift for velferds-forskning*, 5, 1: 2–14.

Atkinson, A.B. (1995) *Public Economics in Action*, Oxford: Oxford University Press.

Atkinson, A.B. (2002) 'Social inclusion and the European Union', *Journal of Common Market Studies*, 40, 4: 625–43.

Atkinson, A.B., Cantillon, B., Markier, E. and Nolan, B. (2002) *Social Indicators: The EU and Social Inclusion*, Oxford: Oxford University Press.

Barbier, J.-C. (2004) 'Systems of social protection in Europe: two contrasted paths to acti-vation and perhaps a third', in J. Lind, H. Knudsen and H. Jørgensen (eds) *Labour and Employment Regulation in Europe*, Bruxelles: P.I.E.-Peter Lang.

Barbier, J.-C. (2005) 'The European employment strategy: a channel for activating social protection', in J. Zeitlin, P. Pochet and L. Magnusson (eds) *The Open Method of Co-ordina-tion in Action: the European Employment and Social Inclusion Strategies*, Brussels: P.I.E.-Peter Lang.

Barnes, C. (1991) *Disabled People in Britain and Discrimination,* London: Hurst.

Barral, C., Paterson, F., Stiker, H.J. and Chauvière, M. (eds) (2000) *L'institution du Handicap,* Presses Universitaires de Rennes.

Bay, A.H. and Pedersen, A.W. (2003) 'The limits of social solidarity: popular attitudes towards basic income in a Nordic welfare State', Working Paper, Oslo: NOVA.

Beck, U. (1992) *Risk Society*, London: Sage.

Beck, U. (1999) *World Risk Society*, Cambridge: Polity Press.

Beck, U. and Beck-Gernsheim, E. (2002) *Individualization: Institutionalised Individualism and its Social and Political Consequences*, London: Sage.

Beck, U. and Willms, J. (2004) *Conversations with Ulrich Beck*, Cambridge: Polity.

Bell, D. (1993) *Communitarianism and its Critics*, Oxford: Clarendon Press.

Bendix, R. and Rokkan, S. (1971) 'The extension of citizenship to the lower classes' (orig. 1962), in M. Dogan and R. Rose (eds) *European Politics: A Reader*, Boston: Little, Brown and Company.

Benhabib, S. (2001) 'Dismantling the Leviathan: citizen and state in a global world', *Responsive Community. Rights and Responsibilities*, 11, 3: 14–27.

Benhabib, S. (2002) *The Claims of Culture, Equality and Diversity in the Global Era*, Princeton: Princeton University Press.

Berlin. I. (1969) 'Two concepts of liberty', in *Four Essays on Liberty*, Oxford: Oxford University Press.

Blunkett, D. (2003) Speech at the conference 'Democracy & Participation Programme: Key Findings and Policy Implications', 24 September 2003, London, UK.

Bohman, J. (1999) 'Deliberative democracy and effective social freedom: capabilities, resources and opportunity', in J. Bohman and W. Regh (eds) *Deliberative Democracy: Essays on Reason and Politics*, Cambridge: MIT Press.

Bohman, J. (2000) *Public Deliberation, Pluralism, Complexity and Democracy*, Cambridge: MIT Press.

Bohman, J. (2004) 'Republican cosmopolitanism', *The Journal of Political Philosophy*, 12, 3: 336–52.

Bönker, F. (2005) 'Changing ideas on pensions: accounting for differences in the spread of the multipillar paradigm in five EU social insurance countries', in P. Taylor-Gooby (ed.) *Ideas and Welfare State Reform in Western Europe*, Basingstoke: Palgrave Macmillan.

Borras, S. and Jacobsson, K. (2004) 'The open method of co-ordination and new governance patterns in the EU', *Journal of European Public Policy*, 11, 2: 185–208.

Brandsen, T., Pavolini, E., Ranci, C., Sitterman, B. and Zimmer, A. (2005) 'The National Action Plan on Social Inclusion: An opportunity for the third sector?', Third Sector European Policy Working Papers 14, London: London School of Economics.

Britton, F. (2001) *Active Citizenship: a Teaching Toolkit*, Abingdon: Hodder & Stoughton.

Brochmann, G. (1997) *Grenser for kontroll: Norge og det europeiske innvandringsregimet*, Bergen: Fagbokforlaget.

Brodkin, E.Z. (1990) 'Implementation as policy politics', in D.J. Palumbo and D.J. Calista (eds) *Implementation and the Policy Process – Opening up the Black Box*, New York: Greenwood Press Inc.

Brown, K.M., Kenny, S., Turner, B.S. and Prince, J.K. (2000) *Rhetorics of Welfare: Uncertainty, Choice and Voluntary Associations*, Basingstoke: Palgrave.

Burke, T.F. (2004) *Lawyers, Lawsuits And Legal Rights*, Berkeley: University of California Press.

Campbell, J. and Oliver, M. (1996) *Disability Politics*, London: Routledge.

Charlesworth, H. and Chikin, C. (2000) *The Boundaries of International Law. A Feminist Analysis*, Manchester: Manchester University Press.

Christensen, A. and Malmstedt, M. (2000) '*Lex Loci Laboris* versus *Lex Loci Domicilii* – an inquiry into the normative foundations of European Social Security Law', *European Journal of Social Security*, 2: 69–111.

Clasen, J. and van Oorschot, W. (2002) 'Changing Principles in European Social Security', *European Journal of Social Security*, 42: 89–115.

Clasen, J. and van Oorschot, W. (2003) 'Work, welfare and citizenship: diversity and variation within European (un)employment policy', in J.G. Andersen, J. Clasen, W. van Oorschot and K. Halvorsen (eds) *Europe's New State of Welfare*, Bristol: The Policy Press.

Cohen, J. (1999) 'Deliberation and democratic legitimacy', in J. Bohman, and W. Regh (eds) *Deliberative Democracy: Essays on Reason and Politics*, Cambridge: MIT Press.

Cowles, G.M., Caporaso, J. and Risse T. (2001) *Transforming Europe. Europeanization and Domestic Change*, Ithaca: Cornell University Press.

Cronqvist, H. and Thaler, R.H. (2004) 'Design choices in privatized social security systems: learning from the Swedish experience', *American Economic Review* (Papers & Proceedings) 94, 2: 424–8.

Crouch, C., Eder, K. and Tambini, D. (eds) (2001) *Citizenship, Markets and the State*, Oxford: Oxford University Press.

Dagger, R. (2002) 'Republican citizenship', in E.F. Isin and B.S. Turner (eds) *Citizenship Studies*, London: Sage.

Dahl, T.S. (1984) 'Women's right to money', in H. Holter (ed.) *Patriarchy in a Welfare Society*, Oslo: Universitetsforlaget.

Danish National Institute on Social Research (2003a) *Somaliere og det danske arbejdsmarked – om netværk, kommunikation og integration*, Workingpaper 13: 2003, Copenhagen: Danish National Institute on Social Research.

Danish National Institute on Social Research (2003b) *Unge indvandrere på kontanthjælp iKøbenhavns Kommune*, Workingpaper 5: 2003, Copenhagen: Danish National Institute on Social Research.

de la Porte, C. and Nanz, P. (2004) 'The OMC – a deliberative-democratic mode of governance? The cases of employment and pensions', *Journal of European Public Policy*, 11, 2: 267–88.

de la Porte, C. and Pochet. P. (eds) (2002) *Building Social Europe Through the Open Method of Coordination*, Brussels: P.I.E.-Peter Lang.

de la Porte, C. and Pochet, P. (2005) 'Participation in the open method of co-ordination. The cases of employment and social inclusion', in J. Zeitlin, P. Pochet and L. Magnusson (eds) *The Open Method of Co-ordination in Action: The European Employment and Social Inclusion Strategies*, Brussels: P.I.E.-Peter Lang.

Dean, H. (1999) 'Citizenship', in M. Powell (ed.) *New Labour, New Welfare State – The Third Way in British Social Policy*, Bristol: Policy Press.

Dean, M. (1995) 'Governing the unemployed self in an active society', *Economy and Society*, 24, 4: 559–83.

Della Porta, D., Kriesi, H. and Rucht, D. (1999) *Social Movements in a Globalizing World*, Basingstoke: Macmillan.

Duffy, K. and Jeliazkova, M. (2005) *Back to the Future? The Implementation Reports on the National Action Plans on Social Inclusion – an EAPN Assessment*, Brussels: European anti-poverty network.

Durkheim, E. (1947) *The Division of Labor in Society* (first published in French 1893), New York: The Free Press.

Dwyer, P. (2000) *Welfare Rights and Responsibilities*, Bristol: Policy Press.

Eberlein, B. and Kerwer, D. (2004) 'New governance in the European Union: A theoretical perspective', *Journal of Common Market Studies*, 42, 1: 121–42.

Edebalk, P.G. and Svensson, M. (2005) *Kundval för äldre och funktionshindrade i Norden*, TemaNord 2005:507, Copenhagen: Nordic Council of Ministers.

Eder, K. (2001) 'Social movement organizations and the democratic order: reorganizing the social basis of political citizenship in complex societies', in C.K. Crouch, K. Eder, and D. Tambini, (eds) *Citizenship, Markets and the State*, Oxford: Oxford University Press.

EDF (1995) *Disabled People's Status in the European Union Treaties – Invisible Citizens,* Brussels: European Disability Forum.

Engström, S. and Westerberg, A. (2003) 'Which individuals make active investment decisions in the new Swedish pension system?', *Journal of Pension Economics and Finance*, 2: 225–45.

Eriksen, E.O. (1996) 'Velferdsstaten og spørsmålet om hvem som skal ha hva', in H. Lorentzen (ed.), *Forståelser av fellesskap: syv artikler om velferdsstatens normative utfordringer*, Oslo: The Norwegian Council of Research.

Eriksen, E.O. (2004) 'Reflexive integration in Europe', Working Paper 04/20, Oslo: ARENA.

Eriksen, E.O., Fossum, J.E. and Menéndéz, A.J. (eds) (2002) *Constitution Making and Democratic Legitimacy*, Report 5/02, Oslo: ARENA.

Ervik, R. (2001) 'Pension reform in Norway, Bergen', Available at: http://ftp.iccr-international.org/spa/penref-d2-no.pdf (accessed 11 June 2003).

Esping-Andersen, G. (1990) *The Three Worlds of Welfare Capitalism*, Cambridge: Polity Press.

Esping-Andersen, G. (1999) *Social Foundations of Postindustrial Economies*, Oxford: Oxford University Press.

Esping-Andersen, G. (2002) 'Towards the good society, once again?' in G. Esping-Andersen, D. Gallie, A. Hemerijck and J. Myles (eds) *Why Do We Need a New Welfare State?*, Oxford: Oxford University Press.

Etzioni, A. (2000) *The Third Way to a Good Society*, London: Demos.

Faulks, K. (2000) *Citizenship*, London: Routledge.

Ferrera, M. (2005) *The Boundaries of Welfare. European Integration and the New Spatial Politics of Social Protection*, Oxford: Oxford University Press.

Ferrera, M. and Hemerijck, A. (2003) 'Recalibrating Europe's welfare regimes', in J. Zeitlin and D.M. Trubek (eds) *Governing Work and Welfare in a New Economy*, Oxford: Oxford University Press.

Føllesdal, A. (1997) 'Do welfare obligations end at the boundaries of the nation state?', in P. Koslowski and A. Føllesdal (eds) *Restructuring the Welfare State. Theory and Reform of Social Policy*, Berlin: Springer-Verlag.

Fox Piven, F. and Cloward, R.C. (1977) *Poor People's Movement*, New York: Pantheon Books.

Fraser, N. (1995) 'From redistribution to recognition? Dilemmas of justice in a post-socialist age', *New Left Review*, 212: 68–98.

Fraser, N. (2003) 'Rethinking recognition: overcoming displacement and reification in cultural politics', in B. Hobson (ed.) *Recognition Struggles and Social Movements*, Cambridge: Cambridge University Press.

Freeman, S. (2002) 'Illiberal libertarians: why libertarianism is not a liberal view', *Philosophy and Public Affairs*, 3, 2: 105–51.

Fusfeld, D.R. (1986) *The Age of the Economist*, 5th edn, Glenview: Scott, Foresman and Company.

Garson, J.-P. and Loizillon, A. (2003) 'The economic and social aspects of migration', paper to conference jointly organised by the European Commission and the OECD, Available at: www.oecd.org (accessed 6 December 2005).

Giddens, A. (1985) *The Nation State and Violence*, Cambridge: Polity Press.

Giddens, A. (1991) *Modernity and Self-Identity*, Cambridge: Polity Press.

Giddens, A. (1998) *The Third Way: The Renewal of Social Democracy*, Cambridge: Polity Press.

Gillion, C., Turner, J., Bailey, C. and Latulippe, D. (eds) (2000) *Social Security Pensions: Development and Reform*, Geneva: ILO.

Glendon, M.A. (1994) 'Rights and responsibilities viewed from afar: the case of welfare rights', *Responsive Community. Rights and Responsibilities*, 4, 2: 33–42.

Goetschy, J. (2003) 'The European employment strategy, multi-level governance, and policy coordination: past, present and future', in J. Zeitlin and D.M. Trubek (eds) *Governing Work and Welfare in a New Economy: European and American Experiments*, Oxford: Oxford University Press.

Goffman, E. (1974) *Frame Analysis*, Boston: North-Eastern University Press.

Goul Andersen, J. (2002) 'Work and citizenship: unemployment and unemployment politics in Denmark, 1980–2000', in J. Goul Andersen and P.H. Jensen (eds) *Changing Labour Markets, Welfare Policies and Citizenship*, Bristol: Policy Press.

Grant, W. (1985) *The Political Economy of Corporatism*, London: Macmillan.

Habermas, J. (1984–87) *The Theory of Communicative Action*, vols. 1–2, Boston: Beacon Press.

Habermas, J. (1994) 'Citizenship and national identity', in B. van Stenbergen (ed.) *The Condition of Citizenship*, London: Sage.

Habermas, J. (1996) *Die Einbeziehung des Anderen. Studien zur politischen Theorie*, Frankfurt a.M: Suhrkamp Verlag.

Hain, W., Lohmann, A. and Lübke, E. (2004) 'Veränderungen bei der Rentenanpassung durch das "RV-Nachhaltigkeitsgesetz"', *Deutsche Rentenversicherung*, 59, 6–7: 333–49.

Hall, S. (1996) 'Introduction: who needs 'identity'?', in S. Hall and P. du Gay (eds) *Questions of Cultural Identity*, London: Sage.

Halleröd, B. (2003) *The Fight Against Poverty and Social Exclusion*. Non-governmental expert report No. 1c-2003, available at: http://ec.europa.eu/employment_social/social_inclusion/docs/sweden_1st_report_final_en.pdf (accessed 26 June 2006).

Halvorsen, R. (2002) 'The paradox of self-organisation among disadvantaged people'. Dissertation, Department of Sociology and Political Science, NTNU, Trondheim.

Halvorsen, R. and Jensen, P.H. (2004) 'Activation in Scandinavian Welfare Policy. Denmark and Norway in a comparative perspective', *European Societies*, 6, 4: 461–83.

Hayek, F.A. (1960) *The Constitution of Liberty*, London: Routledge.

Held, D. (1989) *Political Theory and the Modern State*, Stanford: Stanford University Press.

Hellum, A. (2004) 'Nytt fra likestillingsombudet. Hvorfor kvinnekonvensjonen bør inkorporeres gjennom menneskerettsloven', *Kritisk Juss*, 104, 1: 54–67.

Hering, M. (2004) 'Turning ideas into politics: implementing modern social democratic thinking in Germany's pension policy', in G. Bonoli and M. Powell (eds) *Social Democratic Party Policies in Contemporary Europe*, London: Routledge.

Hicks, A. (1999) *Social Democracy and Welfare Capitalism: A Century of Income Security Policy*, Ithaca: Cornell University Press.

Hietaniemi, M. and Vidlund, M. (eds) (2003) *The Finnish Pension System*, Helsinki: Finnish Centre for Pensions (Eläketurvakeskus).

Hinrichs, K. (1998) *Reforming the Public Pension Scheme in Germany: The End of the Traditional Consensus?*, ZeS-Arbeitspapier Nr. 11/98, Universität Bremen: Zentrum für Sozialpolitik.

Hinrichs, K. (2005) 'New century – new paradigm: pension reforms in Germany', in T. Shinkawa and G. Bonoli (eds) *Ageing and Pension Reform Around the World*, Cheltenham: Edward Elgar.

Hinrichs, K. and Kangas, O. (2003) 'When is a change big enough to be a system shift? Small system-shifting changes in German and Finnish pension policies', *Social Policy and Administration*, 37: 573–91.

Hodson, D. and Maher, I. (2001) 'The open method as a new mode of governance: the case of soft economic policy co-ordination', *Journal of Common Market Studies*, 39, 4: 719–46.

Hvinden, B. (1994) *Divided Against Itself: A Study of Integration in Welfare Bureaucracy*, Oslo: Scandinavian University Press.

Hvinden, B. (2004) 'How to get employers to take on greater responsibility for the inclusion of disabled people in working life?', in B. Marin, C. Prinz, and M. Quiesser (eds) *Transforming Disability Welfare Policies: Towards Work and Equal Opportunities*, Aldershot: Ashgate

Hvinden, B. and Halvorsen, R. (2003) 'Which way for European disability policy?' *Scandinavian Journal of Disability Research*, 5, 3: 296–312.

Hvinden, B., Heikkilä, M. and Kankare, I. (2001) 'Towards activation? The changing relationship between social protection and employment in Western Europe', in M. Kautto *et al.* (eds) *Nordic Welfare States in a European Context*, London: Routledge.

Ingelhart, R. (1997) *Modernization and Postmodernization: Cultural, Economic and Political Change in 43 Countries*, New Haven: Princeton University Press.

Institut für Demoskopie Allensbach (2003) *Wissen um die Altersvorsorge – Allensbacher Studie für die Deutsche Postbank AG*, Allensbach.

Isin, E.N. and Turner, B.S. (2002) 'Citizenship studies: an introduction', in *Handbook of Citizenship Studies*, London: Sage publications.

Jacobsson, K. (2004) 'Soft regulation and the subtle transformation of states: the case of EU employment policy', *Journal of European Social Policy*, 14, 4: 355–70.

Jacobsson K. and Schmid, H. (2002) 'Real integration or just formal adaptation? On the implementation of the national action plans for employment', in C. De la Porte and P. Pochet (eds) *Building Social Europe Through the Open Method of Coordination*, Brussels: P.I.E.-Peter Lang.

Jakhelln, H. and Aune, H. (eds) (2006) *Arbeidsrett.no. Kommentarer til arbejdsmiljøloven*, Oslo: N.W. Damm & Søn.

Jamison, A., Eyeman, R., Cramer, J. and Laessøe, J. (1990) *The Making of the New Environmental Consciousness*, Oxford: Edinburgh University Press.

Janoski, T. and Gran, B. (2002) 'Political citizenship: foundations of rights', in E.F. Isin and B.S. Turner (eds) *Handbook of Citizenship Studies*, London: Sage publications.

Johansson, H. (2001) *I det sociala medborgarskapets skugga. Rätten till socialbidrag under 1980- och 1990-talen*, Lund: Arkivs avhandlingsserie 55.

Johansson, H. (2006) *Svensk aktiveringspolitik och aktivitetsgarantin i nordisk belysning*, ESS Rapport 2006:3. Stockholm: Ministry of Finance.

Johansson, H. and Hvinden, B. (2005) 'Welfare governance and the remaking of citizenship', in J. Newman (ed.) *Remaking Governance: Peoples, Politics and the Public Sphere*, Bristol: Policy Press.

Johnston, H. (1995) 'A methodology for frame analysis', in H. Johnston and B. Klandermans (eds) *Social Movements and Culture*, London: UCL Press.

Julkunen, R. (2001) *Suunnanmuutos* (A Shift in Direction), Tampere: Vastapaino.

Junestav, M. (2004) *Arbetslinjer i svensk socialpolitisk debatt och lagstiftning 1930 – 2001*, PhD dissertation, Uppsala: Acta Universitatis Upsaliensis.

Kagan, R.A. (2001) *Adversarial Legalism*, Cambridge: Harvard University Press.

Kangas, O. and Palme, J. (2005a) 'Social policy and economic development in the Nordic countries: an introduction', in O. Kangas and J. Palme (eds) *Social Policy and Economic Development in the Nordic Countries*, Basingtoke: Palgrave Macmillan.

Kangas, O. and Palme, J. (eds) (2005b) *Social Policy and Economic Development in the Nordic Countries*, Basingstoke: Palgrave.

Katz, H. (1993) 'The decentralization of collective bargaining: a literature review and a comparative analysis', *Industrial and Labour Relations*, 47: 3–13.

Katz, M.B. (2001) *The Price of Citizenship: Redefining the American Welfare State*, New York: Henry Holt and Company.

Katzenstein, K. (1985) *Small States in World Markets: Industrial Policy in Europe*, Ithaca: Cornell University Press.

Kautto, M., Fritzell, J., Hvinden, B., Kvist, J. and Uusitalo, H. (2001) 'Introduction: how distinct are the Nordic welfare states?' in M. Kautto, J. Fritzell, B. Hvinden, J. Kvist and H. Uusitalo (eds) *Nordic Welfare States in the European Context*, London: Routledge.

Kelly, P. (2005) *Liberalism*, Cambridge: Polity.

Keohane, R.O. and Nye Jr., J.S. (2000) 'Introduction', in J.S. Nye Jr. and J.D. Donahue (eds) *Governance in a Globalizing World*, Washington DC: Brookings Institute Press.

Ketscher, K. (2001) 'From marriage contract to labour contract', in K. Nousiainen (ed.) *Responsible Selves*, Dartmouth: Ashgate.

Ketscher, K. (2002) *Socialret*, 2nd ed., Copenhagen: Thomson.

Ketscher, K. (2003) 'Kvindekonventionen gælder i dansk ret', in H. Dam (ed.) *Jura og Historie*, København: Jurist – og Økonomforbundets Forlag.

Keynes, J.M. (1936) *The General Theory of Employment, Interest and Money*, London: Macmillan.

Kiander, J. (2002) 'Onko paluu täystyöllisyyteen mahdollinen?' (Is return to full employment optional?), *Yhteiskuntapolitiikka*, 2/2002: 308–14.

Kildal, N. and Kuhnle, S. (2005). 'Introduction', in N. Kildal and S. Kuhnle (eds) *Normative Foundations of the Welfare State: the Nordic Experience*, London: Routledge.

King, D.S. (1987) *The New Right – Politics, Markets and Citizenship*, London: Macmillan.

Kjønstad, A. (1997) 'Trygderettigheter, Grunnloven og Høyesterett', *Lov og Rett*, 243–292.

Klein, R. and Millar, J. (1995) 'Do-It-Yourself Social Policy', *Social Policy and Administration*, 29: 303–16.

Kleinman, M. (2002) *A European Welfare State? European Union Social Policy in Context*, Basingstoke: Palgrave.

Koopmans, R. (1999) 'Political. Opportunity. Structure. Some splitting to balance the lumping', *Sociological Forum*, 14, 1: 93–105.

Koopmans, R. and Statham, P. (2000) 'Migration and ethnic relations as a field of political contention: an opportunity structure approach', in R. Koopmans and P. Statham (eds) *Challenging Immigration and Ethnic Relations Politics*, Oxford: Oxford University Press.

Kortteinen, M. and Tuomikoski, H. (1998) *Työtön* (Unemployed), Helsinki: Tammi.

Kramvig, B. and Stien, K. (2002a) *Grenseløs verdighet*, Norut Finnmark AS.

Kramvig, B. and Stien, K. (2002b) 'Open Borders – Open Bodies', *NIKK Magasin*, 1: 43–45.

Kymlicka, W. (2002) *Contemporary Political Philosophy*, Oxford: Oxford University Press.

Laclau, E. and Mouffe, C. (1985) *Hegemony & Socialist Strategy: Towards a Radical Democratic Politics*, London: Verso.

Le Grand, J. (2003) *Motivation, Agency, and Public Policy*, Oxford: Oxford University Press.

Leibfried, S. (2005) 'Social policy: left to the judges and the markets?' In H. Wallace, W. Wallace and M.A. Pollack (eds) *Policy-making in the European Union*, 5th edn, Oxford: Oxford University Press.

Leibfried, S. and Pierson, P. (1995) 'Sovereign welfare states: social policy in a multitiered Europe', in S. Leibfried and P. Pierson (eds) *European Social Policy: Between Fragmentation and Integration*, Washington DC: The Brookings Institute.

Leinert, J. (2003) *Altersvorsorge 2003: Wer hat sie, wer will sie? Private und betriebliche Altersvorsorge der 30-bis 50-Jährigen in Deutschland*, Bertelsmann Stiftung, Vorsorgestudien 18, Gütersloh.

Leinert, J. (2004) 'Finanzieller Analphabetismus: Schlechte Voraussetzungen für eigenverantwortliche Vorsorge', *Gesundheits-und Sozialpolitik*, 58, 3–4: 24–30.

Leontieva, A.N. and Sarsenov, K. (2003) 'Russiske kvinner i skandinaviske medier', *Kvinneforskning*, 3: 17–31.

Levitas, R. (1998) *The Inclusive Society? Social Exclusion and New Labour*, London: Macmillan Press.

Lewin, L. (1992) *Samhället och de organiserade intressena*, Stockholm: Nordstedts.

Lindbom, A. (2001) 'De borgerliga partierna och pensionsreformen', in J. Palme (ed.) *Hur blev den stora kompromissen möjlig?*, Stockholm: Pensionsforum.

Lindqvist, R. and Marklund, S. (1995) 'Forced to work and liberated from work – a historical perspective on work and welfare in Sweden', *Scandinavian Journal of Social Welfare*, 4: 224–37.

Lipsky, M. (1980) *Street-Level Bureaucracy*, New York: Russell Sage.

Lister, R. (1990) *The Exclusive Society: Citizenship and the Poor*, London: Child Poverty Action Group.

Lister, R. (2001) 'Towards a Citizen's welfare state: the 3 + 2 'R's of welfare reform', *Theory, Culture & Society*, 18, 2–3: 91–111.

Lister, R. (2003) *Citizenship: Feminist Perspectives*, 2nd edn, Basingstoke: Palgrave Macmillan.

Lister, R. (2004) *Poverty*, Cambridge: Polity.

Lødemel, I. (1997) *Pisken i arbeidslinja: Om iverksetjinga av arbeid for sosialhjelp*, Fafo-rapport 226, Oslo: Fafo.

Lødemel, I. and Trickey, H. (eds) (2001a) *An Offer You Can't Refuse*, Bristol: The Policy Press.

Lødemel, I. and Trickey, H. (2001b) 'A new contract for social assistance', in I. Lødemel and H. Trickey (eds) *An Offer You Can't Refuse: Workfare in International Perspective*, Bristol: The Policy Press.

Loewenstein, G.F. (2000) 'Costs and benefits of health- and retirement-related choice', in S. Burke, E.R. Kingson and U. Reinhardt (eds) *Social Security and Medicare: Individual Versus Collective Risk and Responsibility*, Washington, DC: National Academy of Social Insurance.

Lorentzen, T. and Dahl, E. (2005) 'Active labour market programmes in Norway: are they helpful for social assistance recipients?', *Journal of European Social Policy*, 15, 1: 27–45.

Mabbett, D. and Bolderson, H. (2002) 'Non-discrimination, free movement and social citizenship in Europe: Contrasting provisions for EU-nationals and asylum seekers', in R. Sigg and C. Behrendt (eds) *Social Security in the Global Village*, New Brunswick: Transaction publishers.

Majone, G. (1993) 'The European Community between social policy and social regulation', *Journal of Common Market Studies*, 31, 2: 153–70.

Majone, G. (1997) 'From the positive to the regulatory state: causes and consequences in the mode of governance', *Journal of Public Policy*, 17, 2: 139–67.

Majone, G. (1999) 'Regulation in comparative perspective', *Journal of Comparative Policy Analysis*, 1: 309–24.

Majone, G. (2005) *Dilemmas of European Integration*, Oxford: Oxford University Press.

Maletz, D.J. (2003) 'Making non-citizens: Consequences of administrative centralization in Tocqueville's Old Regime', *Publius*, 22, 2: 17–35.

Marklund, S. and Svallfors, S. (1987) *Dual Welfare: Segmentation and Work Enforcement in the Swedish Welfare System*, Umeå: Research reports from the Department of Sociology, University of Umeå.

Marquand, D. (1991) 'Civic republicans and liberal individualists: the case of Britain', *European Journal of Sociology*, 32, 2: 329–44.

Marschallek, C. (2004) 'Die "schlichte Notwendigkeit" privater Altersvorsorge. Zur Wissenssoziologie der deutschen Rentenpolitik', *Zeitschrift für Soziologie*, 33, 4: 285–302.

Marshall, T.H. (1965) 'Citizenship and social class' (first published 1950), in *Class, Citizenship and Social Development*, New York: Anchor Books.

Mathiesen, T. (1977) *Law, Society and Political Action*, London: Academic Press.

Mayhew, V. (2003) *Pensions 2002: Public Attitudes to Pensions and Saving for Retirement, Department for Work and Pensions*, Research Report No. 193, Leeds: Corporate Document Services.

McAdam, D. (1996) 'Conceptual origins, current problems, future directions', in D. McAdam, J.D. McCarthy and N.Z. Mayer (eds) *Comparative Perspectives on Social Movements. Political Opportunities, Mobilizing Structures and Cultural Framings*, Cambridge: Cambridge University Press.

Mead, L. (1986) *Beyond Entitlement – the Social Obligations of Citizenship*, New York: Anchor Press.

Mead, L. (1997a) 'Citizenship and social policy: T. H. Marshall and poverty', in E.F. Paul, F.D. Miller and J. Paul (eds) *The Welfare State*, Cambridge: Cambridge University Press.

Mead, L. (1997b) *The New Paternalism*, Washington DC: Brookings Institute.

Meehan, E. (1997) 'Political pluralism and European Citizenship', in P.B. Lehning and A. Weale (eds) *Citizenship, Democracy and Justice in the New Europe*, London: Routledge.

Melucci, A. (1996) *Challenging Codes*, Cambridge: Cambridge University Press.

Menéndéz, A.J. (2003) 'The rights foundations of solidarity: social and economic rights in the Charter of fundamental rights of the European Union', Working papers 03/1. Oslo: ARENA.

Menéndéz, A.J. (2005) 'Which social and tax policy for which European Union?', paper presented at SCORE, Stockholm university, June 2005. Available at: www.arena.uio.no/cidel/WorkshopStockholm/FrameworkPaper.pdf (accessed 26 June 2006).

Meyer, N.I., Sørensen, V. and Petersen, K.H. (1978) *Oprør fra midten*, Copenhagen: Gyldendal.

Midré, G. (1995) *Bot, bedring eller brød: om bedømming og behandling av sosial nød fra reformasjonen til folketrygden*, Oslo: Universitetsforlaget.

Mikkola, M. (2000) 'Social rights as human rights in Europe', *European Journal of Social Security*, 2/3, 259–72.

Miller, D. (2000) *Citizenship and National Identity*, Cambridge: Polity Press.

Moses, J.W. (2000) *Open States in the Global Economy*, Basingstoke: Macmillan.

Mósesdóttir, L. (2004) *Policies shaping employment, skills and gender equality in the Iceland labour market*, National report, WELLKNOW – HPSE-CT-2002-00119, available at: www.bifrost. is/wellknow (accessed 30 June 2006).

Mósesdóttir, L. (ed.) (2005) *Policies and Performances. The Case of Austria, Denmark, Finland, the Netherlands, Spain, Hungary and Iceland*, Project report no. 4, WELLKNOW – HPSE-CT-2002-00119, available at: www.bifrost.is/wellknow (accessed 30 June 2006).

Mosher, J.S. and Trubek, D. (2003) 'Alternative approaches to governance in the EU: EU social policy and the European employment strategy', *Journal of Common Market Studies*, 41, 1: 63–88.

Mosley, H. and Sol, E. (2005) 'Contractualism in employment services. A socio-economic perspective', in E. Sol and M. Westerveld (eds) *Contractualism in Employment Services*, The Hague: Kluwer Law International.

Mouffe, C. (1992) 'Democratic citizenship and the political community', in Mouffe, C. (ed.) *Dimensions of Radical Democracy: Pluralism, Citizenship and Community*, London: Verso.

Nervik, J.A. (1997) 'Offentlig politikk og klientløpebaner', dr.polit. thesis, Department of Political Science, Olso: University of Oslo.

Newman, J. (ed.) (2005) *Remaking Governance*, Bristol: Policy Press.

Nozick, R. (1974) *Anarchy, State, and Utopia*, Oxford: Blackwell.

Nussbaum, M. (1992) 'Human function and social justice: In defense of Aristotelian essentialism', *Political Theory*, 20, 2: 202–46.

Nussbaum, M. (2000) *Women and Human Development: the Capabilities Approach*, Cambridge: Cambridge University Press.

Offe, C. (1984) *Contradictions of the Welfare State*, Cambridge: MIT Press.

Offe, C. (1996) *Modernity and the State*, Cambridge: Polity Press.

Oldfield, A. (1990) *Citizenship and Community: Civic Republicanism and the Modern World*, London: Routledge.

Olsen, B., Ventegodt Liisberg, M. and Kjærum, M. (2005) *Personer med funktionsnedsættelser i Danmark*, Copenhagen: Institute for Human Rights.

Olsen, J.P. (2002) 'The many faces of Europeanization', *Journal of Common Market Studies*, 40, 5: 921–52.

Østerud, Ø., Engelstad, F. and Selle, P. (2003) *Makten og demokratiet. En sluttbok fra Makt- og demokratiutredningen*, Oslo: Gyldendal Akademisk.

Palme, J., Bergmark, Å., Bäckman, O., Estrada, F., Fritzell, J., Lundberg, O., *et al*. (2003) 'A welfare balance sheet for the 1990s. Final report of the Swedish Welfare Commission', *Scandinavian Journal of Public Health*, 31, Supplement 60.

Parry, G., Moyser, G. and Day, N. (eds) (1992) *Political Participation and Democracy in Britain*, Cambridge: Cambridge University Press.

Parsons, T. (1967) 'Full citizenship for the Negro American?' (orig. 1965), in *Sociological Theory and Modern Society*, New York: The Free Press.

Parsons, T. (1971) *The System of Modern Societies*, Englewood Cliffs, New Jersey: Prentice-Hall.

Pateman, C. (1970) *Participation and Democratic Theory*, Cambridge: Cambridge University Press.

Pateman, C. (1988) 'The patriarchal welfare state', in A. Gutman (ed.) *Democracy and the Welfare State*, Princeton: Princeton University Press.

Pateman, C. (1989) *The Disorder of Women*, Cambridge: Polity Press.

Pateman, C. (2003) 'Freedom and democratization: why basic income is to be preferred to basic capital', in K. Dowding, J. de Wispelaere and S. White (eds) *The Ethics of Stakeholding*, London: Palgrave.

Pensionsforum (2003) *Pensionsbarometer, September-Oktober 2003*, Stockholm, available at: www.pensionsforum.nu (accessed 10 June 2004).

Phillips, A. (1991) *Engendering Democracy*, Cambridge: Polity Press.

Pierson, P. (2001) 'Post-industrial pressures on mature welfare states', in P. Pierson (ed.) *The New Politics of the Welfare State*, Oxford: Oxford University Press.

Pollack, M.A. (2003) 'The Court of Justice as an agent: delegation of judicial power in the European Union', in *The Engines of European Integration*, Oxford: Oxford University Press.

Queisser, M. (2001) 'Privatization: more individual choice in social protection', in X. Scheil-Adlung (ed.) *Building Social Security*, London: Transaction.

Quinn, G. and Degener, T. (2002) 'A survey of international, comparative and regional disability law reform', in M.L. Breslin and S. Yee (eds) *Disability Rights Law and Policy*, New York: Transnational.

Radaelli, C. (2003) *The Open Method of Coordination. A New Governance Architecture for the European Union*, Report 2003:1, Stockholm: Swedish institute for European policy studies.

Raday, F. (2003) 'Culture, Religion and Gender', *International Journal of Constitutional Law*, 1, 4: 663–715.

Rawls, J. (1971) *A Theory of Justice*, Oxford: Oxford University Press.

Reich, R.B. (1998) *Locked in the Cabinet*, New York: Alfred A. Knopf.

Ringer, F. (1997) *Max Weber's Methodology*, London: Harvard University Press.

Rose, N. (1996) *Inventing Ourselves*, Cambridge: Cambridge University Press.

Rothstein, B. (1992) *Den korporativa staten*, Stockholm: Nordstedts.

Ruzza, C. (2004) *Europe and Civil Society. Movement Coalitions and European Governance*, Manchester: Manchester University Press.

Salais, R. (2003) 'Work and welfare: toward a capability approach', in J. Zeitlin and D.M. Trubek (eds) *Governing Work and Welfare in a New Economy*, Oxford: Oxford University Press.

Salais, R. and Villeneuve, R. (eds) (2005) *Europe and the Politics of Capabilities*, Cambridge: Cambridge University Press.

Salonen, T. and Ulmestig, R. (2004) *Nedersta trappsteget. En studie om kommunal aktivering*, Rapportserie i socialt arbete nr. 1, Växjö: Växjö universitet.

Scharpf, F. (2002) 'The European social model. Coping with the challenges of diversity', *Journal of Common Market Studies*, 40, 4: 645–70.

Schoukens, P. (2002) 'How the European Union keeps the social welfare debate on track: A lawyer's view of the EU instruments aimed at combating social exclusion', *European Journal of Social Security*, 4, 2: 117–50.

Schuck, P.H. (2002) 'Liberal citizenship', in E.F. Isin and B.S. Turner (eds) *Citizenship Studies*, London: Sage.

Scott, W.R. (1992), *Organizations*, Englewood Cliffs: Prentice-Hall.

Sen, A. (2000) 'Social Exclusion: Concept, Application and Scrutiny', Social Development Papers no.1, Manila: Asian Development Bank, Office of Environment and Social Development.

Settergren, O. (2001) 'The automatic balance mechanism of the Swedish pension system – a non-technical introduction', *Wirtschaftspolitische Blätter*, 38: 339–49.

Siim, B. (2000) *Gender and Citizenship: Politics and Agency in France, Britain and Denmark*, Cambridge: Cambridge University Press.

Sindbjerg Martinsen, D. (2003) 'Who has the right to intra European social security? From market citizens to European citizens and beyond', Institute Working Papers Law No. 2003/13, Florence: European University.

Smaadal, T., Hernes. H. and Langberg, L. (2002) *Drømmen om det gode liv, En rapport om utenlandske kvinner gift med norske menn som måtte søke tilflukt på krisesentrene i 2001*, Oslo: Krisesentersekretariatet og Tanaprosjektet.

Smith, R.M. (2002) 'Modern citizenship', in E.F. Isin and B.S. Turner (eds) *Handbook of Citizenship Studies*, London: Sage.

Snow, D.A. and Benford, R.D. (1992) 'Master frames and cycles of protests', in A.D. Morris and C. McClurg Mueller (eds) *Frontiers in Social Movement Theory*, New Haven: Yale University Press.

Sundén, A. (2004) *How Do Individual Accounts Work in the Swedish Pension System?*, Center for Retirement Research at Boston College, Issues in Brief, No. 22, Chestnut Hill.

Sundén, A. (2005) 'How much do people need to know about their pensions and what do they know?', in R. Holzmann and E. Palmer (eds) *Pension Reform: Issues and Prospects for Non-Financial Defined Contribution (NDC) Schemes*, Washington DC: The World Bank.

Supiot, A. (2003) 'Governing work and welfare in a global economy', in J. Zeitlin and D.M. Trubek (eds) *Governing Work and Welfare in a New Economy*, Oxford: Oxford University Press.

Tam, H. (1998). *Communitarianism: A New Agenda for Politics and Citizenship*, New York: New York University Press.

Tarrow, S. (1994) *Power in Movement*, Cambridge: University Press.

Tarrow, S. (2003) *Power in Movement*, 2nd edn, Cambridge: Cambridge University Press.

Taylor, C. (1989) 'The liberal-communitarian debate', in N.L. Rosenblum (ed.) *Liberalism and the Moral Life*, Cambridge: Harvard University Press.

Taylor-Gooby, P. (1999) 'Markets and Motives: Trust and Egoism in Welfare Markets', *Journal of Social Policy*, 28: 97–114.

TemaNord (2005a) *Äldreomsorgsforskning i Norden: En kunskapsöversikt*, TemaNord 2005: 508, Copenhagen: Nordic Council of Ministers.

TemaNord (2005b) *Welfare and Health Services in the Nordic Countries: Consumer Choices*, TemaNord 2005: 575, Copenhagen: Nordic Council of Ministers.

Thaler, R.H. and Benartzi, S. (2004) 'Save more tomorrow: using behavioural economics to increase employee saving', *Journal of Political Economy*, 112, 1: 164–87.

Theodore, N. and Peck, J. (2001) 'Searching for best practice in welfare-to-work: The means, the method and the message', *Policy & Politics,* 29, 1: 81–94.

Thorén, K. (2005) 'Municipal activation policy: A case study of the practical work with unemployed social assistance recipients', IFAU working paper 2005: 20, Uppsala: IFAU.

Tilly, C. (1998) *Durable Inequality*, Berkeley: University of California Press.

Tilly, C. (1999) 'From interaction to outcomes in social movements', in M. Guigni, D. McAdam and C. Tilly (eds) *How Social Movement Matters,* University of Minnesota Press.

Torfing, J. (1999) 'Workfare with welfare: recent reforms of the Danish welfare state', *Journal of European Social Policy*, 9, 1: 5–28.

Torfing, J. (2000) 'Welfare, workfare and the good society', in B. Greve (ed.) *What Constitutes a Good Society?*, Basingstoke: Macmillan Press.

Torfing, J. (2004) *Det stille sporskifte i velfærdsstaten. En diskursteoretisk beslutningsprocessanalyse*, Magtutredningen, Aarhus: Aarhus Universitetsforlag.

Trädgårdh, L. (1997) 'Statist individualism: on the culturality of the Nordic welfare state', in Ø. Sørensen and B. Stråth (eds) *The Cultural Construction of Norden*, Oslo: Scandinavian University Press.

Tuori, K. (2004) 'The many senses of European Citizenship', in K. Nuotio (ed.) *Europe in Search of Meaning and Purpose*, Forum IURIS, Publications of the Faculty of Law, University of: Helsinki, Helsinki.

Turner, B.S. (1990) 'Outline of a theory of citizenship', *Sociology*, 24, 2: 189–217.

Turner, B.S. (2001) 'The erosion of citizenship', *British Journal of Sociology*, 52, 2: 189–209.

Valkenburg, B. and Lind, J. (2002) 'Orthodoxy and reflexivity in international comparative analysis', in R. van Berkel and I. Hornemann Møller (eds) *Active Social Policies in the EU*, Bristol: Policy Press.

van Berkel, R. and Hornemann Møller, I. (eds) (2002) *Active Social Policies in the EU*, Bristol: Policy Press.

van Berkel, R. and Roche, M. (2002) 'Activation policies as reflexive social policies', in R. van Berkel and I. Hornemann Møller (eds) *Active Social Policies in the EU*, Bristol: Policy Press.

van der Mei, A.P. (2003) *Free Movement of Persons Within the European Community: Cross-Border Access to Public Benefits*, Oxford: Hart Publishing

van Oorschot, W. (2006) 'Making the difference in social Europe: deservingness perceptions among citizens of European welfare states', *Journal of European Social Policy*, 16, 1: 23–42.

Vik, K. (1999) *Employers as a Target Group for Disability Policies*, MA thesis in sociology, Trondheim, NTNU.

Vik-Mo, B. and Nervik, J.A. (1999) *Arbeidsplikten i arbeidslinjen*, Report no. 52, Department of Sociology and Political Science, Trondheim: Norwegian University of Science and Technology.

Wallace, W. (1999) 'The sharing of sovereignty', in R. Jackson (ed.) *Sovereignty at the Millennium*, Oxford: Blackwell Publishers.

Walzer, M. (1983) *Spheres of Justice: a Defence of Pluralism and Equality*, New York: Basic Books.

Warburton, J. and Smith, J. (2003). 'Out of the generosity of your heart: are we creating active citizens through compulsory volunteer programmes for young people in Australia?', *Social Policy & Administration*, 37, 7: 772–86.

Wästberg, I.C. (1999) 'The office of the disability ombudsman in Sweden', in M. Jones and L.A. Basser Marks (eds) *Disability, Diversity and Legal Change*, The Hague: Kluwer Law International.

Weber, M. (1949) 'Objectivity in social science and social policy', in *The Methodology of Social Sciences*, New York: Free Press.

Whittle, R. (2000) 'Disability rights after Amsterdam: the way forward', *European Human Rights Review*, 1: 33–48.

Whittle, R. (2002) 'The Framework Directive for equal treatment in employment and occupation: an analysis from a disability rights perspective', *European Law Review*, 27, 2: 303–26.

Whittle, R. (2005) *EU disability policy and the equal opportunity principle. Working for an inclusive society*, EDRC national conference, 15 September 2005, Malta (on file with author).

Williams, F. (1998) 'Agency and structure revisited: rethinking poverty and social exclusion', in M. Barry and C. Hallett (eds) *Social Exclusion and Social Work*, Lyme Regis: Russell House.

Williams, F., Popay, J. and Oakley, A. (1999) *Welfare Research*, London: UCL Press.

Young, I.M. (1990) *Justice and the Politics of Difference*, Princeton: Princeton University Press.

Young, I.M. (2000) *Inclusion and Democracy*, Oxford: Oxford University Press.

Yuval-Davis, N. (1997) *Gender and Nation*, London: Sage.

Zimmermann, B. and Wagner, P. (2004) 'Citizenship and collective responsibility. On the political philosophy of the nation-based welfare state – and beyond', in L. Magnusson and B. Stråth (eds) *A European Social Citizenship? Preconditions for Future Policies from a Historical Perspective*, Bern: Peter Lang Publishing Group.

Zürn, M. (1998) *Regieren jenseits des Nationalstaates*, Frankfurt a.M.: Suhrkamp.

Zürn, M. (1999) 'The state in the post-national constellation – societal denationalization and multi-level governance', Working Paper 35/99, Oslo: ARENA.

Index

For Product Safety Concerns and Information please contact our EU
representative GPSR@taylorandfrancis.com
Taylor & Francis Verlag GmbH, Kaufingerstraße 24, 80331 München, Germany